Pathway to Math 5

Student's Book

Glue your picture here.

Name

Richmond

Richmond

58 St Aldates
Oxford
OX1 1ST
United Kingdom

Pathway to Math Student's Book Level 5

First Edition: March 2016
Eighth Reprint: January 2023
ISBN: 978-607-06-1259-6

Pathway to Math 5 is a collaborative work, created and designed by the Department of Educational Research of Santillana. Richmond adapted the project and created an English version.

Av. Río Mixcoac No. 274, Col. Acacias,
Benito Juárez, C.P. 03240, Ciudad de México

Publisher: Justine Piekarowicz
Editorial Team: Catalina Hernández, Natalia Herrera, Duncan Jones, Jacaranda Ruiz, Milosh Trnka
Pre-Press Coordinator: Daniel Santillán
Cover Design: Lourdes Arroyo
Cover Photograph: ©THINKSTOCK: iStock (Mirexon)
Illustrations: Alejandro Rojas Contreras, Sergio Lantadilla Munizaga, Sergio Quijada Valdés, Carlos Herrera Portilla

Photographs: Archivo Santillana
©Shutterstock.com Natalia Bratslavsky p. 26 (Subterráneo de Nueva York).

Printed in Brazil by Forma Certa

Lote: 774585
Código: 292712596

Introduction

Hi friends!

We are **Spot**  and **Kiki**  and we are here to welcome you to **Pathway to Math**. Follow us on the Pathway to Math, where learning becomes special. Do you want to know why?

- This pathway is full of magic, and everyone is welcome on it. You will find information, texts, pictures and activities presented in a simple and friendly manner. Here you will discover that learning is fun!
- This is a pathway where we can all learn to share and live together. The activities will help us reflect on our values and learn to respect others.

- This is a pathway open to people from all over the world where you can learn interactively with the help of the latest technology.
- This is a pathway full of challenges that involve finding solutions, developing math skills and applying calculation strategies that you and your classmates will work on together.

We will be with you every step of the way!
All you need is curiosity and the desire to learn.

How is your textbook organized?

Pathway to Math 5 is organized into five units. Here is what you will find in each unit.

Initial Pages

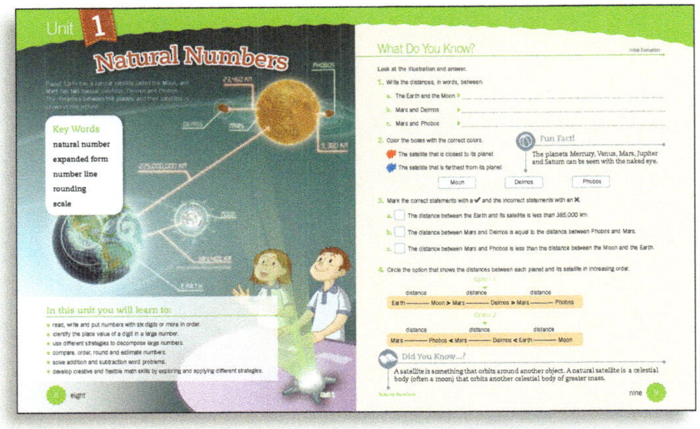

- Number and title of the unit
- Learning objectives
- Initial evaluation

Sections Organized by Learning Objectives

- Connecting
  Observe, read and answer
- Learning
- Practicing
- Analyzing
- Quiz Yourself

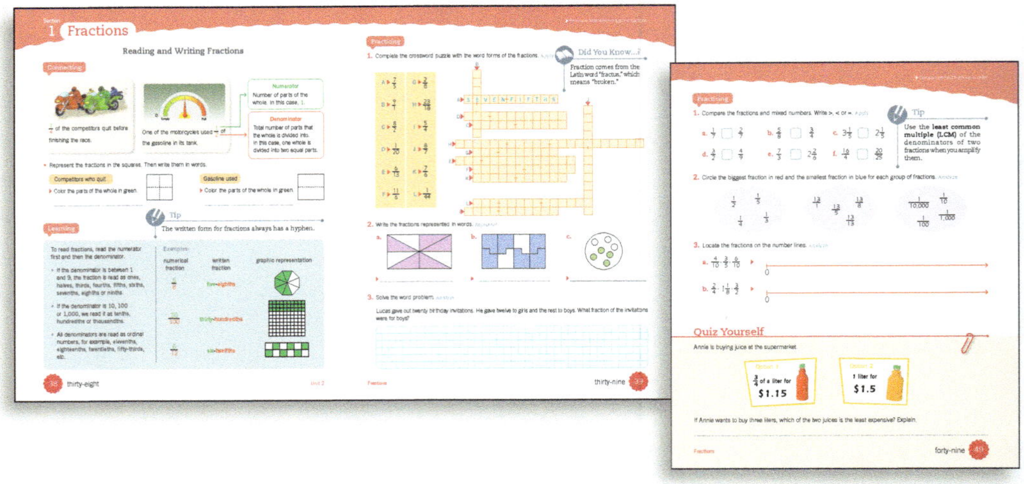

Fun Features

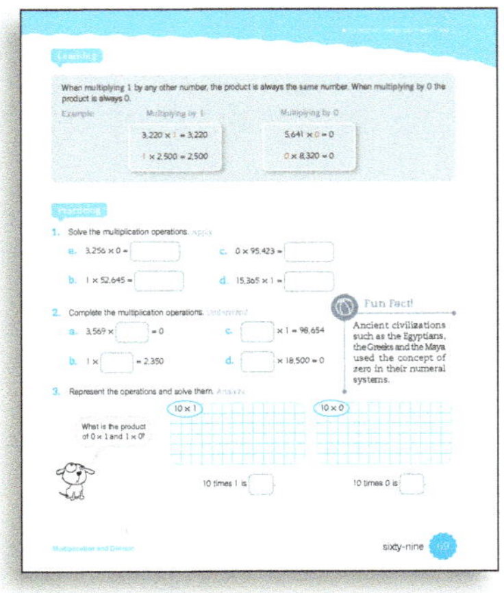

- Education through Values
- Did You Know...?
- Remember!
- Tip
- Word Focus
- Fun Fact!
- Challenge

Evaluation Pages

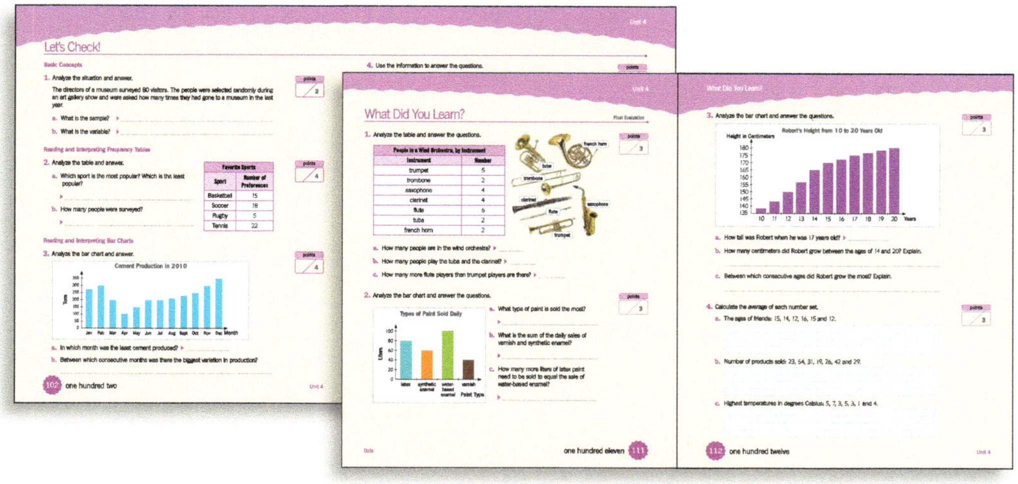

- What Do You Know?
  Initial Evaluation
- Let's Check!
  Intermediate Evaluation
- What Did You Learn?
  Final Evaluation

Special Pages

- Exam Strategies
- Test Study Pages
  Summary and Review

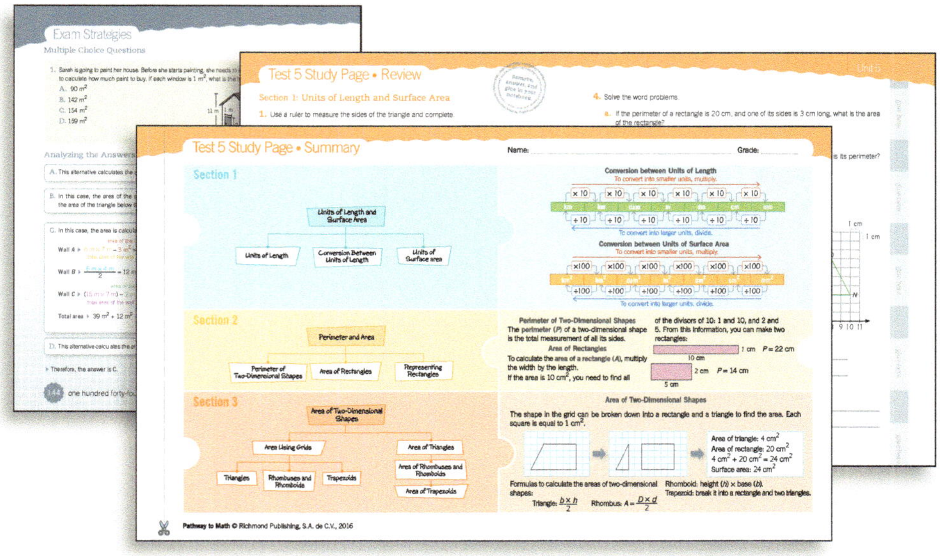

Table of Contents

Unit 1

Natural Numbers

Planet Earth has a natural satellite called the Moon, and Mars has two natural satellites, Deimos and Phobos. The distances between the planets and their satellites is shown in the picture.

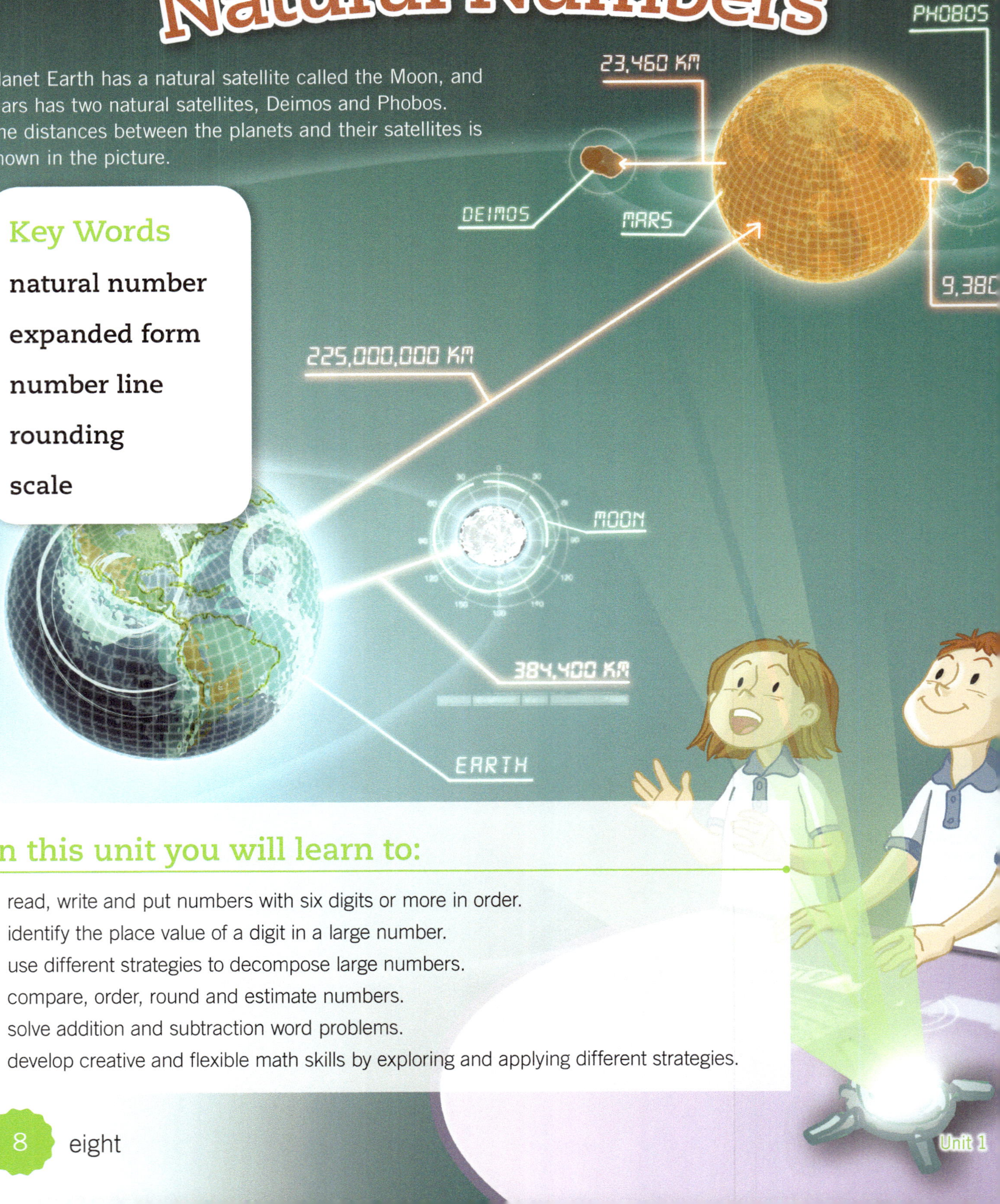

Key Words

- natural number
- expanded form
- number line
- rounding
- scale

In this unit you will learn to:

- read, write and put numbers with six digits or more in order.
- identify the place value of a digit in a large number.
- use different strategies to decompose large numbers.
- compare, order, round and estimate numbers.
- solve addition and subtraction word problems.
- develop creative and flexible math skills by exploring and applying different strategies.

What Do You Know?

Look at the illustration and answer.

1. Write the distances, in words, between:

   a. The Earth and the Moon ▸ ______________________

   b. Mars and Deimos ▸ ______________________

   c. Mars and Phobos ▸ ______________________

2. Color the boxes with the correct colors.

   (orange) The satellite that is closest to its planet

   (blue) The satellite that is farthest from its planet

Moon	Deimos	Phobos

Fun Fact!

The planets Mercury, Venus, Mars, Jupiter and Saturn can be seen with the naked eye.

3. Mark the correct statements with a ✔ and the incorrect statements with an ✖.

   a. ☐ The distance between the Earth and its satellite is less than 385,000 km.

   b. ☐ The distance between Mars and Deimos is equal to the distance between Phobos and Mars.

   c. ☐ The distance between Mars and Phobos is less than the distance between the Moon and the Earth.

4. Circle the option that shows the distances between each planet and its satellite in increasing order.

   Option 1

   Earth —distance— Moon > Mars —distance— Deimos > Mars —distance— Phobos

   Option 2

   Mars —distance— Phobos < Mars —distance— Deimos < Earth —distance— Moon

Did You Know...?

A satellite is something that orbits around another object. A natural satellite is a celestial body (often a moon) that orbits another celestial body of greater mass.

Section 1 Large Numbers

Reading and Writing Natural Numbers

Connecting

Six businesses decided to have a fund-raiser to donate money to an orphanage. The total donated by each business is shown in the table.

Donations by Business						
Business	B1	B2	B3	B4	B5	B6
Total	$183,375	$174,225	$153,740	$155,530	$200,725	$186,525

- Circle the three businesses that collected the least amount of money.

  ▸ B1 ▸ B2 ▸ B3 ▸ B4 ▸ B5 ▸ B6

- Match the numbers with the correct written forms.

Number	**Word Form of the Number**
200,725	One hundred eighty-three thousand, three hundred seventy-five
186,525	Two hundred thousand, seven hundred twenty-five
183,375	One hundred eighty-six thousand, five hundred twenty-five

- The businesses collected a total of $1,054,120. Mark the correct word form with a ✔.

☐ One million, five hundred four thousand, one hundred twenty

☐ One million, fifty-four thousand, one hundred twenty

Tip

In English, we use commas to divide the word form of numbers into millions, thousands and hundreds.

Learning

Natural numbers are one of the first groups of numbers you study. They are the numbers you use every day for counting: 1, 2, 3, 4, 5, 6, …

To **write natural numbers** with many digits, the digits are grouped into sets of three numbers from right to left. Each set is separated by a comma.

Example: 9,507,032,891

9 — billions; 507 — millions; 032 — thousands; 891 — hundreds

To **read natural numbers** you start from the left.

Example: The number 9,507,032,891 is read as nine billion, five hundred seven million, thirty-two thousand, eight hundred ninety-one.

The number you read is called the *word form* of the number.

Practicing

1. Circle the correct numbers. Identify

a. Seventy million, four hundred twenty thousand.

▸ 70,420 ▸ 70,420,000 ▸ 70,420,000,000

b. Eight hundred fifty million, five.

▸ 855,000,000 ▸ 850,005,000 ▸ 850,000,005

c. Two billion, five hundred thirty-two million, eighty-one.

▸ 2,532,000,081 ▸ 2,532,081 ▸ 253,281

2. Write the word forms of the numbers. Interpret

a. 5,230,000 ▸ ______________________________

b. 210,000,125 ▸ ______________________________

c. 2,320,000,001 ▸ ______________________________

3. Write the information in numbers and words. Interpret

a. A human head has approximately 100,000 hairs.

b. A person flexes the joints in their fingers approximately 25,000,000 times in their lifetime.

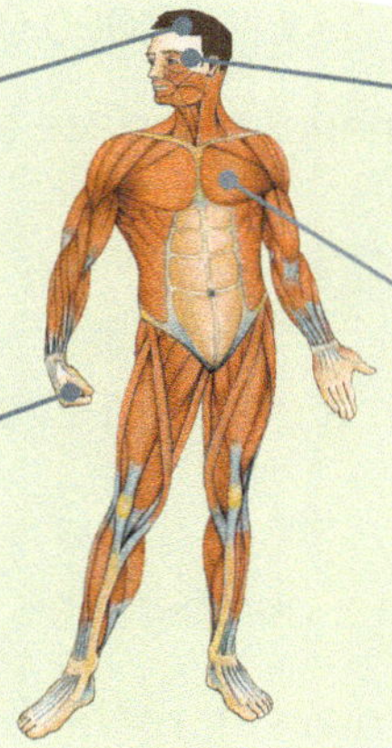

c. You blink approximately 8,000,000 times in one year.

d. The human heart beats more than 40,000,000 times in one year.

Number	Word Form
a. ____________	______________________________
b. ____________	______________________________
c. ____________	______________________________
d. ____________	______________________________

Place Value in Natural Numbers

Connecting

The planet is divided into seven continents. Each has a different surface area that can be expressed in km^2.

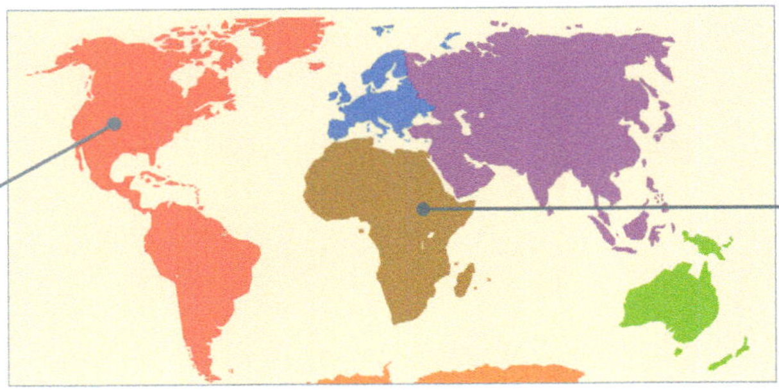

- Complete the table with the area of each continent.

	Ten Millions	Millions	Hundred Thousands	Ten Thousands	Thousands	Hundreds	Tens	Ones
North America								
Africa								

- Mark the value of the green number in Africa's surface area with a ✔.

☐ 300,000 ☐ 3,000,000 ☐ 30,000,000

- Write the value of the red number in North America's surface area. ▸ ____________

Tip

Put a comma every three numbers, starting from the right.

Learning

The value of a digit depends on its position in a number. This is called its **place value**.

Example: In the number 5,417,239,678, the digits have the following place values:

Billions	Hundred Millions	Ten Millions	Millions	Hundred Thousands	Ten Thousands	Thousands	Hundreds	Tens	Ones
B	HM	TM	M	HTh	TTh	Th	H	T	O
5 ,	4	1	7 ,	2	3	9 ,	6	7	8
5,000,000,000	400,000,000	10,000,000	7,000,000	200,000	30,000	9,000	600	70	8

Practicing

1. Write the correct place value for the red digit in each number. Represent

a. 1,743,001,451 ▸ ____________________

b. 1,287,535,450 ▸ ____________________

c. 801,214,564 ▸ ____________________

d. 102,547,462 ▸ ____________________

2. Circle the numbers that fit the descriptions. Apply

a.

The 7 represents 700,000 ones.
587,637,609
13,745,915
9,870,783
709,314,204

b.

The number has 6 HM.
7,394,609,405
516,317,530
26,379,464
8,647,605,435

Remember!

In the number 3**5**4, the digit **5** is in the tens position; this means that its value is *five tens* or 50 *ones*.

3. Write the numbers that fit the descriptions. Analyze

38,967,597 7,905,521,403 9,012,538,707 789,931,250

a. 3 has the highest place value. ▸ ____________________

b. 5 has the smallest place value. ▸ ____________________

c. 1 has a higher place value than 8. ▸ ____________________

d. 7 has a higher place value than 9. ▸ ____________________

4. Solve the word problem. Analyze

Using the number 125,768,245, identify the digits in the tens place and in the ten millions place and increase them both by three. Now, identify the digits in the thousands place and in the hundreds place and halve them both. What number do you get?

Standard and Expanded Forms

Connecting

Dinosaurs existed millions of years ago, before there were any humans.

- Mark the correct statement with a ✓.

  ☐ *Triceratops* existed 67 M years ago.   ☐ *Pterodactyls* existed (100,000,000 + 5,000,000) years ago.

- How long ago did the Stegosaurus live? Circle.

  ▸ 1 HM + 5 TM + 5 M   ▸ 1 × 100,000,000 + 5 × 1,000,000 + 5 × 100,000

Remember!

An **addend** is a number that is added to another addend. The product of an addition operation is called the **sum**.

Learning

There are different ways to decompose numbers.

Standard form: Represent the number as an addition operation in which each addend corresponds to the place value of each digit.

Example: 1,450,000,200 = 1,000,000,000 + 400,000,000 + 50,000,000 + 200

Expanded form: Represent the number as an addition operation in which each addend is the result of multiplying the digit and its place value: 1, 10, 100, 1,000, 10,000, 100,000, etc.

Example: 1,450,000,200 = 1 × 1,000,000,000 + 4 × 100,000,000 + 5 × 10,000,000 + 2 × 100

The number can also be written as:

1,450,000,200 = 1 B + 4 HM + 50 TM + 2 H

Practicing

1. Circle the incorrect expanded forms. Identify

a. 20,000,250

- 20,000,000 + 200 + 50
- 2 × 10,000,000 + 2 × 100 + 5 × 1
- 2 TM + 2 H + 5 T

b. 100,001,001

- 100,000,000 + 100 + 1
- 1 × 100,000,000 + 1 × 1,000 + 1 × 1
- 1 HM + 1 Th + 1 O

c. 8,000,000,700

- 8,000,000,000 + 700
- 8 × 1,000,000,000 + 7 × 100
- 8 B + 7 T

2. Decompose the numbers. Apply

a. 13,006,700 (standard form) ▶ ____________________

b. 4,000,900,001 (expanded form) ▶ ____________________

c. 2,100,050,000 (standard form) ▶ ____________________

3. Decompose the numbers. Analyze

a. 150,900,100 = ____________ HM + 5 TM + ____________ HTh + ____________ H

b. 32,001,500 = 30,000,000 + ____________ + ____________ + 500

c. 2,500,800 = ____________ × 1,000,000 + 5 × ____________ + 8 × ____________

d. 8,000,200,150 = ____________ × ____________ + 2 × 100,000 + 1 × 100 + 5 × 10

Location of Numbers on a Number Line

Connecting

San Francisco is in the north of the state of California. The road sign shows the distances to other cities from San Francisco.

- Mark the city that is farthest from San Francisco with a ✔.

  ☐ Las Vegas ☐ Portland ☐ Reno

- Mark the city that is closest to San Francisco with a ✔.

  ☐ Albuquerque ☐ Portland ☐ Seattle

The distances on the road sign can be represented on a number line.

- Each section of the number line increases by 100 units, which represent 100 km.

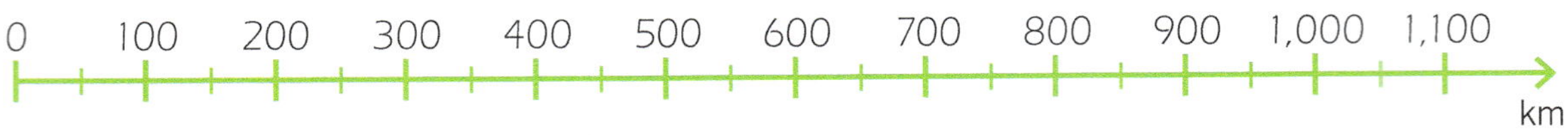

- Write the names of the cities on the number line and connect them to their distances from San Francisco.

San Francisco ____________ ____________ ____________ ____________

____

Learning

The **scale** of a **number line** depends on the the values it represents.

Example: This number line increases by intervals of 3,000 and the numbers 6,000, 12,000, 15,000 and 24,000 are marked.

Practicing

1. There are four dots marked on the number line. Write the numbers that they represent. Identify

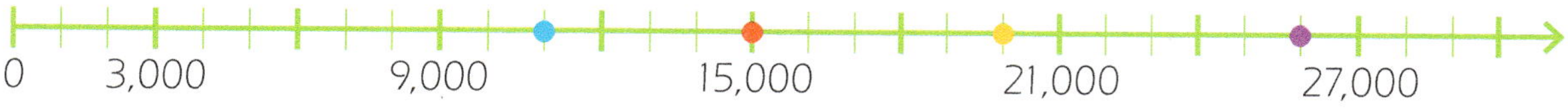

a. ● ▸ ____________ **b.** ● ▸ ____________ **c.** ● ▸ ____________ **d.** ● ▸ ____________

2. Locate and mark the numbers on the number line. Represent

a. 400 **b.** 1,800 **c.** 3,400 **d.** 4,600 **e.** 5,100

3. Match the numbers with their number lines. Relate

a. 15,000, 25,000, 45,000

b. 20,500, 22,500, 23,500

c. 15,000, 20,000, 25,000

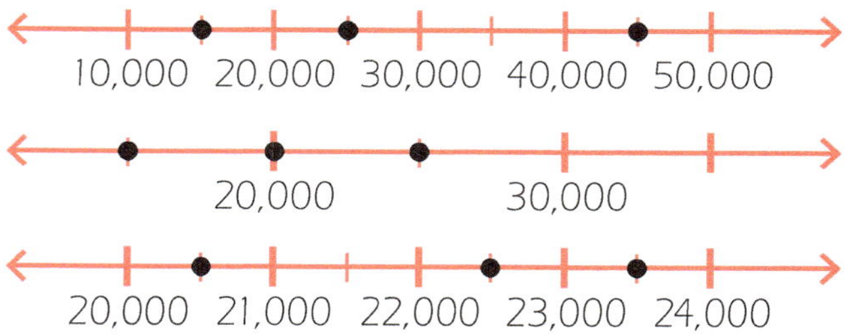

4. Use the number line, below, to mark the heights (in meters) of these buildings. Apply

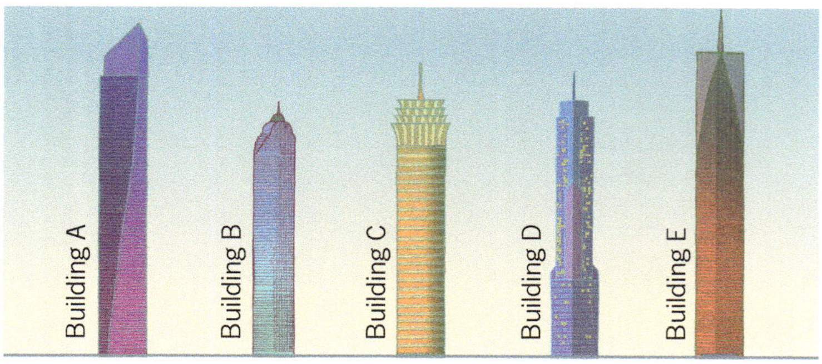

520 m 417 m 445 m 440 m 530 m

Did You Know...?

Very tall buildings are called "skyscrapers" in English because they look like they are almost touching the sky.

Comparing and Putting Natural Numbers in Order

Connecting

A construction company sells two different house designs.

- What place value does 8 have in the price of each house?

  Design 1 ▶ ______________________

  Design 2 ▶ ______________________

- What place value does 5 have in the price of each house?

  Design 1 ▶ ______________________

  Design 2 ▶ ______________________

- To compare the prices of the houses we can compare the place values of the numbers.

Design 1

TM	M	HTh	TTh	Th	H	T	O
0	8	5	1	4	0	0	0

Design 2

TM	M	HTh	TTh	Th	H	T	O
0	8	1	5	4	0	0	0

8 = 8

5 > 1

- So, 8,514,000 > 8,154,000. Therefore, Design 1 is more expensive.

Learning

Methods for Comparing Numbers

When comparing two or more natural numbers with a **different number** of digits, the number with **more digits** is greater.

Example: 2,100,000,000 > 100,000,000

When comparing two or more natural numbers with an **equal number** of digits, compare the digits **in the same positions** from left to right.

Example: 223,450,000 > 221,450,000

3 > 1

Practicing

1. Write a number *greater than* and *less than* the given numbers, using the same number of digits. Apply

a. 1,342,729

less than	greater than

b. 852,325,254

less than	greater than

Remember!

The symbol ">" means **greater than**.
The symbol "<" means **less than**.
The symbol "=" means **equal to**.

2. Compare the numbers. Write <, > or =. Apply

a. 42,548 ☐ 42,584

b. 1,548,325 ☐ 1,600,000

c. 658,584,211 ☐ 658,584,211

d. 1,254,325,325 ☐ 1,254,325

e. 1,635,254 ☐ 1,600,000

f. 1,999,999 ☐ 2,000,000

g. 98,545,111 ☐ 89,545,111

h. 187,024,001 ☐ 187,420,001

3. Write the correct numbers. Analyze

a. A number greater than 1,658,441,221 and less than 2,099,000,000.

▶ ☐

b. A number less than 7 B and greater than 5 M.

▶ ☐

c. A number less than 48 TM and greater than 47,999,998.

▶ ☐

d. The greatest number with 7 digits that has a 6 in the HTh place.

▶ ☐

Sometimes in activities, there is more than one answer.

Rounding and Estimating Natural Numbers

Connecting

www.statista.com

According to a survey by eMarketer, there were 207,200,000 smartphone users in the US in 2016.

- Mark the number that rounds off 207,200,000 to the nearest million with a ✔.

  ☐ 200,000,000 ☐ 20,000,000 ☐ 207,000,000

- If the number of smartphone users doubled in five years, how many users were there in 2011? Circle the correct answer.

  - About 120,000,000
  - About 103,000,000
  - About 400,000,000
  - About 50,000,000

Learning

To make larger numbers easier to work with, you can **round** or **estimate**. Usually, this helps simplify calculations.

- There is no exact method for **estimating** numbers, but it helps to calculate proportions.

  Example: The difference between 550,000,000 and 545,000,300 can be **estimated** to be **about** 5,000,000.

- When **rounding** a number, make sure you know which digit you are rounding to. You can round to the tens, hundreds, thousands or other place values. Then focus on the digit **to the right** of the digit you are rounding.

  - If the number to the right is **greater than** or **equal to 5** (5, 6, 7, 8, 9), you **round up**. You increase the digit by 1 and replace the digits to the right with zeros.

    Example: When rounding 767,054,210 to the HM place.

    767,054,210 → 800,000,000

    6 > 5

  - If the number to the right is **less than 5** (0, 1, 2, 3, 4), you **round down**. The digit you are rounding to stays the same and the digits to the right are replaced with zeros.

    Example: When rounding 354,814,520 to the TM place.

    354,814,520 → 350,000,000

    4 < 5

Practicing

1. Round each number. Apply

a. 8,054,200,187 to the ten millions place ▶ ____________________

b. 1,258,635,260 to the millions place ▶ ____________________

c. 7,540,230,100 to the hundred millions place ▶ ____________________

2. Determine the place values of the rounded off digits. Analyze

	Number		Rounded Number		Place Value
a.	1,520,214,000	▶	1,500,000,000	▶	____________________
b.	8,542,250,540	▶	8,540,000,000	▶	____________________
c.	9,174,870,210	▶	9,000,000,000	▶	____________________

3. Look at the prices and solve by estimating the answer without calculating exactly. Apply

washing machine

$990

stove

$1,990

microwave

$399

a. Estimate the total price of the washing machine and the stove. ▶ ____________________

b. Estimate the total price of the stove and the microwave. ▶ ____________________

c. Estimate the total price of the washing machine and the microwave. ▶ ____________________

Quiz Yourself

Look at the letters. Each letter represents a number.

A = 100,000 + 10,000

B = 2 × 100,000 + 5 × 10,000

C = 5 HTh + 9 TTh

D = 350,000

E = 4 × 100,000 + 5 × 10,000

F = 6 HTh + 7 TTh

- Write the letters and their numbers at appropriate intervals on the number line.

0

Let's Check!

Reading and Writing Natural Numbers

1. Write the numbers from the newspaper headlines.

points ___ / 3

a.

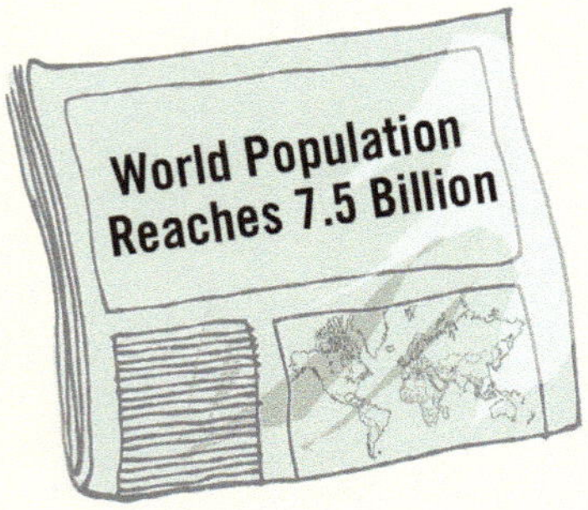

______

b.

______

c.

______

Place Value in Natural Numbers

2. Look at the number and write **T** for **true** and **F** for **false**. Then explain your answers.

points ___ / 3

3,441,658,079

a. ☐ The digit 1 is in the billions place.

Explain: ______________________________

b. ☐ Numbers 0, 7, and 9 are in the thousands, ten thousands and millions places.

Explain: ______________________________

c. ☐ Number 8 is in the thousands place.

Explain: ______________________________

Standard and Expanded Forms

3. Look at the example and then complete the information.

points ___ / 6

	Expanded Form		Standard Form		Natural Number
	2 × 10,000 + 6 × 100	▶	20,000 + 600	▶	20,600
a.	2 × 100,000 + 6 × 10,000	▶	______	▶	______
b.	______	▶	______	▶	2,600,000,000
c.	______	▶	2,000,000,000 + 600,000	▶	______

Location of Numbers on a Number Line

4. Complete the boxes with the correct numbers.

points ___ / 7

18,300,000	14,998,875	22,500,000	8,100,000
1,100,000	4,859,875	28,158,741	

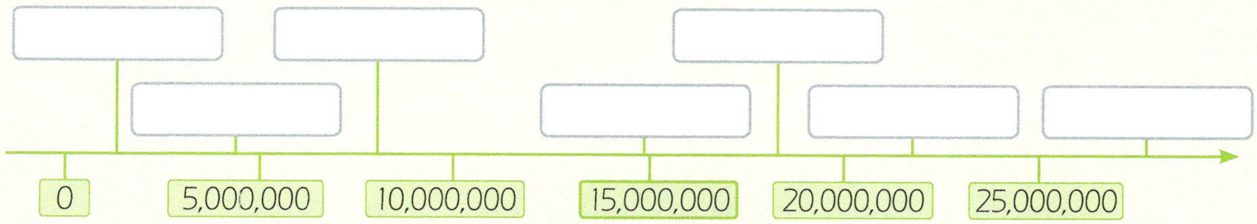

Comparing and Putting Natural Numbers in Order

5. Color the numbers in the correct colors.

points ___ / 7

- (green) Numbers less than 9,999,999
- (blue) Numbers greater than 9,999,999 and less than 999,999,999
- (orange) Numbers greater than 999,999,999

2,647,582	2,647,582,129	13,129,587	
748,586	6,158,381	854,861,397	9,547,301,222

Rounding and Estimating Natural Numbers

6. Look at the table. Round the population of each country to the ten millions place.

points ___ / 5

Approximate Populations of South American Countries

Country	Population
Chile	18,006,000
Peru	31,153,000
Brazil	204,519,000
Argentina	43,132,000
Colombia	48,549,000

Source: Official estimates

a. Chile ▸ ____________________

b. Peru ▸ ____________________

c. Brazil ▸ ____________________

d. Argentina ▸ ____________________

e. Colombia ▸ ____________________

Adding Natural Numbers

Connecting

The table shows the number of people that used bicycles instead of cars over a two-week period.

Bicycle Use	
Week	**Number of People**
1	657,892
2	528,105

Education through Values

Riding your bicycle helps your city reduce pollution and helps you live a healthy lifestyle.

- To calculate the total number of people who used bicycles over the two-week period, you need to add 657,892 and 528,105.

```
  657,892 }
+ 528,105 } addends
 ________
[       ] → sum
```

657,892 + 528,105 = [ ]

(657,892 + 528,105: addends; [ ]: sum)

- In total, ______________ people used bicycles over the two weeks.

Learning

To add two numbers, you combine the **addends** according to their place values. **Ones** are added with **ones**, **tens** with **tens**, **hundreds** with **hundreds**, and so on. The total is the **sum**. Always add from **right to left**.

Example:

	B	HM	TM	M	HTh	TTh	Th	H	T	O	
	7,	6	5	3,	0	5	1,	8	9	2	→ addend
+	2,	1	5	3,	5	7	6,	8	0	7	→ addend
	9,	8	0	6,	6	2	8,	6	9	9	→ sum

1,254,540 + 13,214,100 = 14,468,640

(1,254,540 + 13,214,100: addends; 14,468,640: sum)

Practicing

1. Complete the addition operations. Apply

a.
```
    8,764,210,345
+     312,221,060
-----------------
[              ]
```

b.
```
    2,610,389,678
+   4,981,230,576
-----------------
[              ]
```

c.
```
    5,248,210,029
+   2,367,134,576
-----------------
[              ]
```

2. Solve the word problem. Apply

If someone buys all three items in the picture, how much will they pay?

3. Complete the operations with the missing numbers. Analyze

a.
```
    120,352,105
+ [            ]
---------------
    902,407,105
```

b.
```
  [              ]
+   4,237,158,213
-----------------
    6,053,293,874
```

c.
```
    1,120,352,105
+ [              ]
-----------------
    5,200,357,111
```

Quiz Yourself

Write **T** for **true** or **F** for **false**. Then explain your answers.

a. ☐ If you round to the thousands place, the sum of 234,549 and 273,430 is 507,000.

Explain: ______________________________

b. ☐ 340,709 plus 125,890 is 466,599.

Explain: ______________________________

c. ☐ The sum of 5 M + 4 TTh + 9 H and 270,490,000 is a number between 1 B and 2 HM.

Explain: ______________________________

Section
3 Subtraction

Subtracting Natural Numbers

Connecting

A weekday average of 5,650,000 people use the New York City Subway. The table shows the average numbers of people who used the subway in 2015.

New York City Subway Passengers, 2015	
Average	**Number of Passengers**
Weekday	5,650,610
Saturday	3,309,731
Sunday	2,663,418

Source: www.mta.info

What was the difference between the average numbers of passengers on Saturdays and Sundays?

- Complete the missing information.

		(2)	(12)	(10)		(2)	(11)		
Saturday	▶	~~3~~ ,	~~3~~	~~0~~	~~9~~ , 7	~~3~~	~~1~~	⟶	minuend
Sunday	▶ −	2 ,	◯	6	3 , ◯	1	8	⟶	subtrahend
			6	◯	◯ , 3	1	3	⟶	difference

- Therefore, the difference between the number of passengers that used the subway on Saturdays and Sundays is

______________.

Learning

To **solve a subtraction operation**, the **minuend should be greater than the subtrahend**. Subtraction is done from **right to left** respecting the place value of each digit and **regrouping** when necessary. Study the table to understand regrouping.

borrowing

Example: If the minuend is 3,899,790,289 and the subtrahend is 1,412,425,150, what is the difference?

	B	HM	TM	M	HTh	TTh	Th	H	T	O		
						(8)	(10)					
	3 ,	8	9	9 ,	7	~~9~~	~~0~~ ,	2	8	9	⟶	minuend
−	1 ,	4	1	2 ,	4	2	5 ,	1	5	0	⟶	subtrahend
	2 ,	4	8	7 ,	3	6	5 ,	1	3	9	⟶	difference

Practicing

1. Mark the correct subtraction operations with a ✔ and the incorrect ones with an ✖. Interpret

a.
$$\begin{array}{r} 89{,}504{,}004 \\ -\ 71{,}613{,}514 \\ \hline 17{,}890{,}490 \end{array}$$ ☐

b.
$$\begin{array}{r} 93{,}567{,}841 \\ -\ 84{,}699{,}813 \\ \hline 8{,}968{,}028 \end{array}$$ ☐

c.
$$\begin{array}{r} 32{,}541{,}504 \\ -\ 9{,}563{,}604 \\ \hline 22{,}876{,}900 \end{array}$$ ☐

d.
$$\begin{array}{r} 42{,}861{,}792 \\ -\ 7{,}978{,}791 \\ \hline 34{,}883{,}001 \end{array}$$ ☐

2. Solve the word problems. Apply

a. A pool can hold 2,500,000 liters of water. There are 1,482,500 liters of water in the pool already. How much more water is needed to fill it?

b. A company deposits $54,320,820 into a savings account. Later, it makes two withdrawals of $5,540,000 and $15,980,000. How much money is left in the savings account?

3. Complete the boxes with the values. Then check your answers. Analyze

8,710,495 | 987,534 | 4,256,807 | 5,247,503 | 6,528,326

a. The difference is: 3,462,992

minuend ▶ ☐

subtrahend ▶ ☐

b. The difference is: 3,269,273

minuend ▶ ☐

subtrahend ▶ ☐

The Relationship between Addition and Subtraction

Connecting

The map shows the areas of the Pacific and the Atlantic oceans.

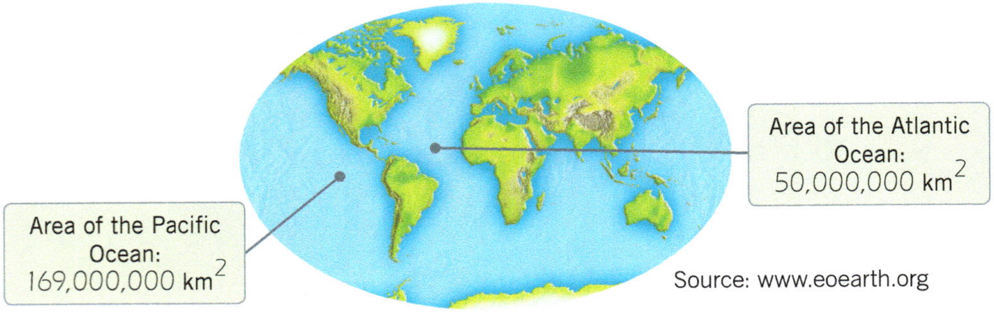

Source: www.eoearth.org

- To calculate the difference between the areas of the Pacific and Atlantic oceans:

	169,000,000	Area of the Pacific Ocean
–	77,000,000	Area of the Atlantic Ocean
	92,000,000	Difference between the areas of both Oceans

The Pacific Ocean is 92,000,000 km^2 greater than the Atlantic Ocean.

- To check if your answer is correct, you can add the answer and the area of the Atlantic Ocean:

	92,000,000	Difference between the areas of both Oceans
+	77,000,000	Area of the Atlantic Ocean
	169,000,000	Area of the Pacific Ocean

Learning

To **check** if the answer to a **subtraction operation** is correct, **add** the **difference** and the **subtrahend**. The answer is the **minuend**.

Example:

Solution	Check your answer
936,214,875	87,087,519
– 849,127,356	+ 849,127,356
87,087,519	936,214,875

To **check** if the answer to an **addition operation** is correct, **subtract** one of the **addends** from the **sum**. The answer is the other **addend**.

Example:

Solution	Check your answer
412,370,985	1,090,913,178
+ 678,542,193	– 412,370,985
1,090,913,178	678,542,193

Practicing

1. Mark the math problem that correctly shows how to check a calculation with a ✔ and the one that does not with an ✖. Understand

a.

```
  127,565,125          183,819,361
+  56,254,236        +  56,254,236
  183,819,361          240,073,597     ☐
```

b.

```
  6,878,447,123        6,343,326,123
–   535,121,000      +   535,121,000
  6,343,326,123        6,878,447,123     ☐
```

2. Complete with the missing numbers. Apply

a.

```
  ☐                       121,215,550
–   124,500,350        + ☐
  ☐                       245,715,900
```

b.

```
  5,915,693,300          8,350,243,500
+ 2,434,550,200        – ☐
  ☐                      ☐
```

3. Solve the word problem. Analyze

A city wants to calculate the amount of glass it has recycled over two years.

paper

354,120,911 kg

glass

_______ kg

plastic

214,111,311 kg

A total of 890,216,432 kg of waste were recycled in two years. How many kilograms of glass were recycled?

Quiz Yourself

The following encoded message was found:

5H456 90U1 372841

```
  6, 8 6 4, 9 W 7, 7 9 C
– S, 4 O 3, N 3 K, 4 Y 3
  4, E 6 R, 2 5 1, A 0 2
```

To solve the hidden message, connect each letter with the correct value in the subtraction operation.

The decoded message is: ______________________________

Exam Strategies

Multiple Choice Questions

1. If the number 2,547,982,100 is rounded up to the millions place and the number 1,245,951,589 is rounded up to the thousands place, what is the difference between the rounded numbers?

A. 1,302,030,511

B. 1,302,048,000

C. 1,302,158,000

D. 1,303,029,511

Analyzing the Answers

A. This answer calculates the difference between both numbers **without rounding**. Although the answer is correct, it is not what was asked for.

B. Rounding 2,547,982,100 to the millions place equals 2,548,000,000.

Rounding 1,245,951,589 to the thousands place equals 1,245,952,000.

The difference is:

```
  7  9 9 10
  2,548,000,000
- 1,245,952,000
  1,302,048,000
```

C. Both numbers are rounded correctly, but the answer is incorrect:

```
  7  10 10 10
  2,548,000,000
- 1,245,952,000
  1,302,158,000
```

D. The numbers are **not rounded correctly**:

When rounding to the millions place the number 2,547,982,100 **is not** 2,548,982,100.

When rounding to the thousands place the number 1,245,951,589 **is not** 1,245,952,589.

1,303,029,511 is not the correct difference.

▸ Therefore, answer **B** is correct.

1. A B C D

What Did You Learn?

Final Evaluation

1. Complete the statements.

points
/ 3

a. The number five billion, two hundred forty-five thousand, seven hundred eighty, in number form is ______________________________.

b. In the number 9,874,635,210, the number 4 is located in the ______________________________ place.

c. In the number 795,210,000, the number 7 is located in the ______________________________ place.

2. Complete the crossword puzzle.

points
/ 6

Across

a. 7 HTh + 8 TTh + 5 H + 2 T + 3 O
b. two hundred thousand, six hundred forty-five
c. 7 HTh + 6 Th + 5 O

Down

d. 500,000 + 30,000 + 2,000 + 80
e. 1 × 100,000 + 5 × 10
f. 4 HTh + 3 Th + 4 T + 6 O

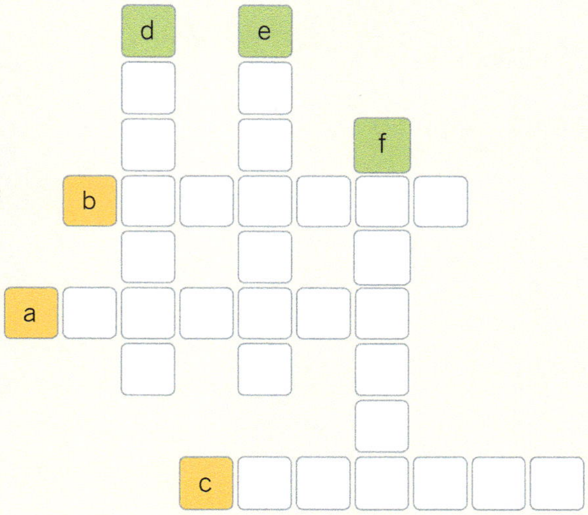

3. Put the numbers in order from greatest to least to find the secret word.

points
/ 2

N	9,000,250,215
G	9,000,100,215
U	9,120,258,215
N	9,020,255,215
I	9,000,300,215
O	9,120,300,215
R	9,120,350,215
D	9,020,250,215

The secret word is ______________________________.

4. Look at the numbers.

points
/ 2

4 2 9 1 8 3 6 5 7

Without repeating digits, write:

a. The greatest number rounded to the nearest hundred millions place. ▶ ____________

b. The smallest number rounded to the hundred thousands place. ▶ ____________

5. Solve the word problem.

points
/ 4

In June, an art museum made $7,660,000 from children's tickets. It made $3,905,000 less from children's tickets than from adult tickets. In July, the museum made $10,850,000 from both child and adult tickets. How much more money did the museum earn in June than in July?

a. What is the question? ▶ ____________

b. Draw a diagram of the problem.

c. Write an operation to solve the problem.

d. Answer ▶ ____________

6. The table shows the population of a town. Complete the chart and answer the question.

points
/ 4

Population of Clinton			
Sex / Age	**Male**	**Female**	**Total**
Under 18	20,058		42,587
18 and older		28,194	56,220
Total	48,084		

What is the difference between the total number of men and the total number of women?
▶ ____________

Mark the correct answers with an ✕.

points
/ 4

7. During a fund-raiser $2,148,387,454 was collected. How would you write the total amount of money raised?

A. Two million, one hundred forty-eight, three hundred eighty-seven, four hundred fifty-four.

B. Two billion, one hundred forty-eight million, three hundred eighty-seven thousand, four hundred fifty-four.

C. Two million, one hundred forty-eight thousand, three hundred eight-seven, four hundred fifty-four thousand.

D. Two billion, one hundred forty-eight million, three hundred eighty-seven, four hundred fifty-four thousand.

8. Which digit is located in the millions place in 658,457,125?

A. 1

B. 5

C. 7

D. 8

9. What is the place value of the red digit in the number 1,458,777?

A. 800

B. 8,000

C. 80,000

D. 800,000

10. Which number matches the expanded form?

20,000,000 + 4,000,000 + 300,000 + 50,000 + 1,000

A. 243,510

B. 2,435,100

C. 24,351,000

D. 243,510,000

points
/ 4

11. Which place value is missing from 365,174,845 in its expanded form?

300,000,000 + 5,000,000 + 100,000 + 70,000 + 4,000 + 800 + 40 + 5

A. 6,000,000
B. 60,000,000
C. 600,000,000
D. 6,000,000,000

12. Which option does not represent 7,542,111?

A. 7 M + 5 HTh + 4 TTh + 2 Th + 1 H + 1 T + 1 O
B. 7,000,000 + 500,000 + 40,000 + 2,000 + 100 + 1
C. 7,000,000 + 500,000 + 40,000 + 2,000 + 100 + 10 + 1
D. $7 \times 1{,}000{,}000 + 5 \times 100{,}000 + 4 \times 10{,}000 + 2 \times 1{,}000 + 1 \times 100 + 1 \times 10 + 1 \times 1$

13. Where is the number 29,000,000 located on the number line?

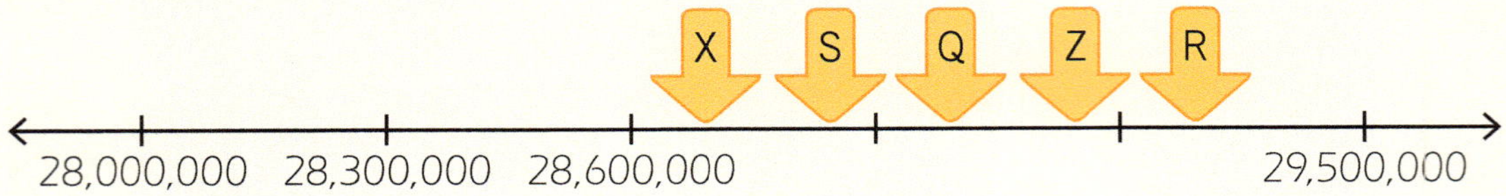

A. Between X and S
B. Between S and Q
C. Between Q and Z
D. Between Z and R

14. X, Y and Z are natural numbers on the number line. Which answer is incorrect?

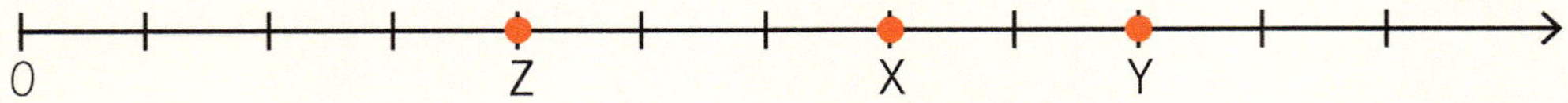

A. $0 < Z$
B. $X > Z$
C. $Y > Z$
D. $Y < Z$

points

/4

15. On which number line is it easiest to identify the number 6,358,144,111?

A. 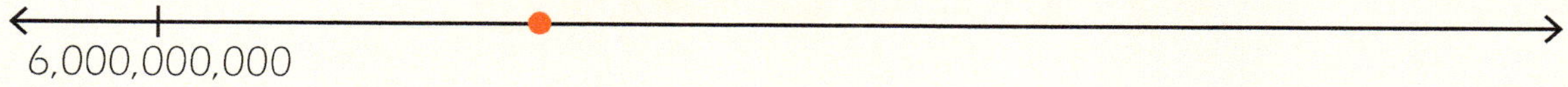

B. 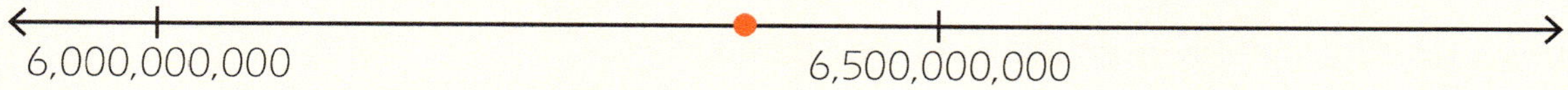

C. 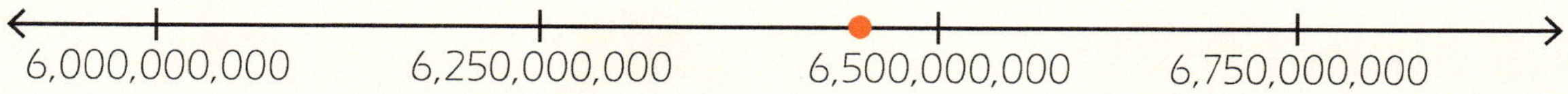

D. 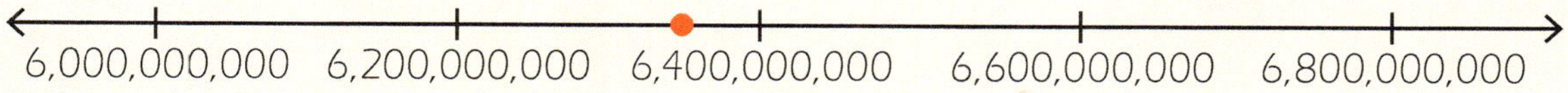

16. Which set of numbers is in decreasing order?

365,100 | 3,548,785,119 | 1,478,300 | 321,145,964

A. 321,145,964, 1,478,300, 3,548,785,119, 365,100

B. 365,100, 1,478,300, 321,145,964, 3,548,785,119

C. 3,548,785,119, 321,145,964, 1,478,300, 365,100

D. 365,100, 321,145,964, 1,478,300, 3,548,785,119

17. Jasmine buys a new car for $45,990 and a motorcycle for $35,990. If she has $90,000 in cash, how much money will she have left over?

A. $8,020

B. $9,020

C. $9,120

D. $18,020

18. Assuming A + B = 25,354 and C = 18,867, what is A + B + C?

A. 33,111

B. 34,221

C. 44,211

D. 44,221

Find Test 1 Study Page

Unit 2

Fractions

Musical notes are symbols that represent sounds and their duration.

Duration of Musical Notes		
Symbol	Duration	Name
𝅝	1 beat	whole note
𝅗𝅥	$\frac{1}{2}$ beat	half note
♩	$\frac{1}{4}$ beat	quarter note
♪	$\frac{1}{8}$ beat	eighth note
𝅘𝅥𝅯	$\frac{1}{16}$ beat	sixteenth note
𝅘𝅥𝅰	$\frac{1}{32}$ beat	thirty-second note

Key Words

simplify

proper fraction

improper fraction

mixed fraction

amplify

equivalent

In this unit you will learn to:

- read, write and classify fractions.
- simplify and amplify fractions to obtain equivalent fractions.
- locate and put fractions in order on a number line.
- solve addition and subtraction operations involving fractions with equal denominators.
- be positive and confident in yourself and your math skills.

What Do You Know?

1. Match each musical symbol with its duration.

Symbol	Duration
	$\frac{1}{4}$
	$\frac{1}{8}$
	$\frac{1}{32}$

Fun Fact!

The duration of a note depends on the *tempo* of the music. *Tempo* is the speed or pace of a piece of music. Think of your favorite song. What is its tempo? How many beats per minute does it have?

2. Look at the example in blue. Then draw the musical symbols that match the representations of their duration.

a.

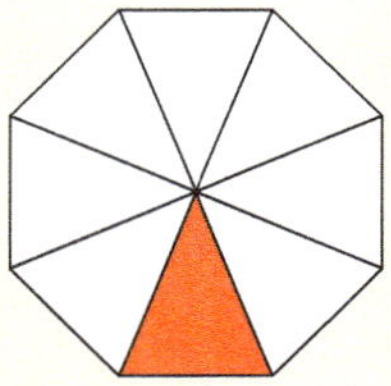

b.

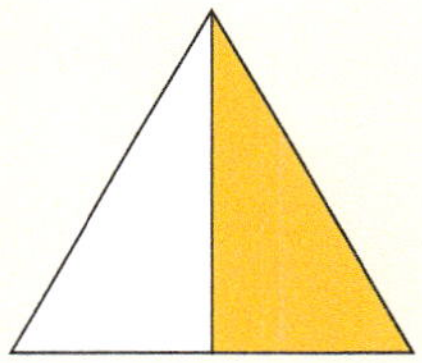

3. Complete the patterns with the duration of the musical symbols.

a. From shortest to longest.

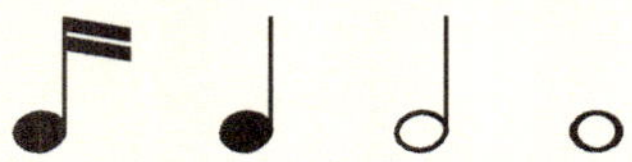

$\frac{1}{16}$ < ☐ < ☐ < 1

b. From longest to shortest.

☐ > $\frac{1}{4}$ > $\frac{1}{8}$ > ☐

Fractions

Reading and Writing Fractions

Connecting

$\frac{1}{4}$ of the competitors quit before finishing the race.

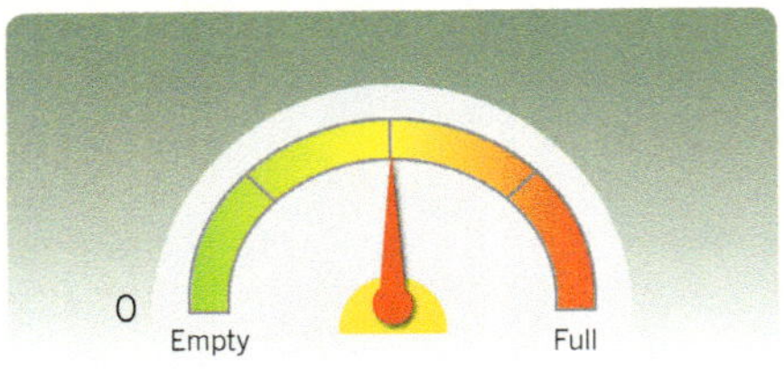

One of the motorcycles used $\frac{1}{2}$ of the gasoline in its tank.

Numerator
Number of parts of the whole. In this case, **1**.

Denominator
Total number of parts that the whole is divided into. In this case, one whole is divided into two equal parts.

- Represent the fractions in the squares. Then write them in words.

Competitors who quit

▸ Color the parts of the whole in green.

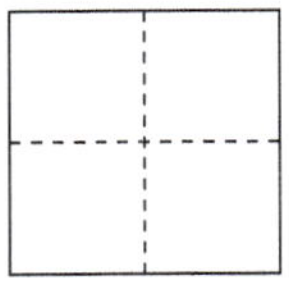

____

Gasoline used

▸ Color the parts of the whole in green.

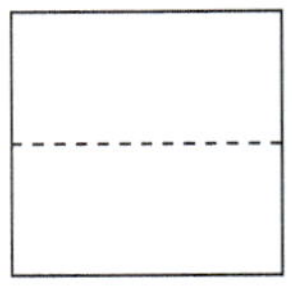

____

Tip

The written form for fractions always has a hyphen.

Learning

To **read fractions**, read the numerator first and then the denominator.

- If the denominator is between 1 and 9, the fraction is read as **ones**, **halves**, **thirds**, **fourths**, **fifths**, **sixths**, **sevenths**, **eighths** or **ninths**.
- If the denominator is **10**, **100** or **1,000**, we read it as **tenths**, **hundredths** or **thousandths**.
- All denominators are read as ordinal numbers, for example, **elevenths**, **eighteenths**, **twentieths**, **fifty-thirds**, etc.

Examples:

numerical fraction	written fraction	graphic representation
$\frac{5}{8}$	**five-eighths**	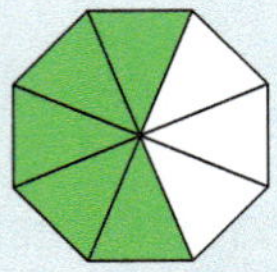
$\frac{30}{100}$	**thirty-hundredths**	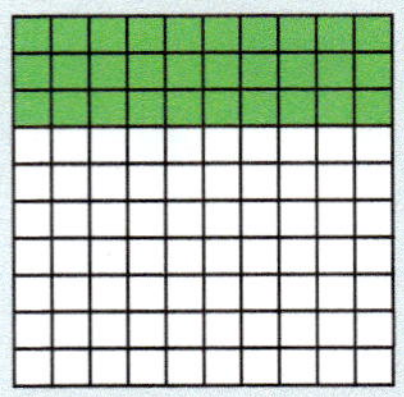
$\frac{6}{12}$	**six-twelfths**	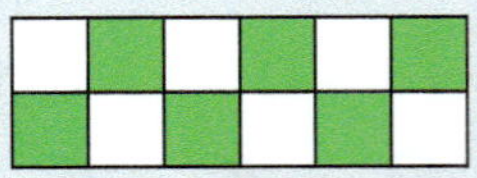

Practicing

1. Complete the crossword puzzle with the word forms of the fractions. Apply

A ▶ $\frac{7}{5}$	G ▶ $\frac{2}{8}$
B ▶ $\frac{9}{1}$	H ▶ $\frac{23}{18}$
C ▶ $\frac{8}{2}$	I ▶ $\frac{5}{4}$
D ▶ $\frac{1}{20}$	J ▶ $\frac{8}{7}$
E ▶ $\frac{6}{13}$	K ▶ $\frac{7}{6}$
F ▶ $\frac{11}{6}$	L ▶ $\frac{1}{44}$

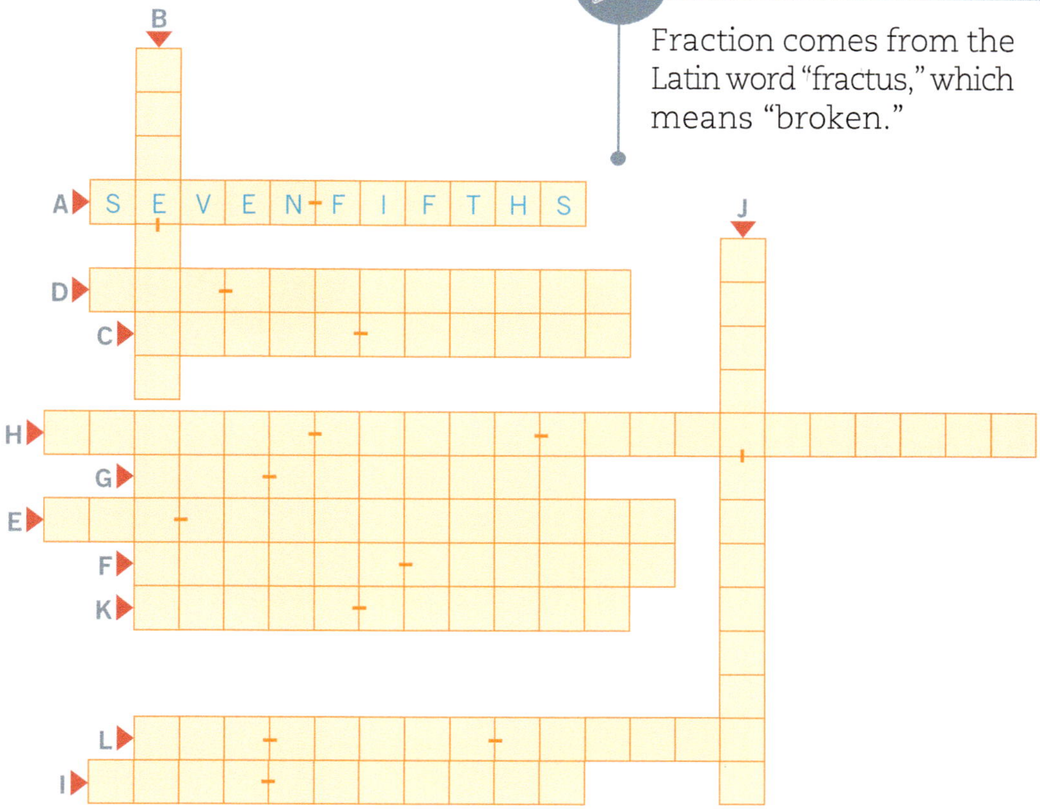

Did You Know...?

Fraction comes from the Latin word "fractus," which means "broken."

2. Write the fractions represented in words. Represent

a.

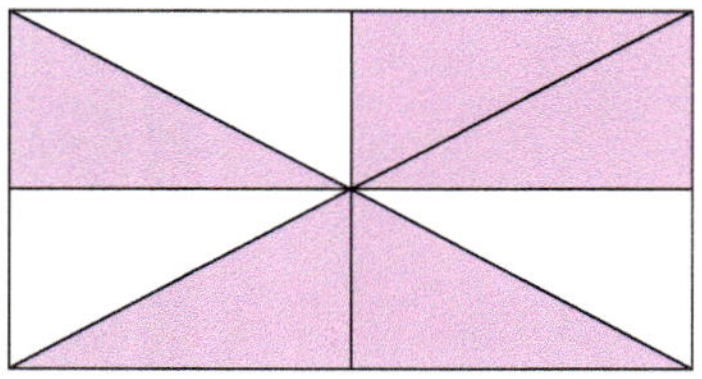

▶ ______________________

b.

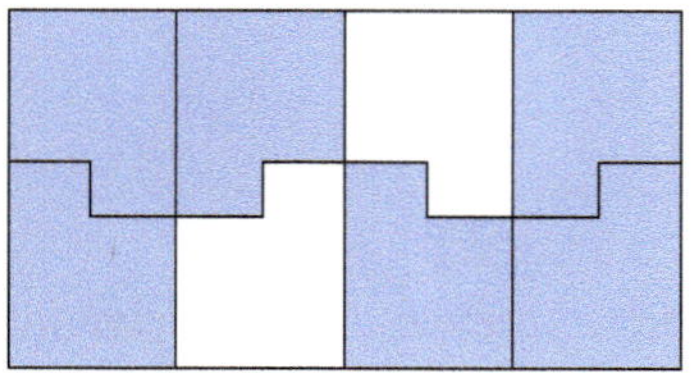

▶ ______________________

c.

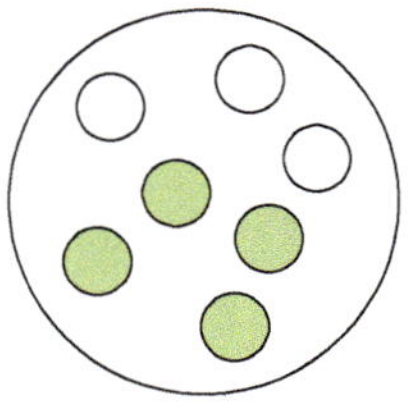

▶ ______________________

3. Solve the word problem. Analyze

Lucas gave out twenty birthday invitations. He gave twelve to girls and the rest to boys. What fraction of the invitations were for boys?

Classifying Fractions

Connecting

Three friends represent fractions on a poster.

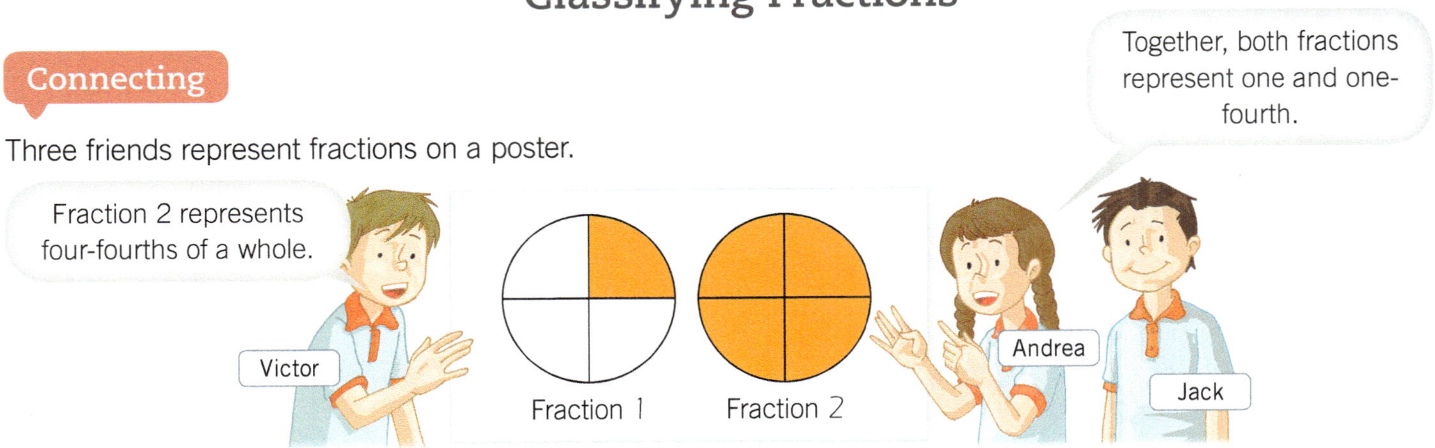

- Mark the correct answer with a ✔.

☐ Victor is wrong. ☐ Andrea and Jack are wrong. ☐ They are all correct.

- The fractions together are written $1 + \frac{1}{4}$ or $1\frac{1}{4}$, which is a mixed fraction.

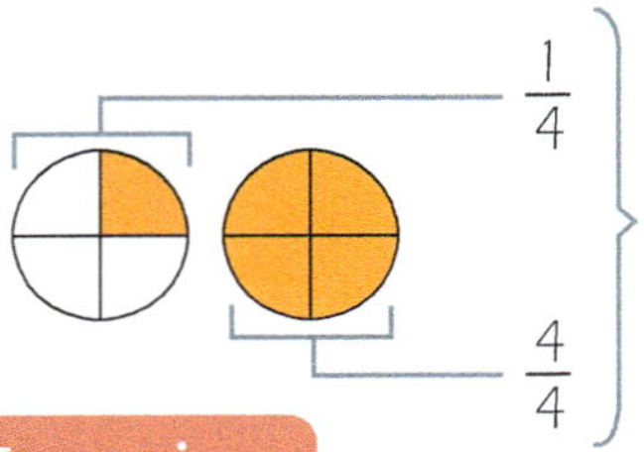

$$1\frac{1}{4} = 1 + \frac{1}{4} = \frac{4}{4} + \frac{1}{4} = \frac{5}{4}$$

Challenge

The population of the whole world is approximately seven billion. Find out the population of your country and calculate what fraction of the Earth's population lives there.

Learning

Fractions can be classified as:

- **Proper**: The numerator is less than the denominator.
- **Whole**: The numerator is equal to the denominator.
- **Improper**: The numerator is greater than the denominator. This type of fraction can be shown as a **mixed** fraction, which has a whole and a remainder.

Examples:

- $\frac{2}{3}$ is a **proper** fraction, since $2 < 3$.
- $\frac{5}{5}$ is a **whole** fraction, since $5 = 5$.
- $\frac{9}{4}$ is an **improper** fraction, since $9 > 4$. To write an improper fraction as a **mixed** fraction you have to divide the numerator by the denominator:

$$9 \div 4 = 2 = 2\frac{1}{4}$$

1 (remainder)

To convert a mixed fraction to an improper fraction you:

$$2\frac{1}{4} = \frac{4 \times 2 + 1}{4} = \frac{8 + 1}{4} = \frac{9}{4}$$

Practicing

1. Classify the fractions. Write **P** for **proper** fractions, **I** for **improper** fractions and **W** for **whole** fractions. Classify

a. $\frac{1}{2}$ ☐ c. $\frac{7}{7}$ ☐ e. $\frac{5}{15}$ ☐ g. $\frac{12}{5}$ ☐

b. $\frac{13}{6}$ ☐ d. $\frac{9}{10}$ ☐ f. $\frac{18}{18}$ ☐ h. $\frac{101}{100}$ ☐

2. Write the mixed and improper fractions that correspond to the representations. Represent

a.

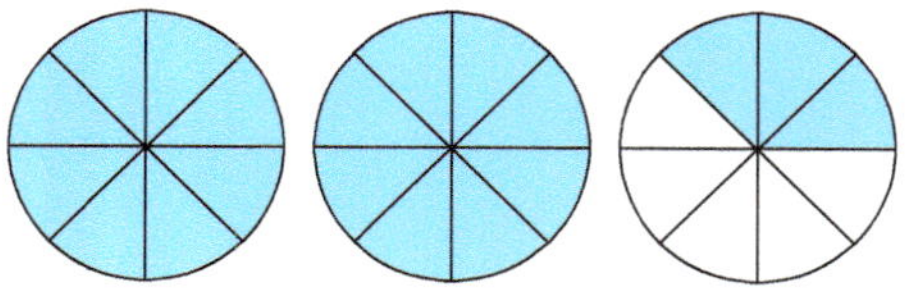

☐ $\frac{☐}{☐}$ = $\frac{☐}{☐}$

b.

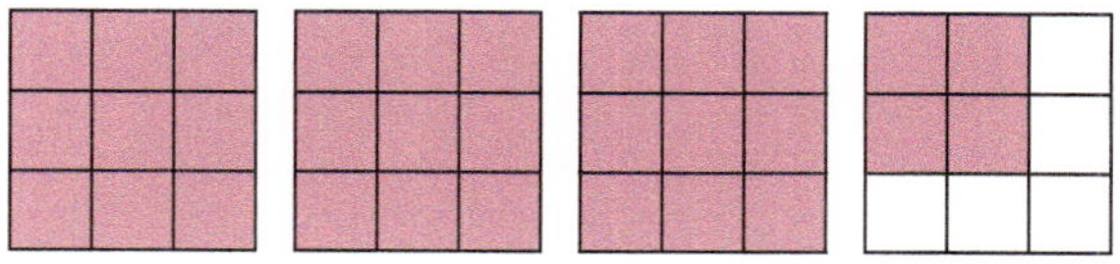

☐ $\frac{☐}{☐}$ = $\frac{☐}{☐}$

3. Write the mixed fractions as improper fractions. Then represent the fractions. Apply

a. $1\frac{1}{6}$ = ☐ ▶

b. $1\frac{3}{5}$ = ☐ ▶

c. $2\frac{1}{4}$ = ☐ ▶

d. $2\frac{1}{3}$ = ☐ ▶

4. Mark the correct answers with a ✔ and the incorrect answers with an ✖. Verify

a. Jerry drank $\frac{8}{3}$ liters of water. Therefore, Jerry drank:

- ☐ Less than one liter of water
- ☐ One liter of water
- ☐ More than one liter of water

b. Margaret ate $\frac{9}{12}$ of a box of candies. Therefore, Margaret ate:

- ☐ Less than one box
- ☐ One box
- ☐ More than one box

Amplifying and Simplifying Fractions

Connecting

Carol and Frank want to know how many blocks they can put away in one minute. Carol put away $\frac{1}{3}$ of the blocks, and Frank put away $\frac{2}{6}$.

- Represent the fraction of the total number of blocks each child put away.

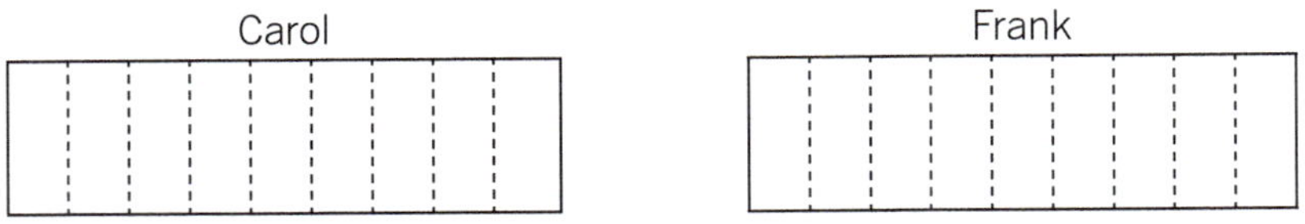

- Who put away the most blocks? ▸ ______________________

- Another child put away $\frac{3}{9}$ of the total number of blocks. How does this relate to the pieces Carol and Frank put away? Look at the representation and explain.

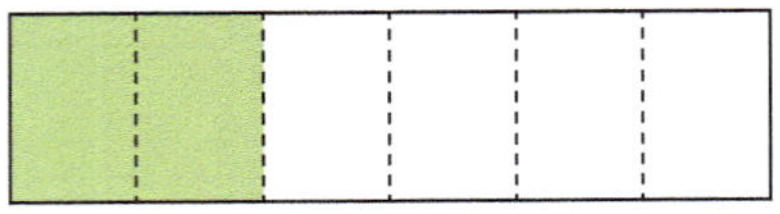

____

____

Learning

To **amplify** (make bigger) a fraction you have to multiply the numerator and denominator by the same number.

Example: To amplify $\frac{2}{5}$ by **3** ▸ $\frac{2}{5} = \frac{2 \times 3}{5 \times 3} = \frac{6}{15}$

Amplification

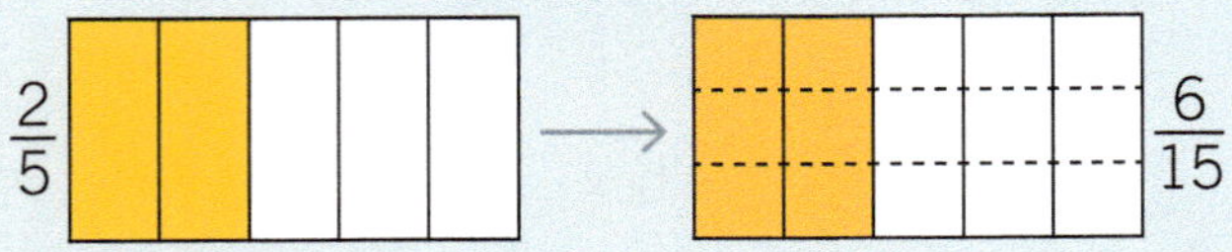

To **reduce** or **simplify** (make smaller) a fraction means to divide the numerator and denominator by the same number – a number greater than 1 and that is a factor of both numbers.

Example: To reduce $\frac{6}{8}$ by **2** ▸ $\frac{6}{8} = \frac{6 \div 2}{8 \div 2} = \frac{3}{4}$

Simplification

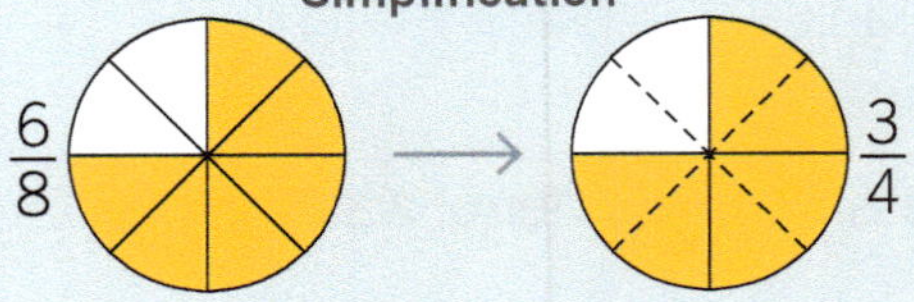

A fraction is in its **simplest form** when it **cannot be simplified** or **reduced** any more. For example, $\frac{2}{5}$ is in its simplest form, since there is no natural number other than 1 that is divisible by 2 and 5.

Practicing

1. Color all the numbers that both the denominator and the numerator are divisible by. Understand

a. $\frac{12}{18}$ ▶ 2 3 4 5 6 7

b. $\frac{15}{75}$ ▶ 2 3 4 5 6 7

2. Write the correct fractions. Apply

a. $\frac{1}{5}$ amplified by 2 ▶

b. $1\frac{3}{9}$ simplified by 3 ▶

c. $\frac{20}{60}$ simplified by 10 ▶

d. $\frac{3}{12}$ amplified by 3 ▶

3. Write the fractions represented. Then write the modified fractions and color the representations. Analyze

a. Amplified by 4

b. Simplified by 3

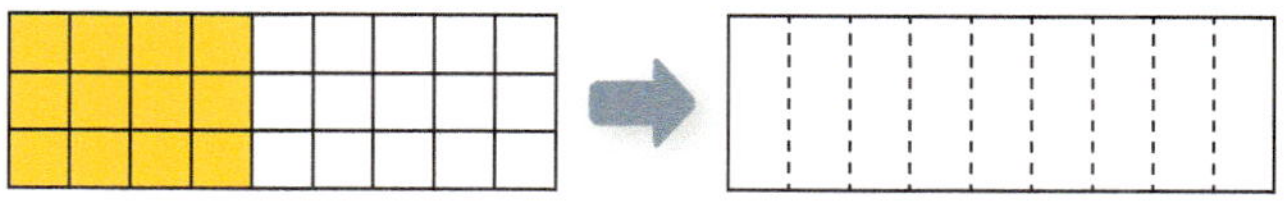

4. Read the problem. Explain who is correct and who is wrong. Analyze

An athlete ran a 400 meter race but stopped running after 200 meters because of a leg injury.

Equivalent Fractions

Connecting

supply bodies with water

You need to keep hydrated when exercising because the body loses water through sweating. The best way to stay hydrated is to drink water. While she was playing basketball, Danielle drank $\frac{1}{4}$ of a water bottle and her friend Caroline drank $\frac{2}{8}$ of the same bottle.

- Which of these numbers can you use to simplify $\frac{2}{8}$?

  2 4 6

- Write the simplified form of $\frac{2}{8}$. ▶ ☐

Remember!

Take a bottle of water with you when you exercise, and stay hydrated.

- What is the total amount of water that Danielle and Caroline drank, as a fraction? ▶ ☐

- If another friend, Claire, drinks $\frac{4}{16}$ of the bottle, does she drink the same amount as Danielle and Caroline? Explain.

____

Learning

Equivalent fractions represent the same part of a whole. You can calculate equivalent fractions by **amplifying** or **simplifying**.

Example: If you **amplify** $\frac{1}{2}$ by 6, you get $\frac{6}{12}$. And, if you **simplify** $\frac{6}{12}$ by 6 you get $\frac{1}{2}$.

- This is represented graphically as:

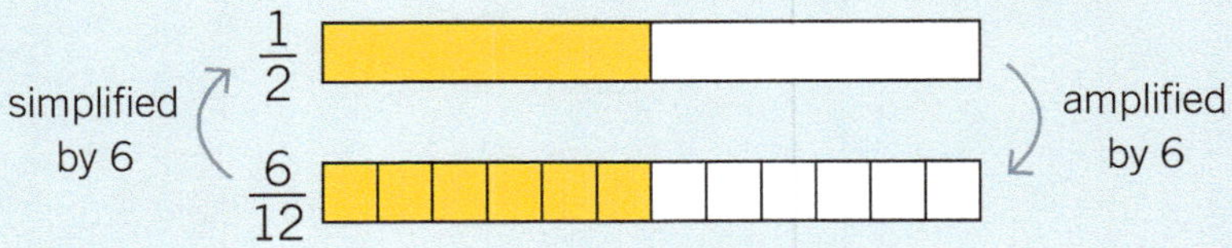

- So, $\frac{1}{2}$ and $\frac{6}{12}$ are **equivalent fractions** that represent the same part of a whole.

Practicing

1. Mark the pairs of fractions that are equivalent with a ✔ and those that are not with an ✖. Understand

a. $\frac{2}{3}$ and $\frac{8}{12}$ ☐ **c.** $\frac{7}{7}$ and $\frac{4}{4}$ ☐ **e.** $\frac{3}{7}$ and $\frac{2}{5}$ ☐

b. $\frac{2}{3}$ and $\frac{10}{30}$ ☐ **d.** $\frac{15}{1}$ and $\frac{1}{15}$ ☐ **f.** $\frac{33}{23}$ and $\frac{3}{2}$ ☐

2. Mark the representations that are not equivalent to $\frac{1}{2}$ with an ✖. Analyze

a.
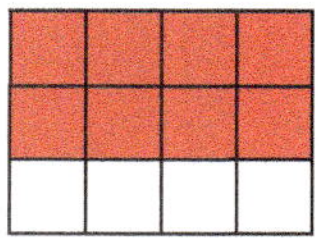
☐

c.

☐

e.
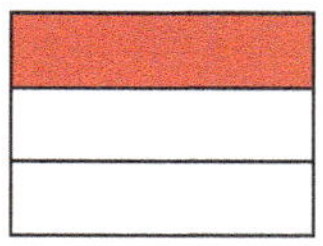
☐

g.
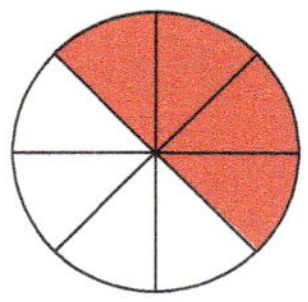
☐

b.
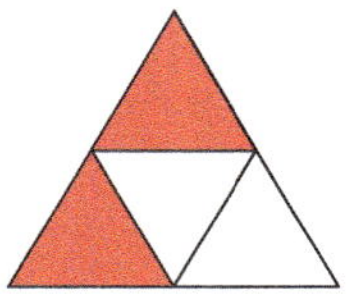
☐

d.
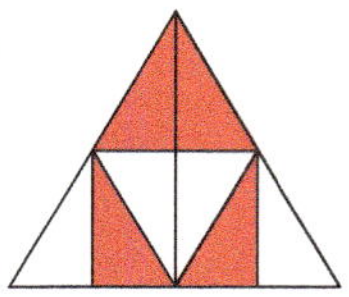
☐

f.
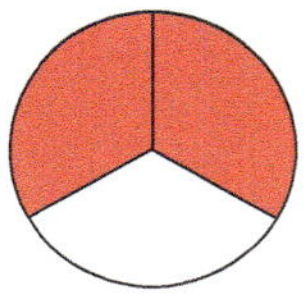
☐

h.
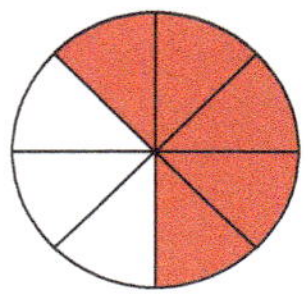
☐

Tip

A useful way to see if a pair of fractions are equivalent is to multiply the numerators and denominators.

If $\frac{a}{b} = \frac{c}{d}$

then $a \times d = c \times b$

Example: $\frac{3}{5} = \frac{15}{25}$

$3 \times 25 = 5 \times 15$

$75 = 75$

3. Circle the equivalent fractions. Analyze

a. Fractions equivalent to $\frac{3}{12}$ ▶ $\frac{1}{3}$ $\frac{2}{4}$ $\frac{1}{4}$ $\frac{2}{8}$

b. Fractions equivalent to $\frac{12}{15}$ ▶ $\frac{2}{5}$ $\frac{4}{5}$ $\frac{8}{10}$ $\frac{16}{40}$

c. Fractions equivalent to $2\frac{1}{3}$ ▶ $\frac{21}{9}$ $\frac{28}{16}$ $2\frac{1}{4}$ $2\frac{5}{15}$

4. Write the fractions represented. Represent

a. Amplify by 2 →

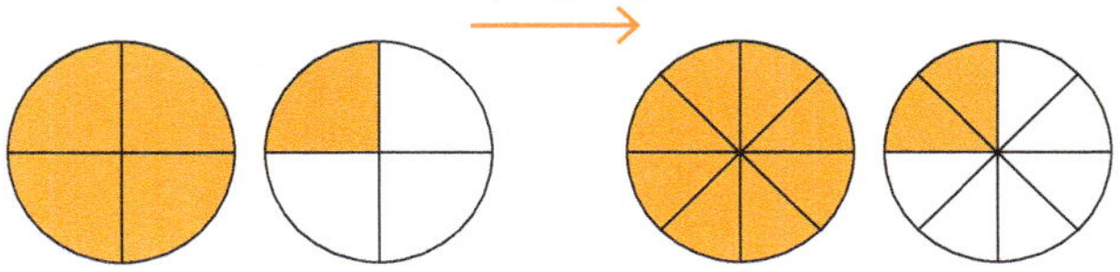

☐ = ☐

b. Simplify by 4 →

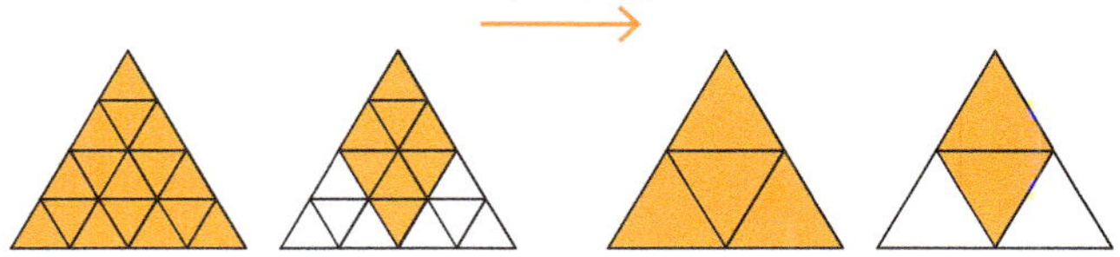

☐ = ☐

Fractions on a Number Line

Connecting

Jamie, Charles and Frank have a paper boat race. Jamie's boat sinks $\frac{3}{5}$ of the way down the stream, Charles' boat sinks $\frac{1}{2}$ of the way down the stream and Frank's boat sinks $\frac{7}{10}$ of the way down the stream.

- Write the fractions that represent the distances traveled by Jamie's and Charles' boats, amplified by 2 and 5, respectively.

  Jamie ▸ ☐ Charles ▸ ☐

- Locate the fractions on the number line. Look at the example.

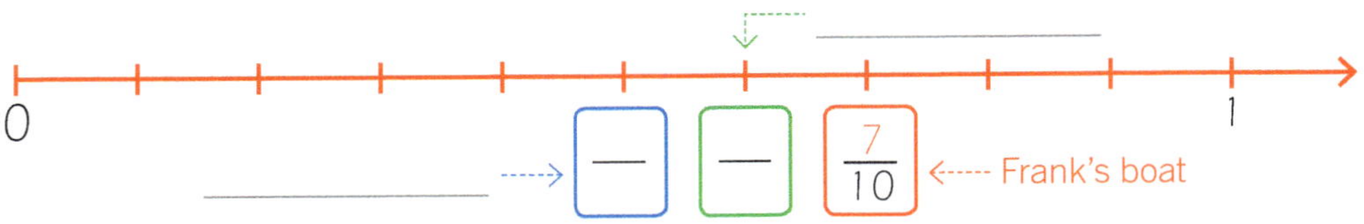

- Why are the fractions $\frac{3}{5}$ and $\frac{1}{2}$ located to the left of $\frac{7}{10}$ on the number line? Explain.

____

Learning

To **locate fractions** on a **number line**, you:

- divide the number line into the same number of equal parts as the denominator, starting with zero.
- begin at zero and count the number of parts in the numerator to locate the position of the fraction.

Proper fractions are always located between 0 and 1 on a number line, and **improper fractions** are located to the right of 1.

Example: $\frac{3}{8}$ on a number line is:

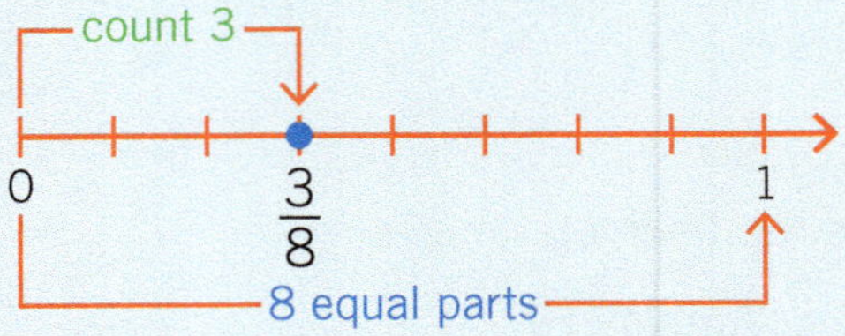

To locate $\frac{5}{3}$ on a number line, you:

$$\frac{5}{3}=\frac{3}{3}+\frac{2}{3}=1+\frac{2}{3}$$

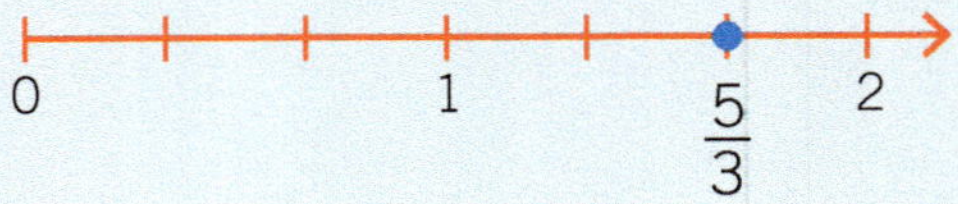

Practicing

1. Write the fractions represented with dots (●) on the number lines. Identify

a. 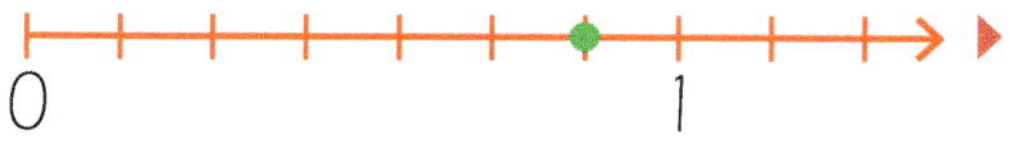

c. 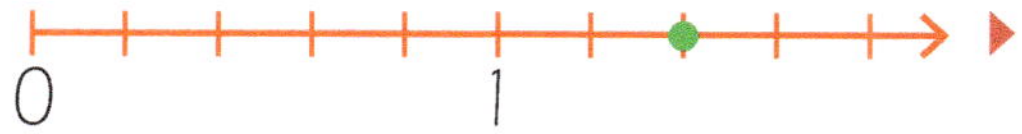

b. 

d. 

2. Locate the fractions on the number lines. Represent

a. $\frac{4}{9}$ 

c. $\frac{7}{8}$ 

b. $1\frac{5}{6}$ 

d. $\frac{7}{4}$ 

3. Locate the fractions on the number line. Analyze

$\frac{3}{6}$ $\frac{6}{4}$ $\frac{7}{12}$ $2\frac{1}{2}$

Tip

To locate fractions with different denominators on a number line, make the denominators equal.

4. Write the fractions represented in the pictures. Then divide the number lines into equal parts and locate the fractions with dots. Represent

a. 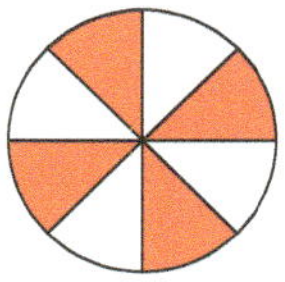 

b. 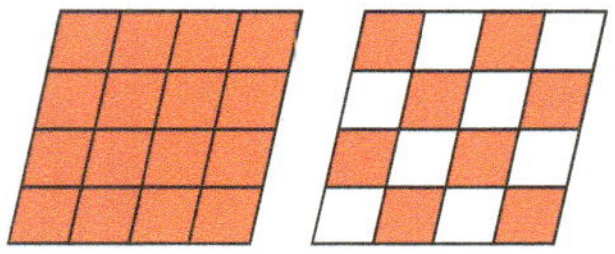 

c. 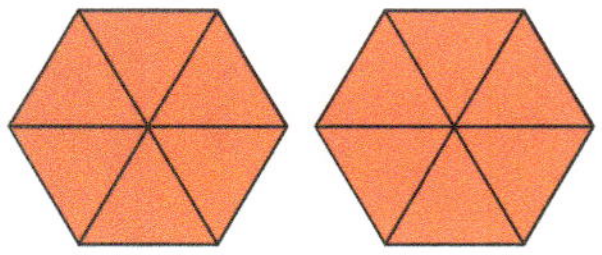 

Comparing and Putting Fractions in Order

Connecting

The discus throw is a track and field event where an athlete throws a heavy, round disk, usually made out of wood and metal. At a competition, an athlete throws $\frac{3}{4}$ of the world record distance in her first throw, and $\frac{8}{10}$ of the world record distance in her second throw.

- Mark the correct answer with a ✔.

  ☐ The athlete was $\frac{1}{4}$ short of the world record distance on her first throw.

  ☐ On her second throw, she was $\frac{1}{10}$ short of the record distance.

- Represent both throws on a number line. Then complete.

0

She threw the discus farther on her ________________ throw.

Learning

If you **compare** two or more fractions with the **same denominator**, the bigger fraction is the one with the larger numerator.

Example: $\frac{7}{4} > \frac{3}{4}$, since $7 > 3$.

To **compare** two or more fractions with **different denominators**, you can **amplify** or **simplify** the fractions so that they have the same denominator, and then compare the numerators.

Example: When comparing $\frac{2}{3}$ with $\frac{3}{4}$, you have to amplify the fractions to represent them with the same denominator.

$$\frac{2}{3} = \frac{2 \times 4}{3 \times 4} = \frac{8}{12} \text{ and } \frac{3}{4} = \frac{3 \times 3}{4 \times 3} = \frac{9}{12}$$

$$\frac{8}{12} < \frac{9}{12} \quad \text{So, } \frac{2}{3} < \frac{3}{4}$$

To put **fractions in order**, use a **number line**.

Example:

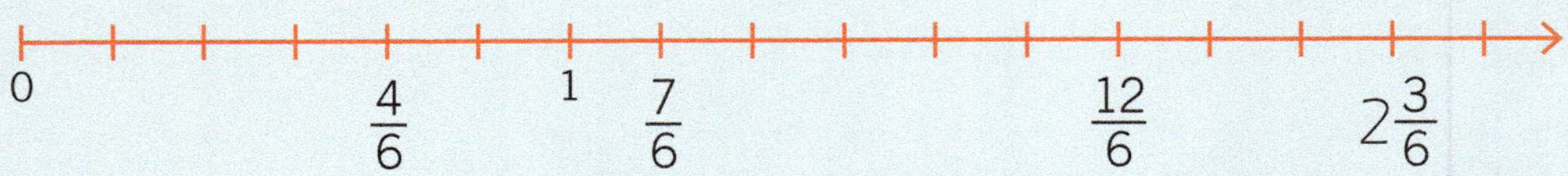

You can put the fractions in increasing order: $\frac{4}{6} < 1 < \frac{7}{6} < \frac{12}{6} < 2\frac{3}{6}$, or decreasing order: $2\frac{3}{6} > \frac{12}{6} > \frac{7}{6} > 1 > \frac{4}{6}$.

Practicing

1. Compare the fractions and mixed numbers. Write >, < or =. Apply

a. $\frac{1}{7}$ ☐ $\frac{2}{7}$ **b.** $\frac{5}{8}$ ☐ $\frac{3}{4}$ **c.** $3\frac{1}{5}$ ☐ $2\frac{1}{5}$

d. $\frac{3}{2}$ ☐ $\frac{4}{9}$ **e.** $\frac{7}{3}$ ☐ $2\frac{2}{6}$ **f.** $\frac{16}{4}$ ☐ $\frac{20}{25}$

Tip

Use the **least common multiple (LCM)** of the denominators of two fractions when you amplify them.

2. Circle the biggest fraction in red and the smallest fraction in blue for each group of fractions. Analyze

$\frac{1}{2}$ $\frac{1}{5}$ $\frac{1}{4}$ $\frac{1}{3}$

$\frac{13}{1}$ $\frac{13}{5}$ $\frac{13}{8}$ $\frac{13}{13}$

$\frac{1}{10{,}000}$ $\frac{1}{10}$ $\frac{1}{100}$ $\frac{1}{1{,}000}$

3. Locate the fractions on the number lines. Analyze

a. $\frac{4}{10}, \frac{3}{5}, \frac{6}{10}$ ▸ 0 ———————→

b. $\frac{2}{4}, 1\frac{1}{8}, \frac{3}{2}$ ▸ 0 ———————→

Quiz Yourself

Annie is buying juice at the supermarket.

Option 1

$\frac{3}{4}$ of a liter for

$1.15

Option 2

1 liter for

$1.5

If Annie wants to buy three liters, which of the two juices is the least expensive? Explain.

Let's Check!

Reading and Writing Fractions

1. Look, read and answer.

points
$\frac{\quad}{2}$

a. Write the fraction that represents the number of students in relation to the number of chairs.

b. Of the total number of cars, what fraction represents the red cars?

Classifying Fractions

2. Circle the fractions in the correct colors according to their types.

points
$\frac{\quad}{9}$

Proper fractions   Improper fractions   Whole fractions

$\frac{1}{2}$ $\frac{7}{5}$ $\frac{88}{8}$ $\frac{99}{100}$ $\frac{342}{80}$ $\frac{5}{27}$ $\frac{32}{2}$ $\frac{12}{12}$ $\frac{24}{1}$

Amplifying and Simplifying Fractions

3. Look at the example. Complete with "amplified" or "simplified." Then write the number the fraction is amplified or simplified by.

points
$\frac{\quad}{6}$

To get $\frac{7}{8}$, the fraction $\frac{14}{16}$ was simplified by 2.

a. To get $\frac{5}{10}$, the fraction $\frac{1}{2}$ was ____________________ by ______.

b. To get $\frac{1}{7}$, the fraction $\frac{7}{49}$ was ____________________ by ______.

c. To get $\frac{216}{36}$, the fraction $\frac{36}{6}$ was ____________________ by ______.

Equivalent Fractions

4. Mark the equivalent fractions with a ✔ and the unequal fractions with an ✖.

points: ___ / 6

a. $\frac{7}{3}$ and $\frac{3}{7}$ ☐

b. $\frac{2}{3}$ and $\frac{20}{30}$ ☐

c. $\frac{4}{9}$ and $\frac{36}{81}$ ☐

d. $\frac{6}{7}$ and $\frac{3}{4}$ ☐

e. $\frac{8}{10}$ and $\frac{4}{5}$ ☐

f. $\frac{15}{35}$ and $\frac{1}{3}$ ☐

Fractions on a Number Line

5. Circle the fractions that are incorrectly located on the number lines.

points: ___ / 3

a.

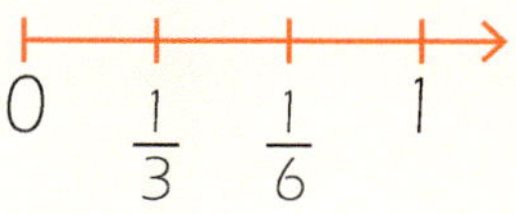

b.

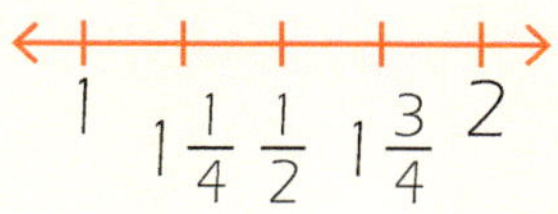

c.

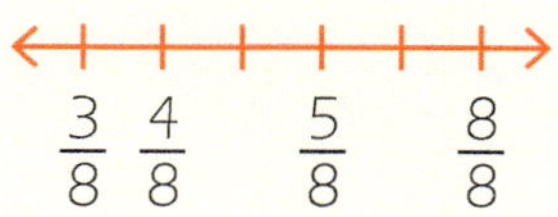

Comparing and Putting Fractions in Order

6. Solve the word problems.

points: ___ / 4

a. In the spring, Ted collected $\frac{3}{4}$ of the strawberries from his field, Mike collected $\frac{3}{6}$ from his field, and Anna collected $\frac{4}{5}$ from her field. Who collected the most and the least strawberries?

b. Aiden wants to paint the gate of his house. There are a few cans of paint in the basement: $\frac{3}{4}$ of a can of blue paint, $\frac{2}{5}$ of brown paint, $\frac{3}{5}$ of yellow paint and $\frac{6}{9}$ of green paint. What color will Aiden paint the gate if he uses the can with the most paint?

Section 2

Operations with Fractions

Addition and Subtraction of Fractions with the Same Denominator

Connecting

Mike walks and runs around the stadium track every day. On Monday, he ran $\frac{1}{4}$ of the track and walked the rest of the way, on Tuesday he ran $\frac{2}{4}$ of the track and on Wednesday he ran $\frac{1}{4}$ of the track.

- Represent the distances Mike ran each day.

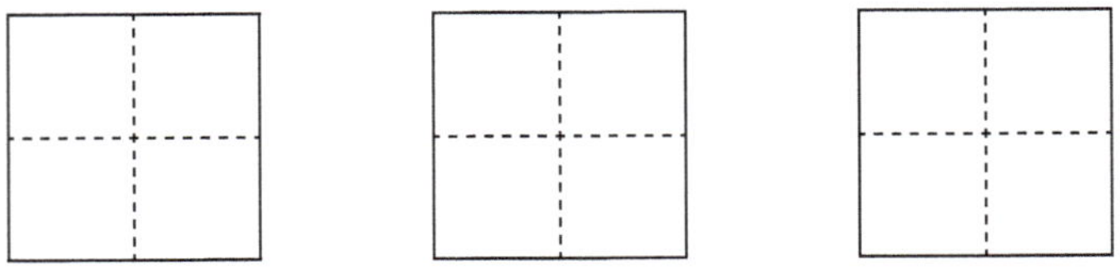

Monday Tuesday Wednesday

- On which day did he run the farthest? ▸ ______________________
- Mark the correct statement with a ✔.

☐ He ran $\frac{3}{4}$ of the track over the three days. ☐ He ran the full track over the three days.

Challenge

Create a word problem with your classmates about your favorite sport. Then go to the playground and act it out to check your answers.

Learning

To solve **addition and subtraction operations with an equal denominator**, you add or subtract the numerators and keep the denominator the same. Then you can simplify the answer to its lowest terms.

Example:

$$\frac{2}{8}+\frac{4}{8}=\frac{2+4}{8}=\frac{6}{8}=\frac{6\div 2}{8\div 2}=\frac{3}{4}$$

Graphic representation:

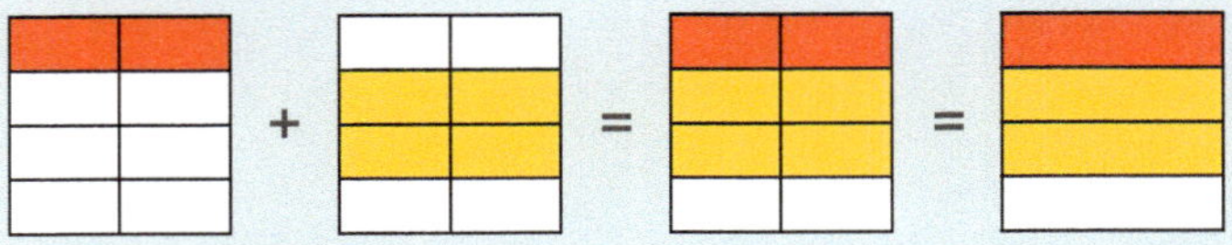

$\frac{2}{8}$ + $\frac{4}{8}$ = $\frac{6}{8}$ = $\frac{3}{4}$

Example:

$$\frac{5}{6}-\frac{1}{6}=\frac{5-1}{6}=\frac{4}{6}=\frac{4\div 2}{6\div 2}=\frac{2}{3}$$

Graphic representation:

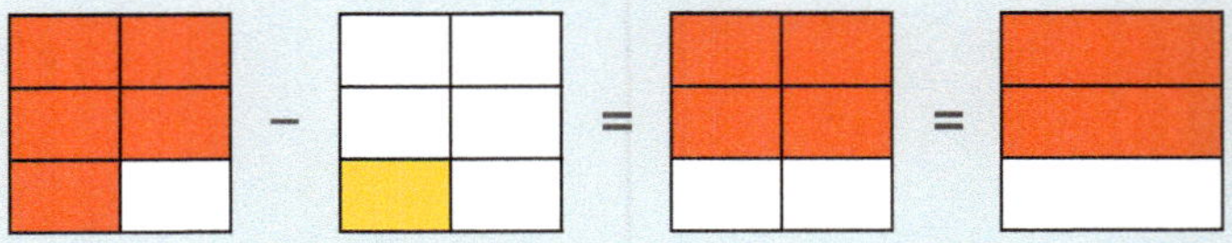

$\frac{5}{6}$ − $\frac{1}{6}$ = $\frac{4}{6}$ = $\frac{2}{3}$

Practicing

1. Look at the example. Write the fractions that correspond to the colors in the pictures. Apply

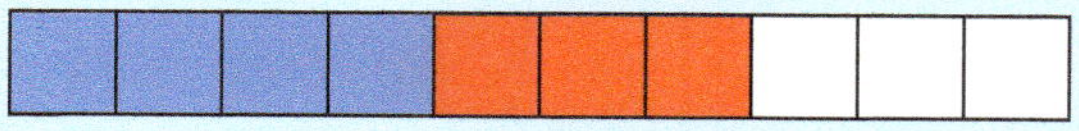

blue ▸ $\frac{4}{10}$

orange ▸ $\frac{3}{10}$

addition

$\frac{4}{10} + \frac{3}{10} = \frac{7}{10}$

a.

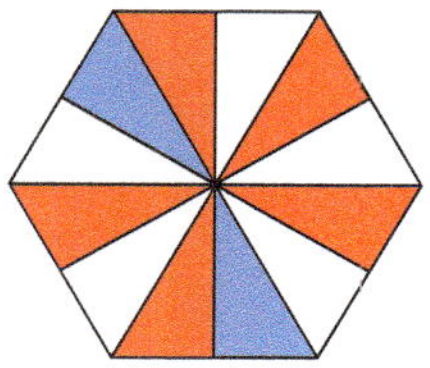

blue ▸ ☐

orange ▸ ☐

addition

☐ + ☐ = ☐

b.

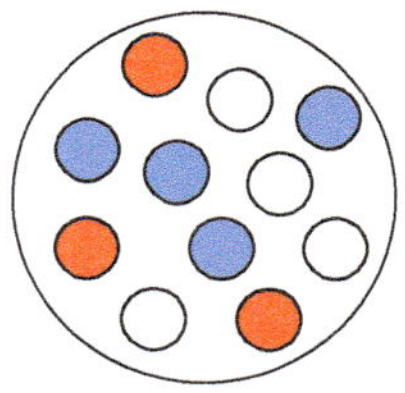

orange ▸ ☐

blue ▸ ☐

subtraction

☐ − ☐ = ☐

2. Complete the operations with the missing fractions. Analyze

a. $\frac{1}{5} + \square = \frac{6}{5}$

b. $\square + \frac{7}{8} = \frac{9}{8}$

c. $\frac{7}{15} + \frac{8}{15} = \square$

d. $\frac{4}{6} - \square = \frac{1}{6}$

e. $\square - \frac{9}{12} = \frac{8}{12}$

f. $\frac{7}{100} - \frac{5}{100} = \square$

3. Solve the word problems. Apply

a. Logan bought four-fifths of a kilogram of cherries and strawberries. If the cherries weigh one-fifth of a kilogram, what fraction of a kilogram do the strawberries weigh?

b. Andrea drank two-fourths of a liter of milk. If her brother drank one-fourth of a liter more than her, how much milk did her brother drink?

Exam Strategies

Multiple Choice Questions

1. Beatrice had \$32,000 in her savings account, and then she withdrew $\frac{2}{5}$ of her money. How much money is left in her savings account?

   A. \$6,400

   B. \$12,800

   C. \$19,200

   D. \$44,800

Analyzing the Answers

A. $\frac{1}{5}$ of Beatrice's savings are calculated. This means you still need to calculate $\frac{2}{5}$ and subtract it from the total.

B. The money corresponding to the withdrawal is calculated:

$$\frac{32{,}000 \times 2}{5} = 12{,}800$$

The final step is missing, in which the money withdrawn is **subtracted** from the total amount.

C. In this case, $\frac{2}{5}$ of the money is calculated and then subtracted from the total amount of money in the savings account.

32,000	⟶	Money in savings account
− 12,800	⟶	Money withdrawn
19,200	⟶	Money left after the withdrawal

D. In this option, the amount withdrawn is calculated, but it is incorrectly added to the initial amount of money in the account.

▸ Therefore, the correct answer is **C**.

1. A — B — C — D

What Did You Learn?

Final Evaluation

1. Color the fractions according to their types.

Whole fraction — Improper fraction — Proper fraction

points ___ / 5

$\frac{9}{10}$ $\frac{2}{5}$ $\frac{4}{4}$ $\frac{11}{10}$ $\frac{15}{12}$

$\frac{10}{6}$ $\frac{12}{3}$ $\frac{4}{2}$ $\frac{7}{8}$ $\frac{13}{13}$

2. Represent the fractions on the number line and then answer.

points ___ / 8

$\frac{1}{5}$, $1\frac{1}{4}$, $2\frac{4}{5}$, $\frac{3}{10}$, $1\frac{1}{3}$

a. Which is the biggest fraction? ▸ ______________________

b. Which is the smallest fraction? ▸ ______________________

c. Write the fractions in decreasing order. ▸ ______________________

3. Color $\frac{1}{6}$ of the cirlces blue, $\frac{3}{8}$ red, $\frac{4}{9}$ green and the rest yellow.

points ___ / 6

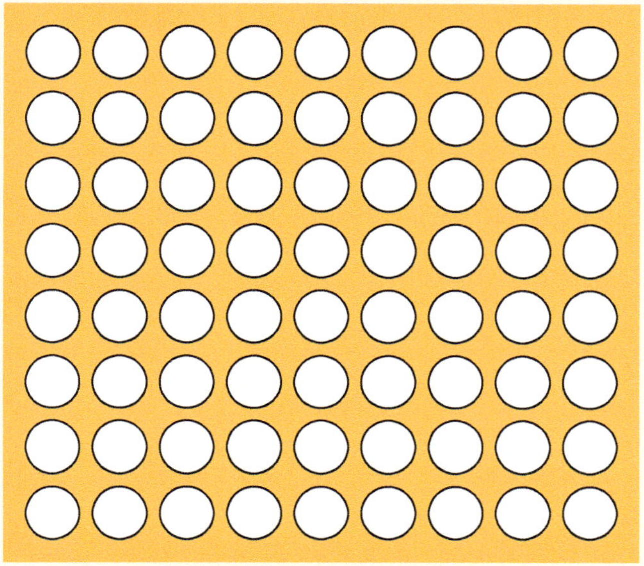

4. Write the fractions that represent the parts in green. (points: /4)

a.

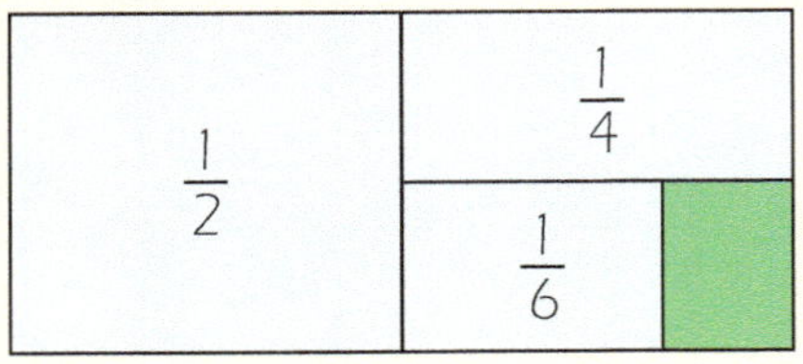

b.

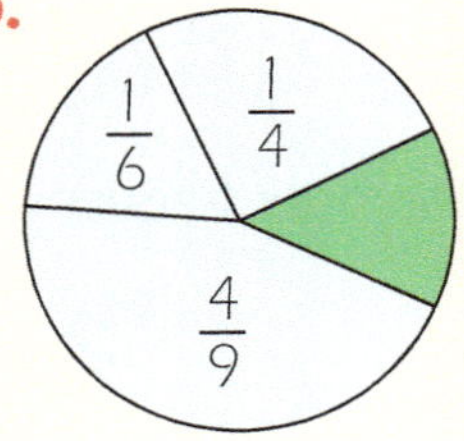

5. Write the mixed and improper fractions of the representations. (points: /6)

a. 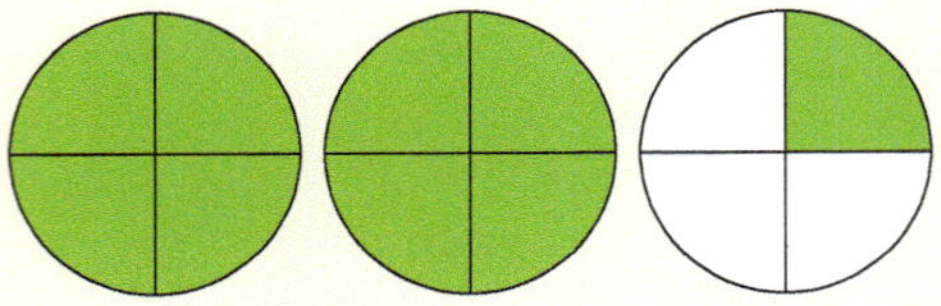

b. 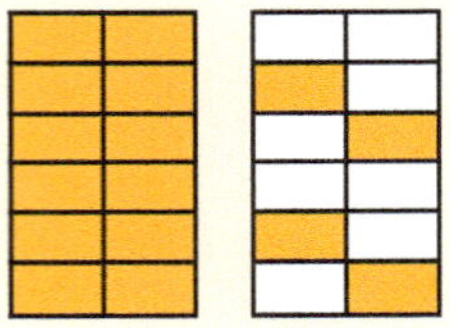

c. 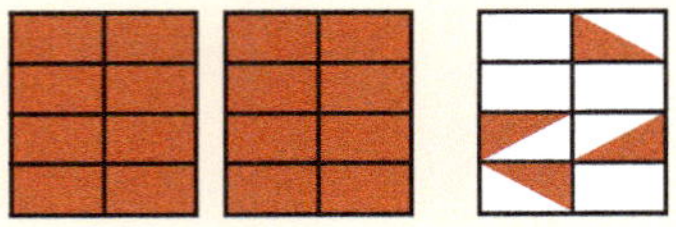

6. Write the mixed fractions for the improper fractions. (points: /6)

a. $\frac{5}{4}$ ▸

c. $\frac{12}{7}$ ▸

e. $\frac{100}{11}$ ▸

b. $\frac{21}{5}$ ▸

d. $\frac{25}{2}$ ▸

f. $\frac{215}{71}$ ▸

Mark the correct answer with an ✕.

points

4

7. Which image does not represent $\frac{1}{4}$?

A. 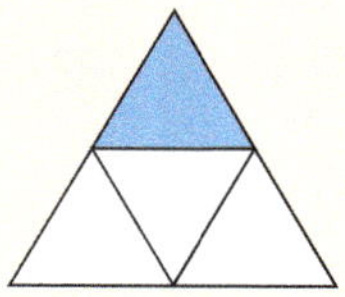

B. 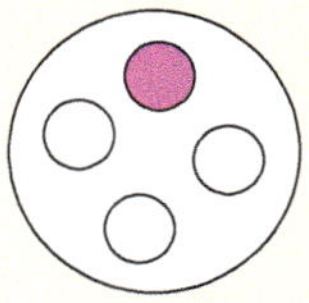

C. 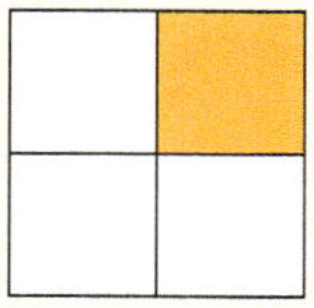

D. 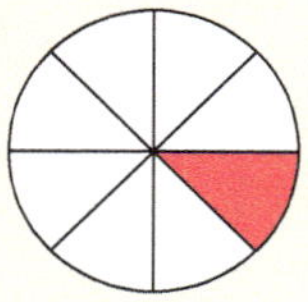

8. What does $\frac{2}{5}$ amplified by 7 equal?

A. $\frac{14}{5}$

B. $\frac{2}{35}$

C. $\frac{14}{35}$

D. $\frac{9}{12}$

9. Which statement is false?

A. Improper fractions can be written as mixed numbers.

B. Improper fractions are always smaller than proper fractions.

C. Proper fractions have a numerator that is smaller than the denominator.

D. Proper fractions can be located between 0 and 1.

10. Which fraction is located between 3 and 4?

A. $\frac{15}{4}$

B. $\frac{4}{3}$

C. $\frac{10}{4}$

D. $\frac{20}{4}$

points

/ 3

11. If you add the colored part of Figure 2 to Figure 1, what fraction does it represent?

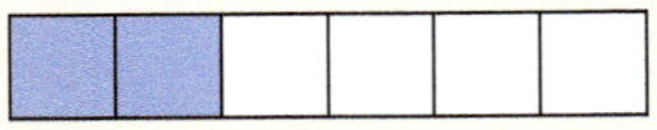

Figure 1

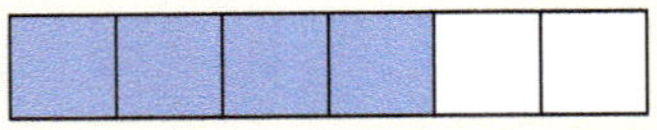

Figure 2

A. $\frac{2}{6}$

B. $\frac{3}{6}$

C. $\frac{6}{6}$

D. $1\frac{2}{6}$

12. Wes gave $\frac{2}{6}$ of his marbles away. He then lost $\frac{1}{4}$ of the marbles he had left. What fraction of the marbles he started with does he have now?

A. $\frac{1}{6}$

B. $\frac{5}{12}$

C. $\frac{7}{12}$

D. $\frac{3}{6}$

13. A bucket of paint is $\frac{3}{4}$ liters full. Chester used $\frac{1}{2}$ a liter to paint a wall and painted the door with the rest. When he was done, he was left with $\frac{1}{8}$ of a liter of paint. How much paint did he use to paint the door?

A. $\frac{2}{8}$

B. $\frac{3}{4}$

C. $\frac{1}{8}$

D. $\frac{3}{8}$

points
/ 4

14. Which denominator goes in the boxes to complete the equality?

$$\frac{7}{\square} + \frac{8}{\square} = \frac{15}{4}$$

A. 2

B. 4

C. 7

D. 8

15. Which is the representation of four-ninths?

A. 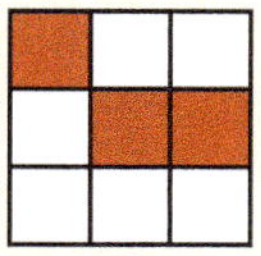

B. 

C. 

D. 

16. Which fraction is in its simplest form?

A. $\frac{2}{4}$

B. $\frac{5}{8}$

C. $\frac{9}{3}$

D. $\frac{7}{42}$

17. Which number line represents $\frac{4}{10}$?

A. 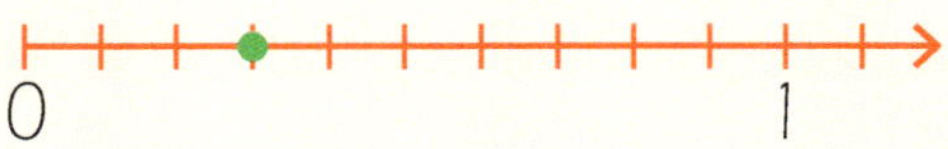

B. 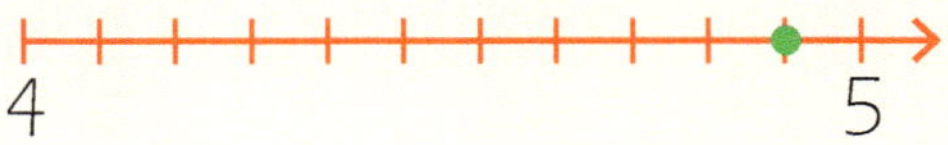

C. 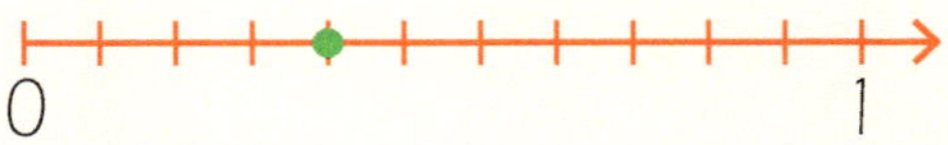

D. 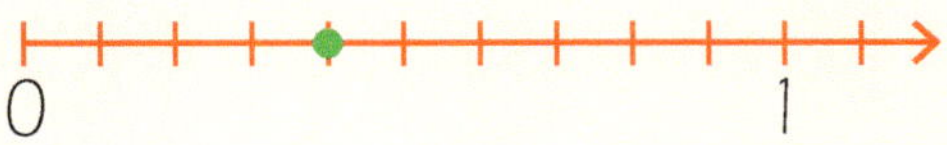

Find Test 2 Study Page

Unit 3

Multiplication and Division

One of the most recycled products in the world is aluminum. Some objects made of aluminum are:

- cans
- container lids
- aluminum foil
- cars

1. Cans are cleaned and crushed to be recycled.

2. The aluminum is melted down and molded into 25,000 kg ingots.

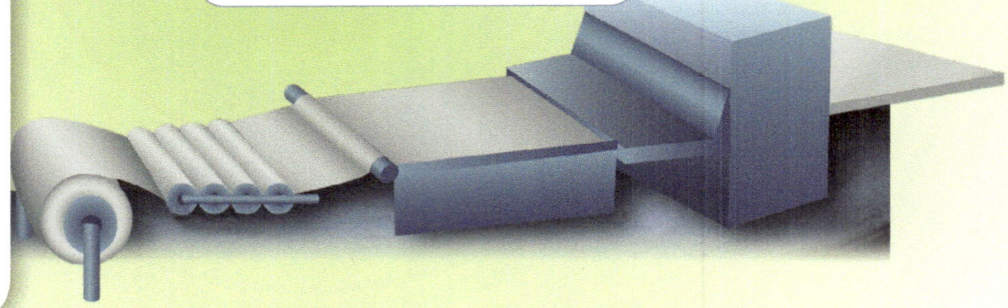

3. The aluminum ingots are melted again and pressed into thin sheets.

4. The aluminum sheets are used to make cans and other products. One kilogram of aluminum can be used to make approximately 67 cans.

Key Words

double

halve

distributive property

strategy

factor

In this unit you will learn to:

- apply mental and written math strategies to solve division and multiplication operations.
- understand the relationship between multiplication and division.
- estimate products and quotients.
- solve multiplication and division word problems.
- use different strategies to solve operations.

What Do You Know?

Use the information on the previous page to answer.

1. Circle the operation that answers how many cans are needed to obtain 500 kilograms of aluminum.

- 500 + 67
- 500 × 67
- 500 – 67
- 500 ÷ 67

2. Complete the table with the number of cans that must be recycled per kilogram of aluminum.

Number of Cans per Kilogram of Aluminum							
Kilograms	1	2	5	10	20	100	1,000
Number of Cans	67						

3. Circle the operation that answers how many ingots 100,000 kilograms of aluminum will produce.

- 100 × 25
- 100 + 25
- 100 ÷ 25
- 100 – 25

4. How many ingots will 200,000 kilograms of aluminum produce? Check the correct answer.

☐ Two ingots ☐ Four ingots ☐ Six ingots ☐ Eight ingots

5. If 201 cans are used to make a sheet of aluminum, how many kilograms are used?

Mental and Written Strategies

Turning Two Factors into Four Factors

Connecting

I have to calculate **45 × 8**, but I'm not sure how... they are big numbers.

You can break the numbers down to make the calculation easier and calculate it as **3 × 15** times **2 × 4**.

45 × 8
3 × 15 × 2 × 4
3 × 30 × 4
90 × 4
360

Remember!

The terms in a multiplication operation are the **factors** and the **product**.

5 × 4 = 20

5, 4 ↓ factors; 20 ↓ product

- How did the boy decompose 8?

  ☐ × ☐ = ☐

- How did the boy decompose 45?

  ☐ × ☐ = ☐

- Is the product of 45 × 8 the same as the product of 3 × 15 × 2 × 4? Explain.

  (Yes) (No), because ______________________________

  ____

- Can 45 be decomposed in another way? (Yes) (No) How? ▸ ☐ × ☐

- Will the product of 45 × 8 be the same if you represent 45 as you decomposed it above? Explain.

  ☐ × ☐ × 2 × 4 = ☐

  (Yes) (No), because ______________________________

  ____

Learning

The strategy of **turning two factors into four factors** can help you solve multiplication operations by **decomposing** each factor.

Examples:

18×25

$2 \times 9 \times 5 \times 5$

$2 \times 45 \times 5$

$90 \times 5 = 450$

So, 18×25 is 450.

250×8

$25 \times 10 \times 2 \times 4$

$25 \times 20 \times 4$

$500 \times 4 = 2{,}000$

So, 250×8 is 2,000.

Practicing

1. Complete the operations using the strategy of turning two factors into four. Apply

a. 30×14

☐ × ☐ × ☐ × ☐

☐ × ☐ × ☐

☐ × ☐ = ☐

b. 28×12

☐ × ☐ × ☐ × ☐

☐ × ☐ × ☐

☐ × ☐ = ☐

2. Solve the operations using the strategy of turning two factors into four. Apply

a. $21 \times 8 =$ ☐ **b.** $24 \times 6 =$ ☐ **c.** $18 \times 30 =$ ☐ **d.** $35 \times 20 =$ ☐

3. Explain the strategy of turning two factors into four in your own words. Analyze

____

____

____

Doubling and Halving

Connecting

To find the product of 5 × 8, I calculated 10 × 4.

Why did you do that?

Look what happens when you represent both of them.

5 × 8 is the same as 5 groups of 8.

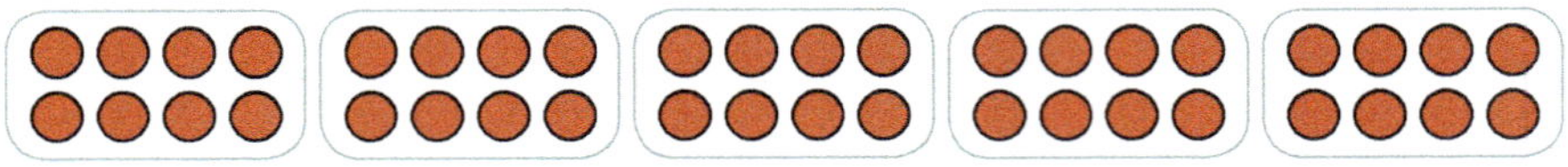

10 × 4 is the same as 10 groups of 4.

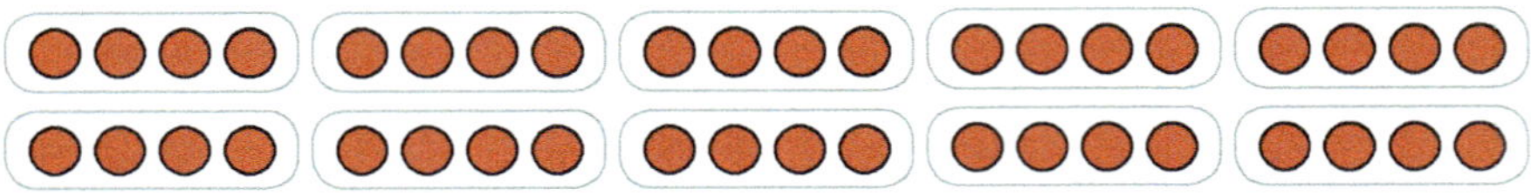

Wow! Now there are double the groups there were before, but with half the elements. And multiplying by ten is easy!

- What is the product of both multiplication operations?

5 × 8 = ☐   10 × 4 = ☐

- How does the first factor in 5 × 8 change in comparison to the first factor in 10 × 4?

____

- How does the second factor in 5 × 8 change in comparison to the second factor in 10 × 4?

____

- Explain the doubling and halving strategy in your own words.

____

____

Learning

The strategy of **doubling and halving** consists of multiplying one factor by two and dividing the other factor by two.

Example: To calculate the product of 8 × 4 you:

1st factor	2nd factor
8 doubled is 16	4 halved is 2
multiply by 2	divide by 2

8 × 4 = 32

16 × 2 = 32

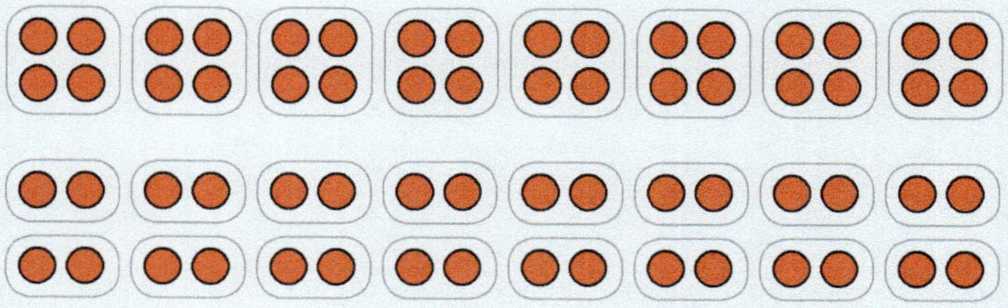

Practicing

1. Calculate the product of each multiplication operation using the doubling and halving strategy. Apply

a. 22 × 2

☐ × ☐ = ☐

b. 16 × 4

☐ × ☐ = ☐

c. 40 × 6

☐ × ☐ = ☐

d. 8 × 150

☐ × ☐ = ☐

Try solving the operations by halving the first factor and doubling the second. Are the results the same?

2. Solve the operations using the doubling and halving strategy. Apply

a. 21 × 4 = ☐

b. 35 × 6 = ☐

c. 4 × 70 = ☐

3. Would this strategy be useful when multiplying 35 × 5? What characteristic must the second factor have? Explain. Analyze

____

____

The Double of Doubles

Connecting

Julie

I have to calculate 25 × 8. To me, that means the same as calculating 50 × 4.

Hmmm. To me, 25 × 8 is the same as 50 × 4, which is also the same as 100 × 2.

Abigail

- What strategy did Julie use? Explain.

____

____

- What do the strategies used by each girl have in common?

____

____

Did You Know...?

Twins are sometimes called doubles of each other. Why do you think that is? What about fraternal twins? Research the difference between identical and fraternal twins.

Learning

The multiplication strategy of **doubling doubles** consists of multiplying one factor by two and dividing the other factor by two, two **consecutive** times.

consecutive: one after the other

1st factor	2nd factor	
15	**8**	15 × 8 = 120
double of 15 is	half of 8 is	
30	**4**	30 × 4 = 120
double of 30 is	half of 4 is	
60	**2**	60 × 2 = 120

60: The double of doubles

Practicing

1. Complete the operations using the double of doubles strategy. Apply

a. 25×12

☐ × ☐

☐ × ☐ = ☐

b. 20×20

☐ × ☐

☐ × ☐ = ☐

c. 15×24

☐ × ☐

☐ × ☐ = ☐

d. 40×22

☐ × ☐

☐ × ☐ = ☐

Try solving the operations by halving the first factor and doubling the second factor two consecutive times. Are the products different?

Quiz Yourself

Read and answer.

To find the product of **30** × **16** I did this:

30 × **16**

10 × **3** × **2** × **8**

10 × **3** × **2** × **2** × **4**

- What is the name of the strategy the boy used?

____

____

- Find the product of 30 × 16 by breaking down the factors using the strategy that helps you calculate the answer the fastest.

Multiplication with 0 and 1

Connecting

- Represent the multiplication operations using ●.

0 × 15

1 × 15

0 times 15 is ☐.

1 times 15 is ☐.

- How can you represent 1 × 7,200? Explain.

____

____

- How can you represent 0 × 7,200? Explain.

____

____

- Based on your calculations, are Jim's answers correct?

(Yes) (No), because ______________________________

____

Learning

When **multiplying 1** by any other number, the product is always the **same** number. When **multiplying by 0** the product is always **0**.

Example:

Multiplying by 1

3,220 × 1 = 3,220

1 × 2,500 = 2,500

Multiplying by 0

5,641 × 0 = 0

0 × 8,320 = 0

Practicing

1. Solve the multiplication operations. Apply

a. 3,256 × 0 = ☐

b. 1 × 52,645 = ☐

c. 0 × 95,423 = ☐

d. 15,365 × 1 = ☐

2. Complete the multiplication operations. Understand

a. 3,569 × ☐ = 0

b. 1 × ☐ = 2,350

c. ☐ × 1 = 98,654

d. ☐ × 18,500 = 0

Fun Fact!

Ancient civilizations such as the Egyptians, the Greeks and the Maya used the concept of zero in their numeral systems.

3. Represent the operations and solve them. Analyze

What is the product of 0 × 1 and 1 × 0?

10 × 1

10 times 1 is ☐.

10 × 0

10 times 0 is ☐.

Multiplication Strategies

Connecting

A class of 5th graders are collecting cardboard for their school. They know that the school can sell the cardboard for \$9 per kilogram. If the students collect 221 kilograms of cardboard, how much will the school make?

221×9
$(200 + 20 + 1) \times 9$
$(200 \times 9) + (20 \times 9) + (1 \times 9)$
$1,800 + 180 + 9$
$= 1,989$

The school will make \$1,989.

$$
\begin{array}{r}
221 \\
\times \quad 9 \\
\hline
9 \\
180 \\
+\ 1,800 \\
\hline
1,989
\end{array}
$$

The school will make \$1,989.

- How did the boy calculate the money the school will make? Explain his strategy.

____

____

- How did the girl calculate the money the school will make? Explain her strategy.

____

____

- What is the difference between the two strategies? Explain.

____

____

- Which strategy would you use to calculate 342 × 7? Why?

____

____

Learning

You can use different strategies to solve multiplication operations.

Decomposing: One of the factors is decomposed according to its place values, and each addend in the operation is multiplied by the remaining factor.

243×2

$(200 + 40 + 3) \times 2$

$(200 \times 2) + (40 \times 2) + (3 \times 2)$

$400 + 80 + 6 = 486$

Addition in column: The place value of each number in the first factor is multiplied by the second factor.

$$\begin{array}{r} 243 \\ \times\ \ 2 \\ \hline 6 \\ 80 \\ +400 \\ \hline 486 \end{array}$$

Practicing

1. Solve the multiplication operations using both strategies. Apply

a. Decomposing

413×6

(______ + ______ + ______) × ______

(______ × ______) + (______ × ______) + (______ × ______)

______ + ______ + ______ = ______

Addition in column

$$\begin{array}{r} 413 \\ \times\ \ 6 \\ \hline \square \\ \square \\ +\ \square \\ \hline \square \end{array}$$

b. Decomposing

264×3

(______ + ______ + ______) × ______

(______ × ______) + (______ × ______) + (______ × ______)

______ + ______ + ______ = ______

Addition in column

$$\begin{array}{r} 264 \\ \times\ \ 3 \\ \hline \square \\ \square \\ +\ \square \\ \hline \square \end{array}$$

Applying the Distributive Property Using Addition

Connecting

Three 5th grade classes are going to share sandwiches at their end-of-semester party. If each class brings 24 ham sandwiches and 12 cheese sandwiches, how many sandwiches will there be in total? Peter and Lauren calculated the total number in different ways.

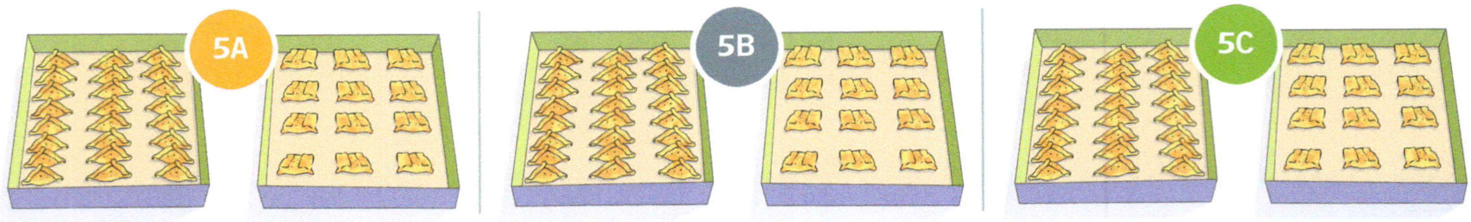

Peter

The three classes brought 24 ham sandwiches and 12 cheese sandwiches.

$(3 \times 24) + (3 \times 12)$

$72 + 36$

$= 108$

In all, there were 108 sandwiches to share.

Lauren

There are three classes, and each of them brought 24 ham sandwiches and 12 cheese sandwiches.

$3 \times (24 + 12)$

3×36

$= 108$

In all, there were 108 sandwiches to share.

- What operations did each student solve? Write them in the order they did them.

Peter

▸ ______________________

____

____

Lauren

▸ ______________________

____

____

- If Peter and Lauren used different strategies, why did they get the same answer? Explain.

____

____

Learning

The **distributive property in multiplication** allows one factor to stay the same while the other is represented as an **addition operation**. This strategy can help you calculate multiplication operations.

$$5 \times (230 + 450)$$

factor 1 ← 5 | (230 + 450) → factor 2

Using this strategy will give you the same results if:

First, you solve the addition operation, and then you multiply the factors.

$5 \times (230 + 450)$
5×680
$= 3{,}400$

First, you multiply each addend with the first factor and, then you add the results.

$(5 \times 230) + (5 \times 450)$
$1{,}150 + 2{,}250$
$= 3{,}400$

Practicing

1. Circle the factor in and the factor expressed as an addition operation in . Identify

 a. $2 \times (354 + 368)$ b. $(589 + 197) \times 6$

2. Complete the operations using the distributive property. Understand

 a. $2 \times (200 + 100) = (2 \times$ ______ $) + (2 \times$ ______ $)$

 b. $(350 + 189) \times$ ______ $= (350 \times 3) + ($ ______ $\times 3)$

 c. $(652 \times 4) + ($ ______ $\times 4) = (652 + 98) \times$ ______

Remember!

Parentheses allow us to organize operations. When there are parentheses, you should always solve the operation inside them first.

Fun Fact!

The origin of the "sandwich" dates back to 1762 when John Montagu, the 4th Earl of Sandwich, ordered for meat to be served between two slices of bread because he wanted something easy and quick to eat. Soon after that, people started ordering "the same as Sandwich," and that is how the sandwich became popular.

3. Solve the operations using the distributive property. Apply

a. 4 × (125 + 700) = (______ × ______) + (______ × ______)

4 × ______ = ______ + ______

______ = ______

b. (295 × 5) + (590 × 5) = (______ + ______) × ______

______ + ______ = ______ × ______

______ = ______

Word Focus

To distribute means to spread or divide something. How does the idea relate to the strategy?

4. Read the word problem and solve it. Analyze

Tanya and Simon are organizing a healthy snack for eight classes. Each class will bring apples and oranges. They have calculated the number of apples and oranges in different ways:

Tanya

Each of the eight classes has collected 12 apples and 18 oranges.

8 × (12 + 18)

Simon

Each of the eight classes collected 12 apples and each of the eight classes collected 18 oranges.

(8 × 12) + (8 × 18)

Did Tanya and Simon get the same results? Calculate and explain.

Tanya

Simon

Yes No , because ______________________________

____

5. Use the information below to write two versions of the same word problem. Interpret

Information: There are three groups of girls and boys.
There are 14 girls and 16 boys in each group.

Sophie

$3 \times (14 + 16)$

Danny

$(3 \times 14) + (3 \times 16)$

Quiz Yourself

Read the word problem and answer.

A shopping mall has four stories. On each story there are twelve clothing stores, four technology stores and three toy stores. How many stores are there all together?

The problem can be solved with:
$(4 \times 12) + (4 \times 4) + (4 \times 3)$

It can also be solved with:
$4 \times (12 + 4 + 3)$

- Is the girl using the distributive property to solve the word problem? Explain.

Yes No , because ____________________

Let's Check!

Mental and Written Strategies

1. Solve the multiplication operations using different strategies.

points
/ 4

a. Turning two factors into four

36×25

☐ × ☐ × ☐ × ☐

☐ × ☐ × ☐

☐ × ☐

= ☐

b. Doubling and halving

25×20

☐ × ☐

= ☐

c. Turning two factors into four

49×21

☐ × ☐ × ☐ × ☐

☐ × ☐ × ☐

☐ × ☐

= ☐

d. The double of doubles

15×28

☐ × ☐

☐ × ☐ = ☐

Multiplication with 0 and 1

2. Mark the strategy you would use for each problem with a ✔.

points
/ 2

a. Five artists are invited to an art exhibition. Each of them will display three paintings and one sculpture. How many sculptures will be displayed?

- ☐ multiplying by 0
- ☐ multiplying by 1

b. A fruit stand sells apples for $8 a kilogram, bananas for $6 a kilogram and oranges for $5 a kilogram. At the end of the day, they have sold 12 kilograms of apples, 18 kilograms of bananas and no oranges. How much did they make from selling oranges?

- ☐ multiplying by 0
- ☐ multiplying by 1

Multiplication Strategies

3. Solve the operation using both strategies.

points ___ / 2

Decomposing

564 × 6

(_____ + _____ + _____) × _____

(_____ × _____) + (_____ × _____) + (_____ × _____)

_____ + _____ + _____ = _____

Addition in column

$$\begin{array}{r} 564 \\ \times \quad 6 \\ \hline \square \\ \square \\ + \ \square \\ \hline \square \end{array}$$

Applying the Distributive Property using Addition

4. Solve the word problem in two different ways using the distributive property.

points ___ / 2

Marcy wants to make some necklaces. If each necklace has 18 red beads and 12 green beads, how many beads does she need to make nine necklaces?

Information ▸ ______________________________

____

Strategy 1

Strategy 2

Answer ▸ ______________________________

____

Division with 1

Connecting

Natalie's and Martin's grandmother gave Natalie a gift bag with 12 hair clips. In a second gift bag, she had 24 colored pencils for her grandchildren to share equally.

- Circle the pencils that belong to Natalie in orange. Circle the pencils that belong to Martin in blue. How many groups did you make? How many pencils are there in each group?

___

- Write a division operation to represent the calculation.

☐ ÷ ☐ = ☐

- Circle the hair clips in green. How many hair clips did each child get? How many groups did you make?

___

- Write a division operation to represent the calculation.

☐ ÷ ☐ = ☐

Learning

When the divisor in an operation is 1, the quotient will always be the same as the dividend. In other words, when **dividing any number by 1** the number will stay the same.

Examples:

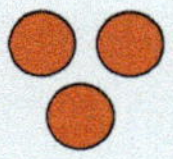

▶ If you have one group of elements and you divide it by 1, the result is the same number. ▶ 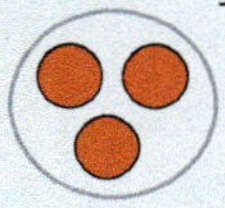

Therefore, 3 ÷ 1 = 3.

In the operation 2,352 ÷ 1, the quotient is 2,352.

Remember!

The terms of a division operation are:

25	÷	5	=	5
↓		↓		↓
dividend		divisor		quotient

Practicing

1. Complete the division operations. Understand

a. ____ ÷ 1 = 56,324

b. 98,999 ÷ ____ = 98,999

c. 13,258 ÷ 1 = ____

d. 20,000 ÷ ____ = 20,000

e. ____ ÷ 1 = 45,400

f. ____ ÷ 1 = ____

2. Mark the word problem that could be solved by dividing by 1 with a ✔. Compare and Contrast

- A fund-raising event collected $150,000 to give to two charities. How much will each charity receive? ☐
- A fund-raising event collected $150,000 to give to one charity. How much will that charity receive? ☐
- A fund-raising event collected $100,000 for one charity and $50,000 for a second charity. What is the total amount that the charities will receive? ☐

The Relationship between Multiplication and Division

Connecting

A 5th grade teacher asks her students to represent some situations.

- Represent each situation as a multiplication or division operation.

____ × ____ = ____

____ ÷ ____ = ____

____ ÷ ____ = ____

- How are the three situations related? Explain.

____

____

Learning

The **relationship between multiplication and division** is that two division operations can be created from one multiplication operation.

Example:

$25 \times 3 = 75$ → $75 \div 3 = 25$

$25 \times 3 = 75$ → $75 \div 25 = 3$

The three operations use the same three numbers: 75, 35 and 3.

Practicing

1. Complete the multiplication and division operations. Apply

There are eight boxes with 25 balls in each. How many balls are there in total?

☐ × ☐ = ☐

↑ number of boxes | ↑ number of balls in each box | ↑ total number of balls

In the toy store, there are ☐ balls divided equally into boxes. If there are 25 balls in each box, how many boxes are there?

☐ ÷ ☐ = ☐

In the toy store, there are ☐ balls divided equally into eight boxes. How many balls are there in each box?

☐ ÷ ☐ = ☐

Section 4

Multiplication and Division Word Problems

Estimating Products and Quotients

Connecting

During a school's anniversary week, there was a Movie Afternoon every day. Two teachers are counting the number of students that attended one afternoon.

- Which teacher, Teacher 1 or Teacher 2, estimates the number of students? Explain.

____

____

- That afternoon there was a two-for-the-price-of-one **promotion** (an offer) on tickets. If the tickets cost $4, how would each teacher calculate the money collected?

Teacher 1

Teacher 2

Learning

When **estimating products and quotients**, the factor or the dividend that has more than one digit is rounded to the nearest ten or hundred. Then the operation is calculated to get an estimated answer.

Example: **Estimate the product of 253 × 3.**

253 is rounded to the nearest tens, 250.

250 × 3 = 750

253 × 3 is approximately 750.

Example: **Estimate the quotient of 58 ÷ 2.**

58 is rounded to the nearest tens, 60.

60 ÷ 2 = 30

58 ÷ 2 is approximately 30.

Practicing

1. Match the operations to the rounded operations used to estimate them. Understand

a.	354 × 7	360 × 7
b.	358 × 7	80 ÷ 2
c.	82 ÷ 2	90 ÷ 2
d.	88 ÷ 2	350 × 7

Challenge

Think about daily situations that involve rounding. Write about three of them and discuss them with your classmates.

2. Round the terms in the operations to the nearest tens to estimate the answers. Apply

a. 324 × 2

b. 165 ÷ 5

Word Problems

Connecting

- What operation will answer the woman's question? Explain.

____

____

- Represent the operation the woman needs to use to solve the problem.

Answer ▶ ______________________________

____

- What operation will answer the man's question? Explain.

____

____

- Represent the operation the man needs to use to solve the problem.

Answer ▶ ______________________________

____

Learning

To solve **multiplication and division word problems** you need to answer a question related to the problem.

Read the **word problem** and the **question**.	A class of 36 students is divided into groups of 3. How many groups of students are there?
Then identify the **information** that will help you solve the question.	36 students. 3 groups.
Determine the **operation** and calculation **strategy**.	$36 \div 3$ $(30 \div 3) + (6 \div 3)$ $10 + 2 = 12$
Answer the question.	There are twelve groups.

Practicing

1. Identify the information that will help you to answer the word problems. Understand

a. Marcy bought four plants to decorate her house. Each plant cost $8.50. How much money did Marcy spend?

Information ▸ ____________________

b. In a store, there are three racks with the same number of sweaters on them. There are 45 sweaters in all, 20 are black and 25, white. How many sweaters are on each rack?

Information ▸ ____________________

c. A bus ride costs $3.30. A family of six, two of which are women, get on the bus. How much do the women pay for a ride?

Information ▸ ____________________

2. Identify the important information in the word problems. Mark the operations needed and solve them. Apply

a. A car uses seven liters of gas to travel 91 kilometers. How many kilometers can the car travel with one liter of gas?

Information ▸ ______________________________

____

☐ multiplication ☐ division

Answer ▸ ______________________________

b. A paper company charges customers for each delivery of 500 kilograms of paper. If they made six deliveries this month, how many kilograms of paper did they deliver?

Information ▸ ______________________________

____

☐ multiplication ☐ division

Answer ▸ ______________________________

c. A shopping mall has five floors with the same number of stores on each floor. If there are a total of 85 stores, how many stores are there on each floor?

Information ▶ ______________________________

____

☐ multiplication ☐ division

Answer ▶ ______________________________

Quiz Yourself

Read and answer.

There are approximately 60 apples in each basket. How many apples can we estimate there are in total?

- What does the teacher mean by approximately 60 apples? Explain.

____

____

- Estimate the total number of apples.

Information ▶ ______________________________

____

Answer ▶ ______________________________

Exam Strategies

Multiple Choice Questions

1. A school is collecting cans to recycle. Each class has a goal of collecting 135 cans each month. If there are nine classes and each class reaches its goal, how many cans will the school collect in one month?

A. 15
B. 972
C. 1,115
D. 1,215

Analyzing the Answers

A. In this case, the information has been divided instead of multiplied.

$$135 \div 9 = 15$$

B. When using the addition in column strategy you should consider the place value of each digit. In this case, the digit 3 has a place value of 30.

30 × 9 is 270, not → 27

$$\begin{array}{r} 135 \\ \times\ 9 \\ \hline 45 \\ 27 \\ +\ 900 \\ \hline 972 \end{array}$$

C. In this case, the remainder was not considered in the addition.

//1 → 270

$$\begin{array}{r} 135 \\ \times\ 9 \\ \hline 45 \\ 270 \\ +\ 900 \\ \hline 1,115 \end{array}$$

D. The operation was solved correctly.

$$\begin{array}{r} 135 \\ \times\ 9 \\ \hline 45 \\ 270 \\ +\ 900 \\ \hline 1,215 \end{array}$$

▸ Therefore, the correct answer is **D.**

1. A B C D

What Did You Learn?

Final Evaluation

1. Solve the operations using different strategies.

points /6

Turning Two Factors into Four

a. 36 × 64

□ × □ × □ × □

□ × □ × □

□ × □

= □

b. 49 × 9

□ × □ × □ × □

□ × □ × □

□ × □

= □

Doubling and Halving

c. 18 × 4

□ × □

= □

d. 25 × 6

□ × □

= □

The Double of Doubles

e. 8 × 12

□ × □

□ × □

= □

f. 25 × 36

□ × □

□ × □

= □

2. Solve the operations by decomposing them according to the place values of the terms.

points
/ 4

a. 315 × 4

(______ + ______ + ______) × 4

(______ × 4) + (______ × 4) + (______ × 4)

______ + ______ + ______ = ______

c. 659 × 3

(______ + ______ + ______) × ______

(______ × 3) + (______ × 3) + (______ × 3)

______ + ______ + ______ = ______

b. 65 × 5

(______ + ______) × 5

(______ × 5) + (______ × 5)

______ + ______ = ______

d. 99 × 9

(______ + ______) × 9

(______ × 9) + (______ × 9)

______ + ______ = ______

3. Solve the operations by using addition in column.

points
/ 4

a.

$$\begin{array}{r} 849 \\ \times\ \ 5 \\ \hline \square \\ \square \\ +\ \square \\ \hline \square \end{array}$$

c.

$$\begin{array}{r} 234 \\ \times\ \ 3 \\ \hline \square \\ \square \\ +\ \square \\ \hline \square \end{array}$$

b.

$$\begin{array}{r} 531 \\ \times\ \ 4 \\ \hline \square \\ \square \\ +\ \square \\ \hline \square \end{array}$$

d.

$$\begin{array}{r} 646 \\ \times\ \ 6 \\ \hline \square \\ \square \\ +\ \square \\ \hline \square \end{array}$$

4. Read the word problem and answer.

points
/ 2

Ruth and John have to calculate the number of students participating in a competition.

Ruth

The competition has four categories. In each category there are eleven girls and ten boys participating.

$4 \times (11 + 10)$

John

Eleven girls are participating in four categories. There are ten boys participating in four categories.

$(4 \times 11) + (4 \times 10)$

Will Ruth and John get the same answer? Calculate and explain.

Ruth

John

Yes No, because ______________________________

____

5. Use the information to create two versions of the same word problem that can be solved using the operations given.

points
/ 2

Information: Five groups of cars.
15 red cars and 18 blue cars.

____
____
____
____
____

$5 \times (15 + 18)$

____
____
____
____
____

$(5 \times 15) + (5 \times 18)$

Mark the correct answer with an ✖.

points
/ 3

Use the information in the picture to answer **questions 6, 7 and 8**.

6. If a woman buys two broccoli stalks, how much will she pay?

stem of a plant

A. $9

B. $8.11

C. $8

D. $2

7. No cabbage was sold for two days. What operation represents the amount of money collected for the sale of this vegetable?

A. $4.50 × 2

B. $4.50 × 0

C. $6.50 + $4.00

D. $6.50 – $4.00

8. Marie bought a stalk of celery. How much money did she spend?

A. $6.50

B. $6.51

C. $8.50

D. $1.30

Use the information from the word problem to answer **questions 9, 10 and 11**.

points
/ 3

Parents from a 5th grade class are organizing a field trip to a museum outside the city. They have considered these expenses for the whole trip.

Museum Admission Tickets	\$990
Bus (round trip)	\$1,750
Lunches and snacks	\$3,700

round trip: travel to a place and back again

9. If you round the costs of the admission tickets, the bus fares and the food to the greatest place values, they would be:

A. 990, 1,800 and 3,700

B. 900, 1,000 and 3,000

C. 1,000, 2,000 and 4,000

D. 1,000, 1,800 and 4,000

10. If you round the sum of the cost of the admission tickets, the bus fares and the food to the greatest place value, what is the total cost?

A. 4,900

B. 6,000

C. 6,440

D. 7,000

11. If you round the cost of the admission tickets, the bus fares and the food to the nearest ten, they would be:

A. 990, 1,750 and 3,700

B. 1,000, 1,800 and 3,700

C. 1,000, 1,800 and 3,800

D. 1,000, 1,760 and 3,800

Find Test 3 Study Page

Unit 4

Data

One day, during science class, Ms. Graham taught the students about how we use water in our homes. The class decided to take action and do some research on how they could reduce the amount of water they use at home. First, they calculated how much water they use during one week.

In this unit you will learn to:

- recognize the basic elements of a statistical study.
- read and interpret data represented in frequency tables and in bar charts.
- calculate the averages of data represented in bar charts.
- identify the advantages and disadvantages of using averages.
- approach problem solving in a creative and flexible manner.

Key Words

average

frequency

population

sample

statistics

What Do You Know?

Answer using the information from Ms. Graham's science class.

1. What is the title of the bar chart? ▸ ______________________________

2. What do the bars in the bar chart represent? Explain.

____

____

3. Mark with a ✔ if the statements are correct and an ✖ if they are incorrect.

a. ☐ The horizontal axis of the chart represents the different types of water use.

b. ☐ From the chart you can calculate the total amount of water use.

c. ☐ Every bar in the chart should have the same width.

d. ☐ Every bar in the chart should have the same height.

4. Ms. Graham's class worked on a plan for reducing the percentage of water used in their bathrooms at home. Look at the information in the table and complete the bar chart.

Water Used In Bathrooms	
Day	**Amount of Water (%)**
Monday	47%
Tuesday	40%
Wednesday	38%
Thursday	30%
Friday	25%

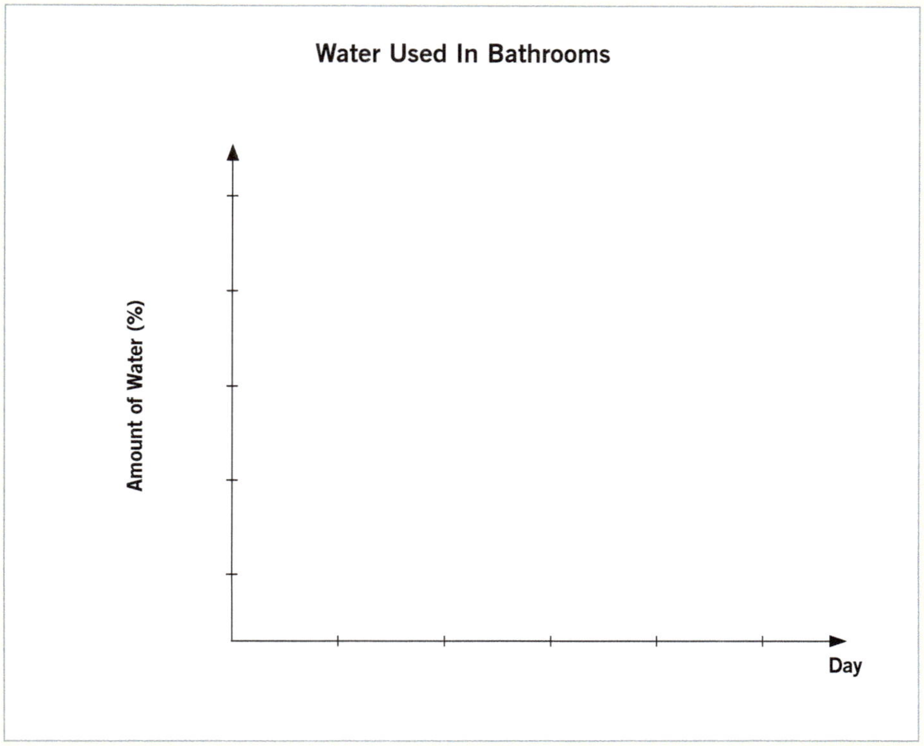

Section 1 Statistics

Basic Concepts

Connecting

no pattern or method

A factory that makes matches produces 1,000 boxes of matches every day. Each box contains 40 matches. To be able to analyze the daily production, the quality control team selects a **random** sample of 30 boxes to check the number of matches that each box contains.

The quality control team collected these results from the random sample:

39	40	42	38	40	40	40	39	38	37	40	41	42	40	40
40	40	41	36	40	36	41	43	43	40	41	41	40	40	40

- Why do you think the selection of boxes was random?

____

- What was analyzed in the sample of boxes? ______________________________

- Mark the objective of the analysis with a ✔.

☐ To find out the exact number of matches produced daily.

☐ To find out if the number of matches in each box is the same.

Learning

Statistics is a branch of mathematics dealing with the collection, analysis, interpretation and presentation of **numerical data. Data for a study** is often collected through surveys. When it is not possible or practical to survey a **large population**, you can use data from a smaller subset of the population, called a **sample**. A **variable** is the quantity that you are measuring in the survey.

Example:

- **Study:** To improve students' eating habits, a school decides to survey 50 students, selected at random, to find out how many times a week they eat junk food.
- **Objective:** To propose strategies to improve students' eating habits.
- **Data:** The information on the number of times students eat junk food.
- **Population:** The total number of students in the school.
- **Sample:** 50 students selected at random.
- **Variable:** The number of times the students eat junk food in a week.

Practicing

1. Read the studies and complete the information. Interpret

a. Researchers want to know the different sports children in the capital city play to design a campaign to promote exercise. They choose 70 boys and 70 girls to survey at random.

Population ▶ ______________________________

Sample ▶ ______________________________

Variable ▶ ______________________________

Data ▶ ______________________________

Objective ▶ ______________________________

b. To improve customer service at a department store, the managers decide to survey 60 people who are shopping at the store on one day.

Population ▶ ______________________________

Sample ▶ ______________________________

Variable ▶ ______________________________

Data ▶ ______________________________

Objective ▶ ______________________________

2. Read the information and then answer the questions. Analyze

A **qualitative** variable corresponds to a description or a characteristic of the population or sample. For example, *hair color* or *favorite sport*, are qualitative variables.

A **quantitative** variable corresponds to a numerical characteristic of the population or sample that can be measured. For example, *age* or *height*, are quantitative variables.

a. How would you classify the variable of "weight" in a study of people? Explain.

____

b. How would you classify the variable "fruit" in a study about favorite fruits? Explain.

____

Reading and Interpreting Frequency Tables

Connecting

In a survey, 60 people were asked about the number of computers they have at home. The table shows the survey results.

How Many Computers Do You Have at Home?	
Number of Computers	**Number of People**
0	5
1	26
2	19
3	10

- What data is represented in this table? Explain.

____

____

- Which values represent the number of computers?

____

- What piece of data has the highest frequency in the survey results? Explain.

____

____

Learning

A **frequency table** shows data in an organized way. The basic elements of a frequency table are: **population**, **sample**, **variable**, **category** and the **frequency** each variable is repeated.

Example: The table shows the preferred colors for a class shirt.

Preferred Colors	
Color	**Frequency**
green	3
blue	12
yellow	14
orange	8

Population and sample: In this case, because the group is small, the whole population was surveyed. The population corresponds to the total number of students in the class.

Variable: Color.

Categories of the variable: Green, blue, yellow and orange.

Frequency: The number of times that each variable is repeated. The frequency of green is 3, of blue is 12, of yellow is 14 and of orange is 8.

Practicing

1. Identify and describe the statistical elements in the table. Then answer the questions. Interpret

A math teacher shows her students a table with the grades they got on their last test.

Grades on the Test					
Grade	6	7	8	9	10
Number of Students	2	5	15	7	2

Tip

In a study that surveys an entire population there is no sample.

a. Population ▶ ______________________

Sample ▶ ______________________

Variable ▶ ______________________

Data ▶ ______________________

Objective ▶ ______________________

b. How many students took the test? ▶ ________ students

c. How many students got a grade less than 8? ▶ ________ students

2. Make a frequency table to organize the data. Then analyze it and answer the questions. Apply

Number of people that live in an apartment building.

3 4 1 2 1 4 3 3 2 3 4 5 1 2 3 3 3 4 5 2 4 3 1 1 3 4 0 1 2 2 3 5 5 3 2 5 3 4 5 2 1 0

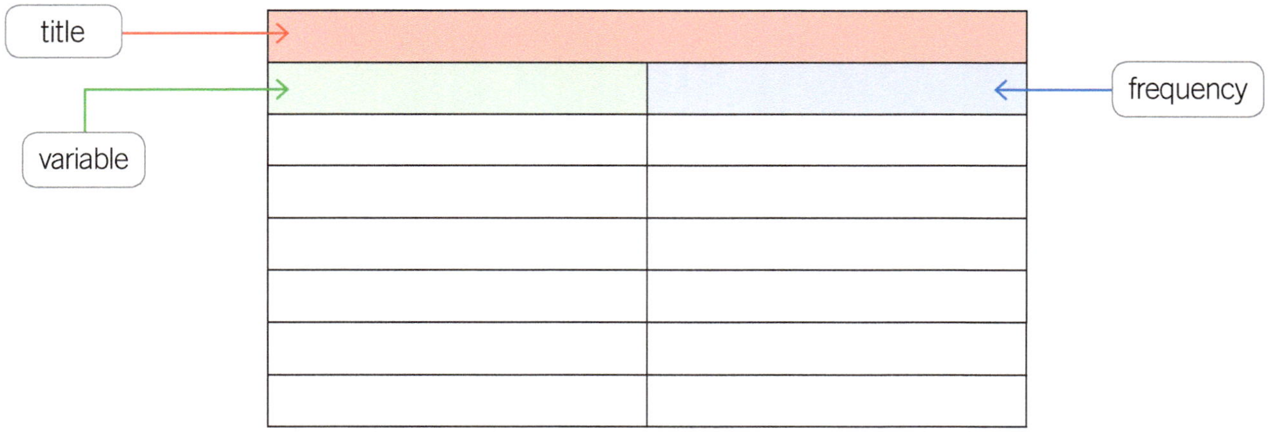

a. How many apartments are occupied? ▶ ______________________.

b. How many apartments are there in total? ▶ ______________________.

c. How many people live in the building? ▶ ______________________.

Reading and Interpreting Bar Charts

Connecting

At a school students are offered fruit during recess to help promote a healthy diet. To evaluate the campaign, the school made a bar chart with the data from the first five months of the school year.

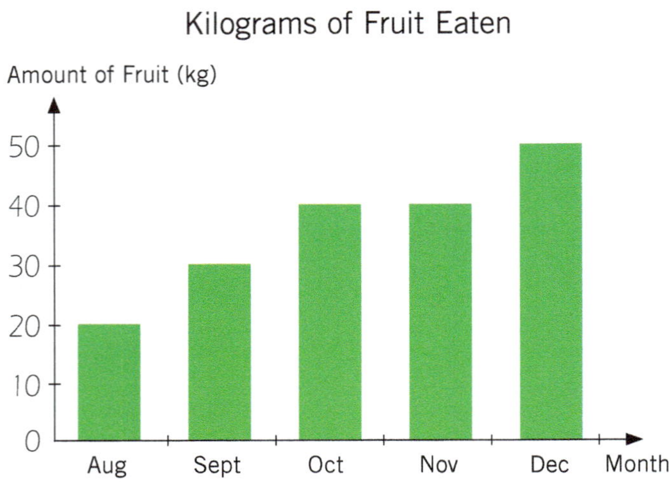

- What do the bars represent?

- In which month was the most fruit eaten?

- In which month was the least fruit eaten?

- Can you tell if the campaign has been successful by looking at the bar chart? Why or why not?

Learning

Bar charts help you to visualize data quickly and clearly. To read the information in the chart, look at the length of the **rectangular bars**. The bars represent the quantitative and qualitative **variables** studied. The bars can be **vertical** or **horizontal** depending on the variables represented in the axes. The **x-axis** is the horizontal line and the **y-axis** is the vertical line.

Example: At a high school, the student council was chosen in an election. For this election, five lists were created with the names of the different candidates for the different positions. To predict the results of the election, a survey was made using a random sample of 50 students.

On the bar chart you can interpret that List 4 got the most votes in the survey, with 17 votes.

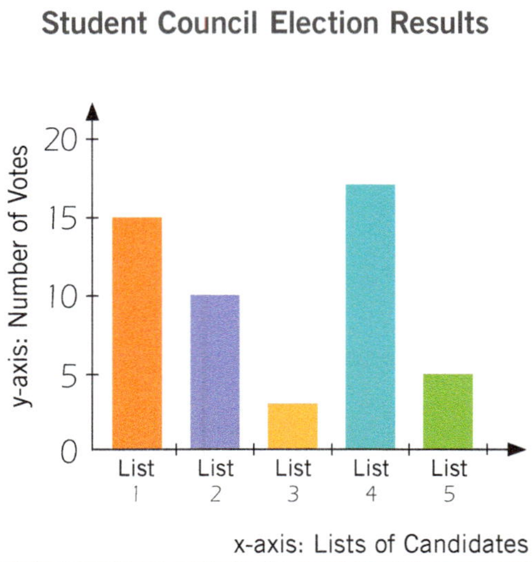

Practicing

1. Analyze the bar chart. Then answer the questions. Analyze

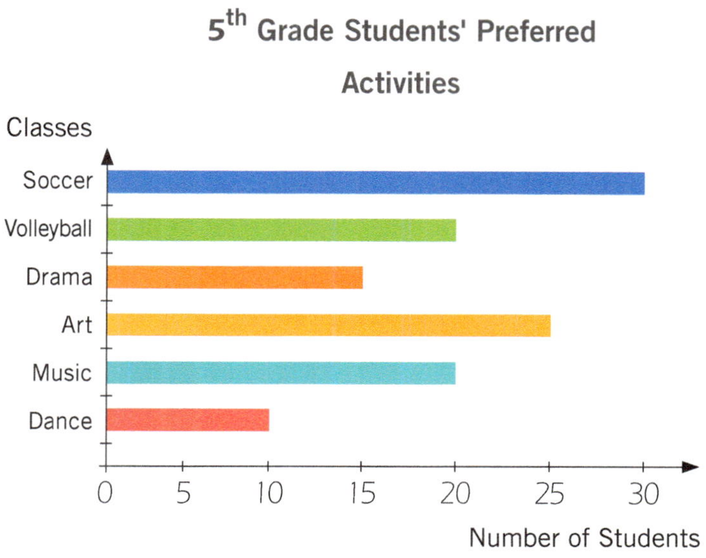

a. How many students prefer Drama class?

▶ ______________________

b. Which class was preferred by most students?

▶ ______________________

c. How many more students preferred Soccer class than Dance class?

▶ ______________________

d. What is the objective of this study? Explain.

____

____

2. Analyze the bar chart. Then answer the questions. Analyze

The chart shows the results of a survey to find out how effective a healthy foods program is in a cafeteria.

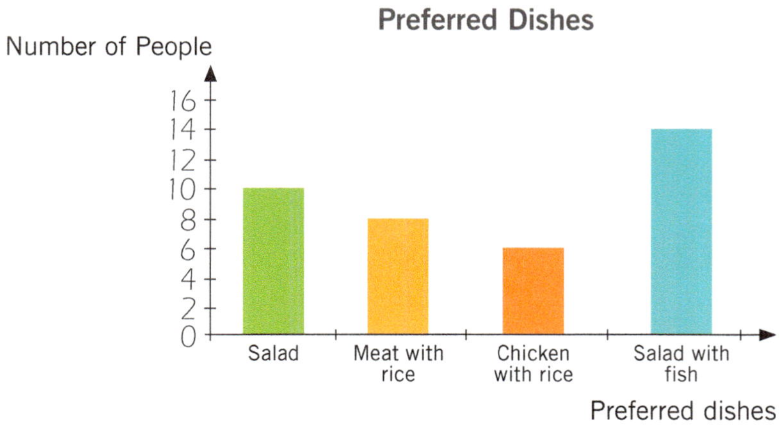

Education through Values

Remember to eat a balanced diet in order to grow up strong and healthy.

a. How many people participated in the survey? ▶ ______________________

b. Which dish was the least popular? ▶ ______________________

c. How many more people chose Salad with fish than Chicken with rice? ▶ ______________________

d. Do you think the healthy foods program is effective or not?

____

____

Let's Check!

Basic Concepts

1. Analyze the situation and answer.

points
/ 2

The directors of a museum surveyed 80 visitors. The people were selected randomly during an art gallery show and were asked how many times they had gone to a museum in the last year.

a. What is the sample? ▸ ______________________

b. What is the variable? ▸ ______________________

Reading and Interpreting Frequency Tables

2. Analyze the table and answer.

points
/ 4

a. Which sport is the most popular? Which is the least popular?

▸ ______________________

b. How many people were surveyed?

▸ ______________________

Favorite Sports	
Sport	**Number of Preferences**
Basketball	15
Soccer	18
Rugby	5
Tennis	22

Reading and Interpreting Bar Charts

3. Analyze the bar chart and answer.

points
/ 4

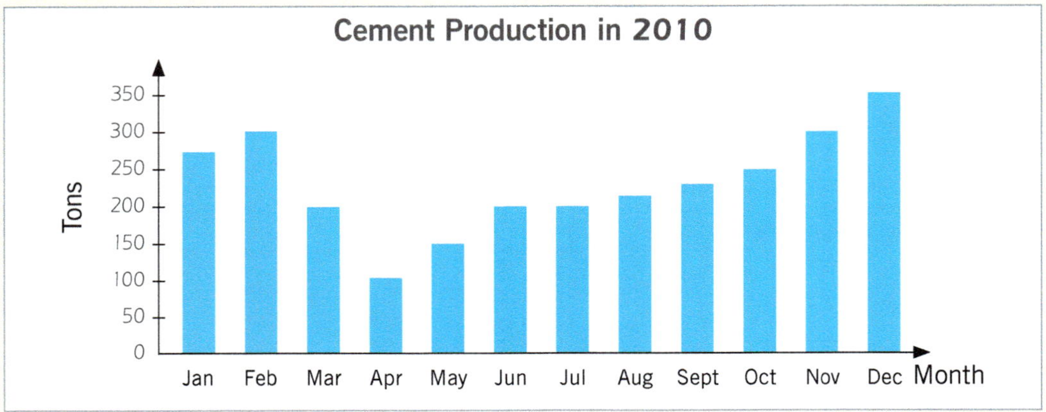

a. In which month was the least cement produced? ▸ ______________

b. Between which consecutive months was there the biggest variation in production?

____

4. Use the information to answer the questions.

points
/ 4

A park ranger is doing an annual survey of trees in a zone of a national park.

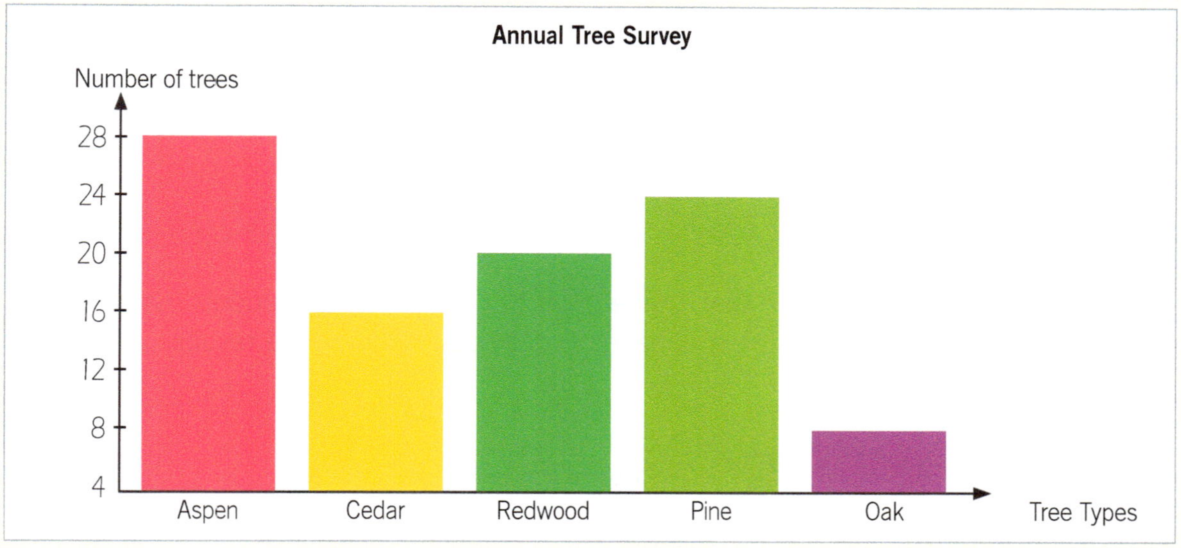

a. How many trees are there in total in this zone of the park? ▸ ____________________

b. What is the most common tree type in this zone? ▸ ____________________

5. Analyze the bar chart and then answer the questions.

points
/ 3

The 5th grade decided to collect some food to donate to a local charity. The bar chart shows how many children donated in a week. Each child donated once.

a. How many children are there in the class?

▸ ____________________

b. Which day had the least donations?

▸ ____________________

c. Write an appropriate title for the bar chart.

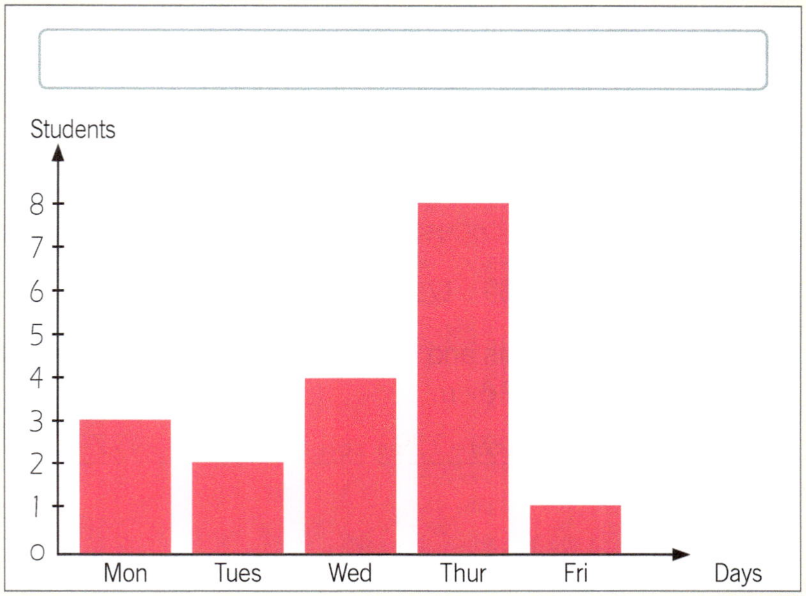

Calculating Averages

Connecting

These are the grades that two 5th grade classes got on their final exam.

5A: 5, 5, 5, 8, 6, 10, 6, 7, 10, 6, 7, 7, 8, 6, 7, 6, 7, 8, 7, 8, 7, 6, 7, 10, 8, 7, 10, 6

5B: 6, 9, 8, 8, 8, 8, 9, 10, 9, 8, 8, 9, 9, 10, 9, 8, 7, 7, 6, 9, 7, 8, 10, 10

Johnny thinks that 5B has better grades than 5A because his class has eight 8s and the other class only has five.

Peter says that if you add all of the grades of 5A, and then divide them by the number of students that took the exam, this will give them the class **average**. If the same is done to 5B, they can compare the results.

- Calculate the sum of all the grades for each class.

  Sum of the grades for 5A ▸ ☐ Sum of the grades for 5B ▸ ☐

- Then divide the sums by the total number of students in each class that took the final exam.

  ☐ ÷ 28 = ☐

  ☐ ÷ 24 = ☐

Therefore, 5A got [higher / lower] grades than 5B on the final exam.

Tip

Regularly refer back to the objective of a word problem to help you focus on what you need to find out.

Learning

The **average** or **arithmetic mean** corresponds to the sum of the numerical values of a variable divided by the total number of data.

Example: This data corresponds to the heights, in centimeters, of a group of soccer players.

174 169 179 184 175 168 177 182 176 181 178 174 179 182 186

If you add the heights and divide the results by the total number of players, you will find that the **average** height of the players is 177.6 cm.

$$\textbf{Average} = \frac{174+169+179+184+175+168+177+182+176+181+178+174+179+182+186}{15} =$$

$$\frac{2{,}664}{15} = 177.6$$

Practicing

1. Calculate the average for each group of data. Apply

a. 4, 5, 7, 10, 12

b. 4, 6, 8, 13, 16, 40, 35, 54

c. 45, 54, 63, 103, 110

d. 500, 400, 200, 350, 450

2. Determine the missing numbers needed to calculate the averages in yellow. Analyze

a. 8, 8, 8, 8, 8, 8, 8, ________ = 8

b. 12, 3, 4, 5, 7, ________ , 9, 8 = 6

c. 7, 6, 12, ________ , 8, 17, 3 = 8

d. ________ , 100, 110, 240 = 125

3. Solve the word problems. Apply

a. The ages of five friends are 13, 15, 13, 12 and 12. What is the average age of the group?

b. The table shows the vegetable sales at a store. What is the number of vegetables sold on average?

Vegetables Sold

Vegetable	Number Sold
Lettuce	18
Carrots	9
Onions	15
Broccoli	9

c. These are Jenny's grades in math: 9, 7, 7 and 8. What grade does she need to get on the next test to have an 8 as her final average grade?

Using Bar Charts to Calculate Averages

Connecting

The bar chart shows the amount of copper (in kilograms) that is extracted daily from a mine.

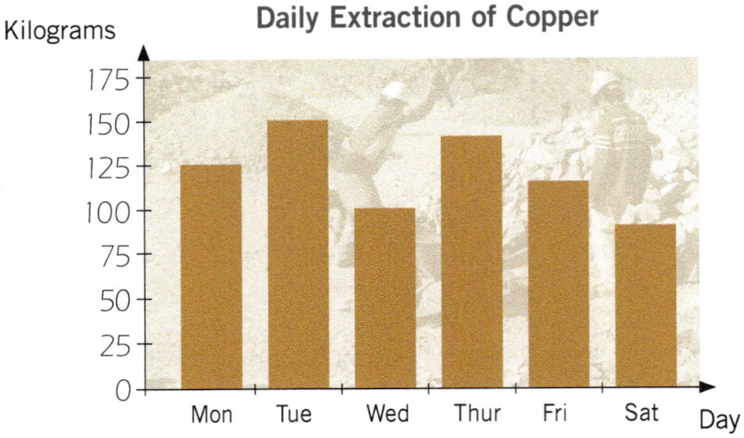

- To calculate the average, use the operation: $\frac{125 + 150 + 100 + 140 + 115 + 90}{6} = \frac{\square}{\square} = \square$
- During one week, the mine extracted an average of ☐ kilograms of copper per day.

Learning

To calculate the **average of data** on a bar chart, you should add the values of the variable (represented by the rectangular bars), and then divide the value by the total amount of data.

Example:

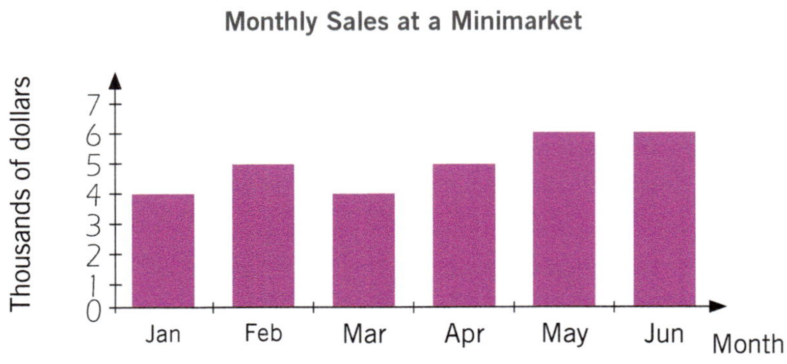

$$\text{Average} = \frac{4{,}000 + 5{,}000 + 4{,}000\ \ 5{,}000 + 6{,}000 + 6{,}000}{6} = \frac{30{,}000}{6} = 5{,}000$$

The **monthly average** sale at the minimarket is $5,000.

Practicing

1. Calculate the averages. Apply

a. On average, how many $1 coins were collected by each friend?

b. On average, how many tools are made daily?

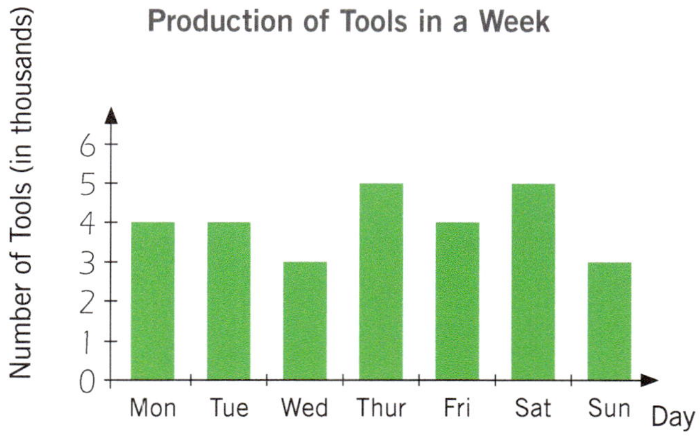

c. What is the average number of sandwiches made at a cafeteria every day?

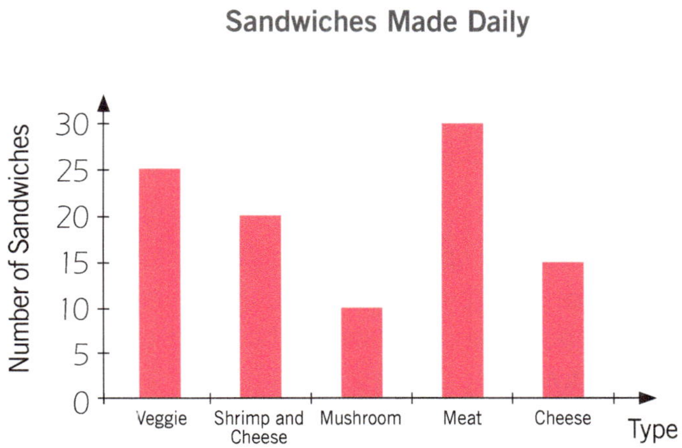

Advantages and Disadvantages of Averages

Connecting

A tourist wanted to travel across Canada. He was informed that the average temperature in July is 22° C, so he only packed light clothing. However, when he reached Inukjuak, the temperature was 7° C.

- Prove that the average of all the temperatures shown in the table is 22° C.
- Was the average temperature for the month of July a good indicator of the low temperature in Inukjuak? Mark your answer.

Yes No

Average Temperatures in Ten Canadian Cities in July	
City	**Temperature**
Vancouver	22° C
Edmonton	23° C
Yellowknife	20° C
Inukjuak	27° C
Winnipeg	26° C
Ottawa	26° C
Montreal	26° C
Toronto	27° C
Halifax	23° C
St. John's	20° C

Learning

The **average** of a group of data has its advantages and disadvantages.
For example:

Advantages

- It is the most common numerical value used to represent a collection of data.
- It is expressed in the same units as the variables.
- It is one number.
- It changes based on any variation in the data.

Disadvantages

- You cannot calculate the average of qualitative (non-numerical) data.
- It is greatly affected by very small or very high values, which change its ability to accurately represent the data set.

Example: In reference to the situation above we can conclude that the advantages and disadvantages of calculating an average temperature are:

Advantages

- The average of 22° C has the same unit of measurement as the temperatures recorded.
- There is no other number that represents the average of the temperatures.
- If you add another city and the average rises to 24° C, we know that the city added has a higher temperature.

Disadvantages

- If the data recorded was the type of climate each city has, an average could not be calculated since the data would not be numerical.
- The average temperatures in July did not help the tourist take the necessary precautions during his visit to Canada, since the average does not show the high and low temperatures for each city.

Practicing

1. Mark the correct statements with a ✔ and the incorrect statements with an ✖. Then explain. Evaluate

a. ☐ If the average age of ten people is 27 years, then all of the people are older than 10.

Explain: ______________________________

b. ☐ Robert is 15 years old and is 165 cm tall. His soccer team has an average height of 158 cm. This means he is the tallest in the group.

Explain: ______________________________

c. ☐ During a fund-raising event, a company collected an average of $50,000 each year for ten years. This year their average was $51,000; therefore, they did better this year.

Explain: ______________________________

2. Analyze the situation and answer the questions. Analyze

The scores of a basketball team in their first five games of the season were: 65, 48, 63, 59 and 80.

a. What is their average score?

b. If the score of their last game changes the average to 54 points, what can you state about the score of the last game?

____

Quiz Yourself

The average of the surface area of 999 farms is 2,000 m². If a new 200,000 m² farm is added, the new average is 2,198 m². On the other hand, if the average of the surface area of 9 farms is 2,000 m² and you add a 200,000 m² farm, the new average will be 21,800 m².

- Why do you think the new 200,000 m² farm affects each data group differently?

____

Exam Strategies

Multiple Choice Questions

1. Choose the most appropriate names for the x- and y-axes, respectively.

A. Frequency and Number of Students

B. Subjects and Number of Students

C. Subjects and Preferences

D. Number of Students and Subjects

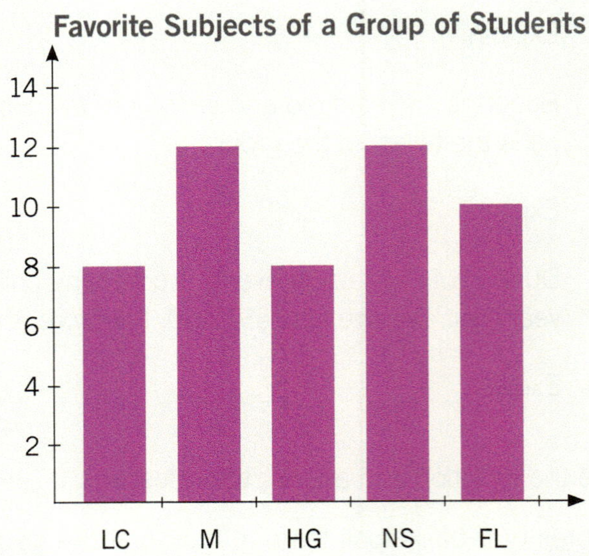

LC	▸ Language and Communication
M	▸ Mathematics
HG	▸ History, Geography and Social Studies
NS	▸ Natural Science
FL	▸ Foreign Language

Analyzing the Answers

A. Both the frequency and the number of students are titles related to the y-axis.

B. The favorite subjects are shown on the x-axis, so the first title is appropriate. The frequency is on the y-axis. Since it is calculated by the number of students who choose each subject, the title "Number of Students" is also appropriate.

C. Since the information on the y-axis is numbers, the second title in this option would not be appropriate.

D. The subjects are on the x-axis, not the y-axis, and the numbers of students who chose their favorite subject are on the y-axis, not the x-axis.

▸ Therefore, **B** is correct.

1. A — B — C — D

What Did You Learn?

Final Evaluation

1. Analyze the table and answer the questions.

points /3

People in a Wind Orchestra, by Instrument	
Instrument	**Number**
trumpet	5
trombone	2
saxophone	4
clarinet	4
flute	6
tuba	2
french horn	2

a. How many people are in the wind orchestra? ▶ ________

b. How many people play the tuba and the clarinet? ▶ ________

c. How many more flute players than trumpet players are there? ▶ ________

2. Analyze the bar chart and answer the questions.

points /3

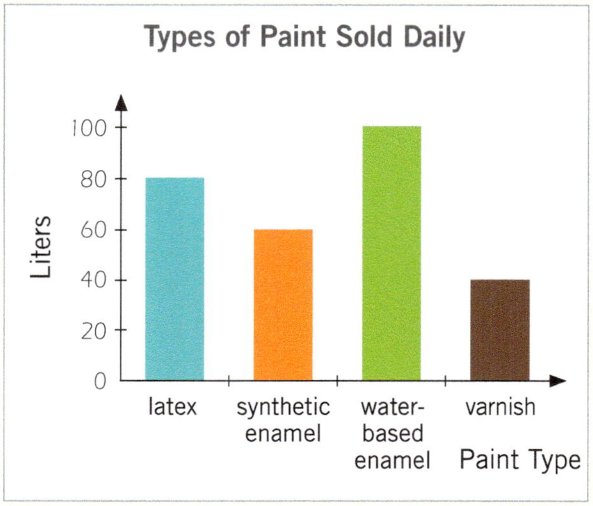

a. What type of paint is sold the most?

▶ ________________________

b. What is the sum of the daily sales of varnish and synthetic enamel?

▶ ________________________

c. How many more liters of latex paint need to be sold to equal the sale of water-based enamel?

▶ ________________________

3. Analyze the bar chart and answer the questions.

points
/ 3

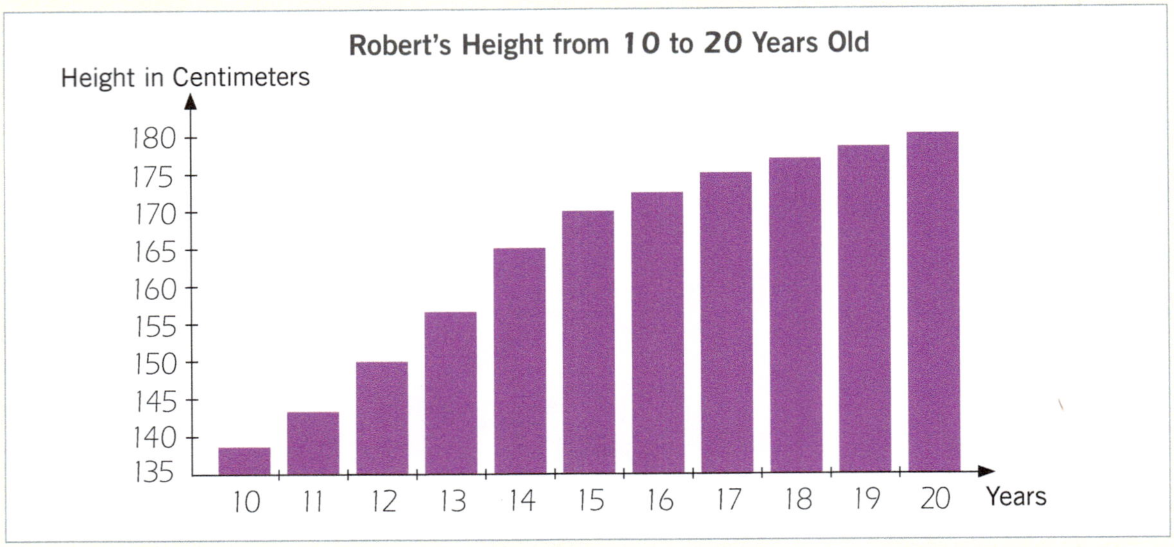

a. How tall was Robert when he was 17 years old? ▸ ______________

b. How many centimeters did Robert grow between the ages of 14 and 20? Explain.

____

c. Between which consecutive ages did Robert grow the most? Explain.

____

4. Calculate the average of each number set.

points
/ 3

a. The ages of friends: 15, 14, 12, 16, 15 and 12.

b. Number of products sold: 23, 54, 31, 19, 26, 42 and 29.

c. Highest temperatures in degrees Celsius: 5, 7, 3, 5, 3, 1 and 4.

Mark the correct answer with an ✕.

points

/ 4

Use the information to answer **questions 5 and 6**.

A school surveyed 40 parents on how many hours they study with their children weekly. The objective of this survey was to find out what extra resources may be needed and suggest teaching strategy workshops for parents.

5. What is the population of the study?

A. Students' parents.

B. Parents' teaching strategies.

C. The 40 parents surveyed.

D. The number of hours that parents study with their children.

6. What is the objective of the survey?

A. Compile data.

B. Propose study strategies and resources.

C. Survey 40 parents.

D. Increase the number of hours that students study.

7. Look at the information in the table. How many groups with more than two children went to the movies?

A. 8

B. 12

C. 16

D. 28

Groups of People Who Went to the Movies	
Children per Group	**Number of Groups**
1	20
2	12
3	8
4	5
5	3

8. Using the data in the table, which statement is true?

A. Five groups of people went to the movies with three children.

B. Fifteen children saw the movie.

C. Forty-eight groups went to the movies.

D. The variable in this study is the number of people.

9. According to the bar chart, how many cats need to go to the veterinarian to equal the total number of horses and dogs that go?

points
1

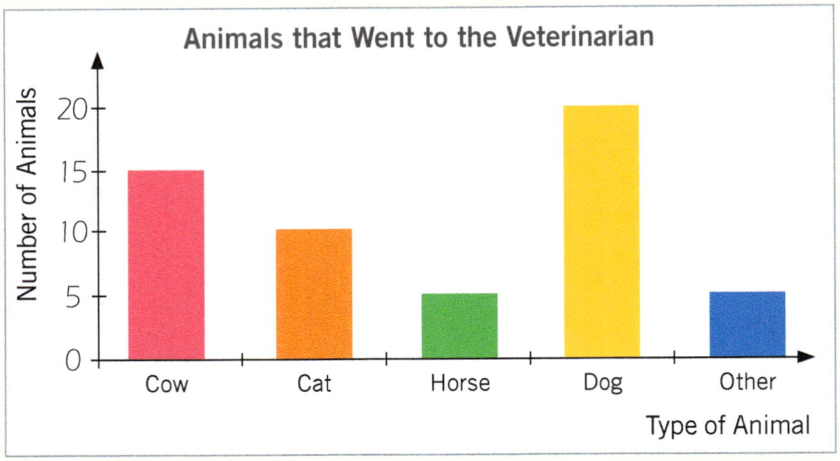

A. 5
B. 15
C. 25
D. 30

Analyze the bar chart and answer **questions 10 and 11**.

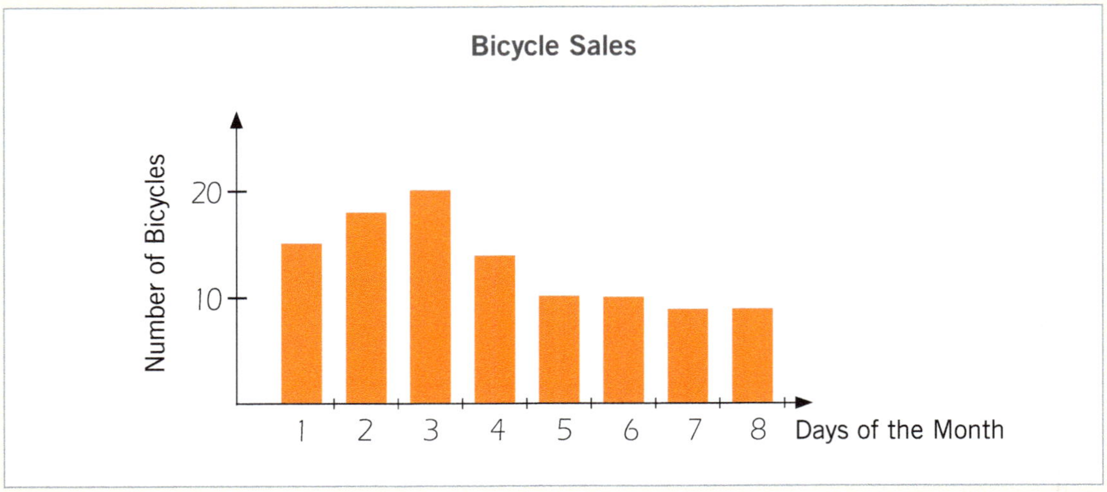

10. How many more bicycles were sold on the third day than on the fifth day?

points
2

A. 6
B. 10
C. 16
D. 22

11. Based on the bar chart, which statement is false?

A. The highest number of bicycles was sold on the third day.

B. Less bicycles were sold on the first day than on the third day.

C. The biggest difference in sales between two consecutive days was between days 5 and 6.

D. Overall, bicycle sales decreased with time.

Look at the table and answer **questions 12 and 13**.

12. What is the difference, in meters, between the day Richard ran the most and the day he ran the least?

A. 6,351 m

B. 4,828 m

C. 4,666 m

D. 3,143 m

13. How many meters did Richard run in total during the week?

A. 30,349 m

B. 31,349 m

C. 31,359 m

D. 31,389 m

Distance Run by Richard in One Week	
Day	**Meters**
Monday	4,154
Tuesday	3,984
Wednesday	2,985
Thursday	1,300
Friday	5,147
Saturday	6,128
Sunday	7,651

points

/2

Find Test 4 Study Page

Unit 5 Measurement

Important Facts

New Zealand is an island nation in the southwestern Pacific Ocean. It is made up of two large islands and numerous smaller ones. The two main islands are separated by a distance of 22 km. The country is approximately 1,600 km long and 400 km wide, with a total surface area of 268,000 km^2. It has a coastline of 15,000 km.

North Island	South Island
The smaller of the two main islands has a surface area of 113, 729 km^2. It is the most populated island in the country, with a population of 3,500,000.	This New Zealand island has the largest surface area: 150, 437 km^2. Its population is 1,076,000.

New Zealand is situated 1,500 km east of Australia. Its most important cities are Auckland, Wellington, Hamilton and Christchurch.

In this unit you will learn to:

- measure length using standard units of measurement.
- convert units of length.
- calculate the perimeter of two-dimensional shapes.
- represent and calculate the surface area of a rectangle.
- calculate the surface area of triangles, rhombuses, rhomboids and trapezoids.
- develop an interest and curiosity for math.

Key Words

perimeter

rhombus

rhomboid

trapezoid

What Do You Know?

Initial Evaluation

Use the information on the previous page to answer the questions.

1. The approximate time it takes to drive from Auckland to Wellington is eight hours. The distance between the cities is 643 km. How many minutes does it take to travel between these two main cities?
(Remember: 1 hour is 60 minutes)

2. Mark the correct statements with a ✔ and the incorrect statements with an ✖.

a. ☐ The distance between Australia and New Zealand is greater than the total length of New Zealand.

b. ☐ The sum of the surface areas of the two main islands is equal to the total surface area of the country.

c. ☐ The distance from New Zealand to Australia is greater than the coastline of New Zealand.

d. ☐ The width of New Zealand is equal to 400,000 m.

3. 1,000,000 m^2 is equal to 1 km^2. How can you convert the surface area of New Zealand into m^2? Explain.

4. Why are kilometers used to express the width of the country and not meters? Explain your answer.

Tip

The small number 2 to the right of units of measurement, such as m^2, is read as "squared" for example, 3 m^2, is read "three meters squared."

Section 1

Units of Length and Surface Area

Units of Length

Connecting

Use a ruler to measure the segments and then answer the questions.

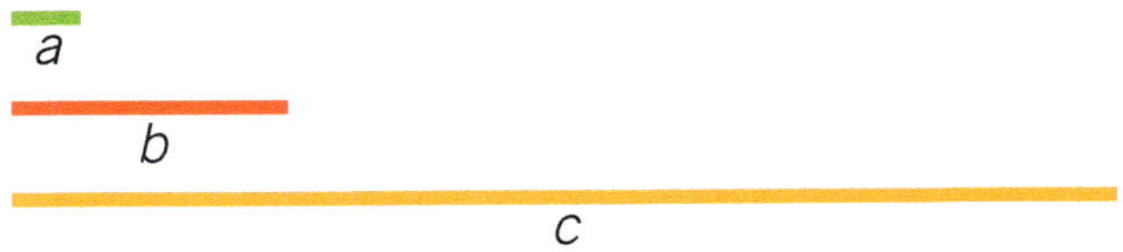

- Complete with the length of each segment.

Segment *a* ▶ ________ cm   Segment *b* ▶ ________ cm   Segment *c* ▶ ________ cm

- Circle the segment that has a measurement that corresponds to a decimal number.

▶ Segment *a*   ▶ Segment *b*   ▶ Segment *c*

- Mark the correct statement(s) with a ✔ and the incorrect statement(s) with an ✖.

☐ Segment *b* is one-fourth the length of segment *c*.

☐ Segment *a* is one-fourth the length of segment *c*.

Challenge

The longest bridge in the world, the Danyang-Kunshan Grand Bridge in China, is 164,800 m long. How many cm is that? Find out which is the longest bridge in your continent and convert its distance into centimeters.

Learning

A **meter (m)** is the basic unit of measurement used in the Metric System.

- Here are some unit equivalences:
  - ▶ kilometer (km) = 1,000 m
  - ▶ hectometer (hm) = 100 m
  - ▶ decameter (dam) = 10 m
  - ▶ decimeter (dm) = 0.1 m
  - ▶ centimeter (cm) = 0.01 m
  - ▶ millimeter (mm) = 0.001 m

Example: A student is 1 meter, 50 cm tall. You can also write this as 1.5 m or 150 cm.

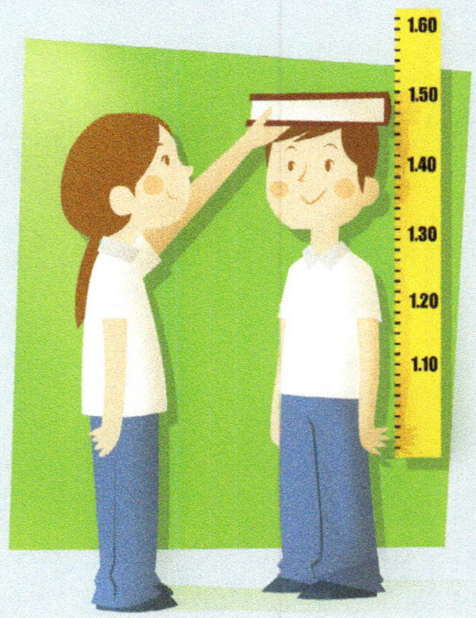

Practicing

1. Use a ruler to measure the objects. Then complete the measurements and answer the question. Analyze

a.

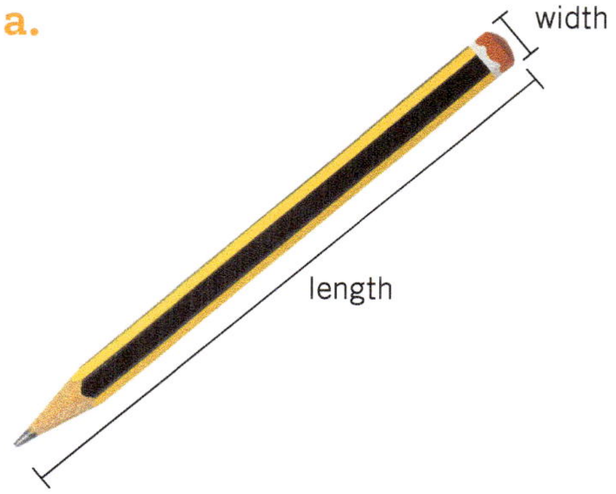

Length ▸ ____________ cm

Width ▸ ____________ cm

b.

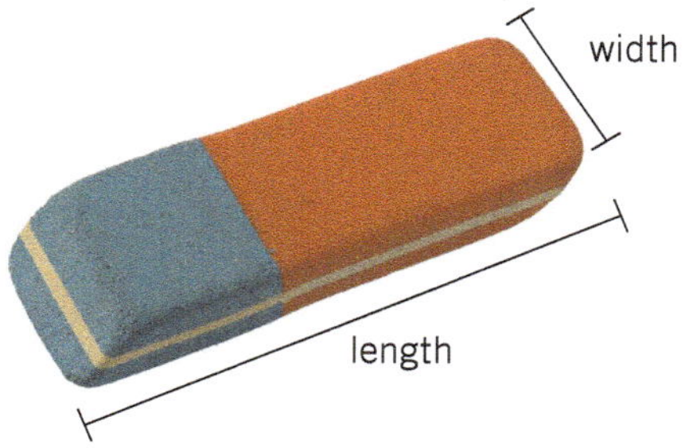

Length ▸ ____________ mm

Width ▸ ____________ mm

c.

Height ▸ ____________ cm

Width ▸ ____________ cm

- If you were to measure the real objects, would the measurements be similar? Explain.

____

____

2. Solve the word problems. Analyze

a. To calculate the distance between two cities, what unit of measurement would you use? Explain.

____

____

b. If you measure the width and length of your math notebook, which unit is more appropriate to use: meters, centimeters or millimeters? Explain.

____

____

c. Does your textbook only have a length and a width? What other measurements are missing? Discuss with your classmates and answer.

____

____

Conversion Between Units of Length

Connecting

Hamilton is located approximately 146 km from Auckland. If Sandy is in Auckland and she rides her bike 1,000 meters to get to the bus station for her trip to Hamilton, how many meters does she travel in total?

- Using the unit equivalence:

1 kilometer (km) = 1,000 meters (m)

- Circle the correct conversion.

  - 146 km = 1,460 m
  - 146 km = 14,600 m
  - 146 km = 146,000 m

- Mark the correct answer with a ✔.

  - ☐ Sandy travels 147,000 m.
  - ☐ Sandy travels 152 000 m.
  - ☐ Sandy travels 146,100 m.

Learning

To convert units of length, a meter (m) can be used as a reference. A meter can be subdivided into smaller units by dividing it by 10 (dm), by 100 (cm) and by 1,000 (mm); it can also be multiplied by 10 to obtain dam, by 100, to obtain hm, and by 1,000 to obtain km.

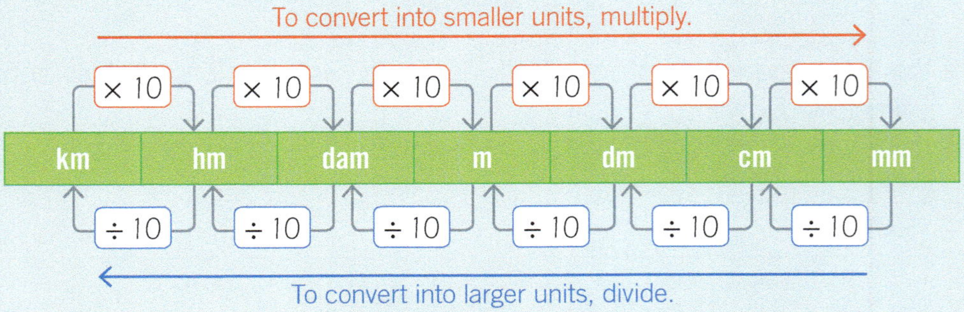

Examples:

- 8 km = 8,000 m, because 8 m × 1,000 = 8,000 m
- 25 dam = 250 m, because 25 m × 10 = 250 m
- 9,300 m = 9.3 km, because 9,300 m ÷ 1,000 = 9.3 km
- 250 m = 25 dam, because 250 m ÷ 10 = 25 dam

Practicing

1. Look at the example. Write the operations necessary to convert the units of measurement. Analyze

From dam to cm, multiply by 1,000.

a. From cm to m, ______________________ by ________.

b. From km to dm, ______________________ by ________.

c. From km to m, ______________________ by ________.

d. From mm to hm, ______________________ by ________.

2. Convert each distance traveled into meters. Circle the shortest distance. Apply

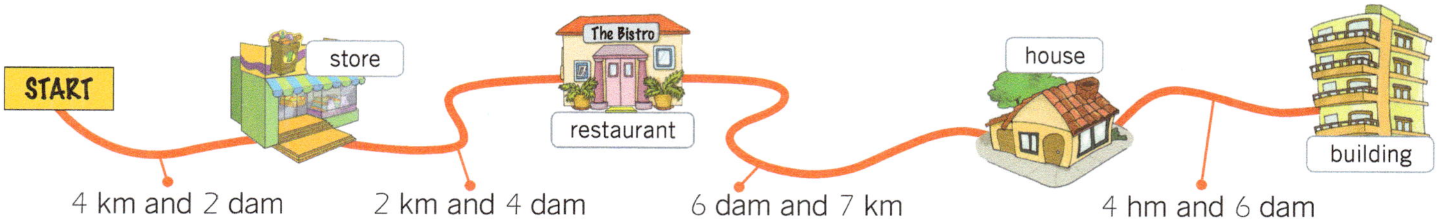

a. From the start to the store. ▶ ____________

b. From the store to the restaurant. ▶ ____________

c. From the restaurant to the house. ▶ ____________

d. From the house to the building. ▶ ____________

3. Read the word problems and answer. Analyze

a. The length of a track is 400 m. How many times would a person need to run around the track in a 10 km race?

b. Last year Lauren was 1.58 m tall, and this year she is 1.65 m tall. How many centimeters did she grow in the last year?

4. Explain which strategy you would use to express 7.52 m in millimeters and kilometers. Discuss with your classmates. Analyze

____

____

Units of Surface Area

Connecting

Stewart Island is the third biggest island in New Zealand and has a surface area of 1,746 km^2.

Fiordland National Park on New Zealand's South Island has an area of 12,500 km^2.

- Mark the correct statement with a ✔.

☐ Stewart Island has a smaller surface area than Fiordland National Park.

☐ Fiordland National Park has a surface area greater than 13,000 km^2.

Learning

- A **square meter (m^2)** is the basic unit used to measure area in the metric system. Its name comes from a square whose sides all measure 1 meter.

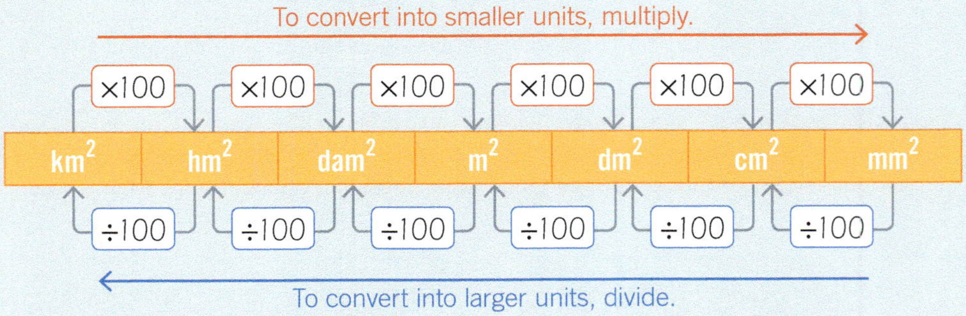

Examples:

- 1 square kilometer (km^2) equals 1,000,000 m^2.
- 1 square hectometer (hm^2) equals 10,000 m^2.
- 1 square decameter (dam^2) equals 100 m^2.
- 1 square decimeter (dm^2) equals 0.01 m^2.
- 1 square centimeter (cm^2) equals 0.0001 m^2.
- 1 square millimeter (mm^2) equals 0.000001 m^2.

Practicing

1. Trace the most appropriate surface area unit for the place shown in each image. Then explain your answer. Identify

a.

cm^2 m^2 km^2

Explanation ▶ ______________________________

____

b.

cm^2 m^2 dam^2

Explanation ▶ ______________________________

____

2. Circle the largest measurements of surface area in red and the smallest in blue. Analyze

a.

51,000 cm^2

4.9 hm^2

5,200 dm^2

0.5 km^2

b.

9 dam^2

9 m^2

9 km^2

9 hm^2

c.

800 km^2

3,000 hm^2

650 mm^2

30 m^2

Quiz Yourself

Jacob needs to cover an 18 m^2 wall with wallpaper. He sees these two offers in different stores.

Wallpaper House

Dimensions: 50 cm × 150 cm

3 for 2 special,
only $55.00

All Walls

Dimensions: 1 m × 3 m

2 for 1 special
only $75.00

Which of the two sale prices is better for Jacob? Explain.

____

Section

2 Perimeter and Area

Perimeter of Two-Dimensional Shapes

Connecting

Danny, Andrew, Kylie and Vanessa used some rope to make a large square. Each side of the square measures 10 m. How many meters of rope did they need to make the square?

- Check the correct option.

☐ The sides of the square have different lengths.

☐ The sides of the square have the same length.

- Complete the statement with *square* or *add*.

To calculate the total length in meters of the ________________, you should ________________ the lengths of the ropes that form it.

- Mark the correct answer with a ✔.

☐ They needed 20 m of rope. ☐ They needed 40 m of rope.

Learning

The **perimeter (*P*)** of a two-dimensional shape is the total measurement of all its sides.

Example 1:

- Calculate the perimeter of a rectangle with these measurements.

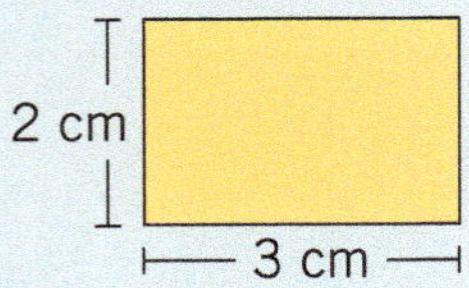

The opposite sides have the same length, so the sides can be labeled like this:

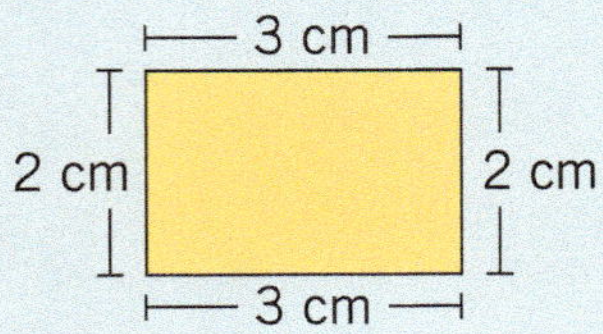

So, the perimeter is:
(*P*) = 3 cm + 3 cm + 2 cm + 2 cm = 10 cm

Example 2:

- If the perimeter of a rectangle is 20 cm, and one of its sides is 3 cm, what is the measurement of the other sides?

The problem can be represented like this:

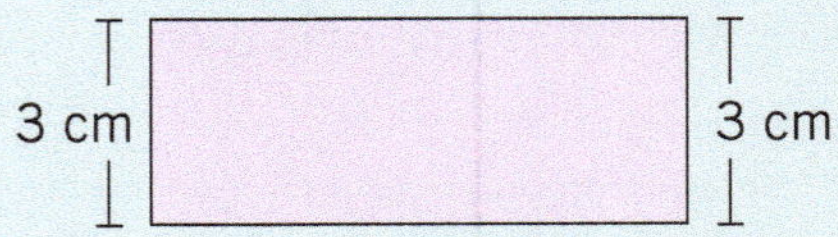

The other sides equal 14 cm together. Since those sides are equal in length, each one measures 7 cm.

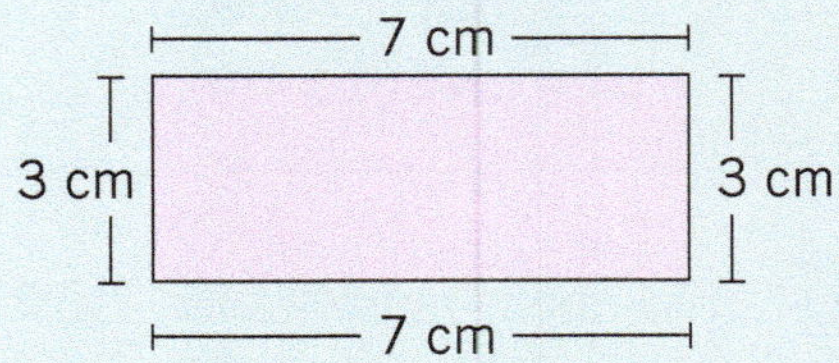

Practicing

1. Calculate the perimeters (*P*) of the quadrilaterals. Apply

a.

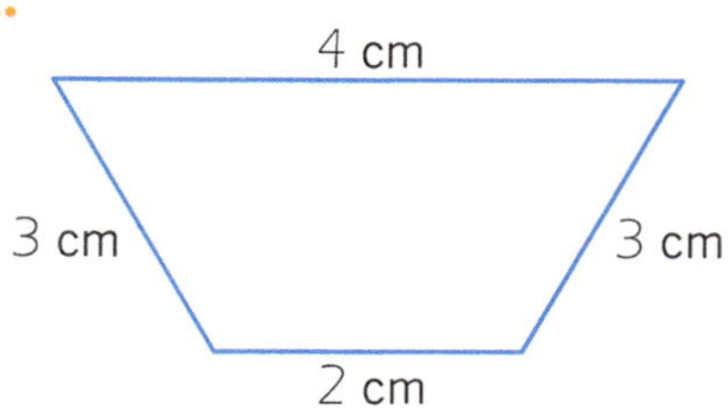

P = ____________ cm

b.

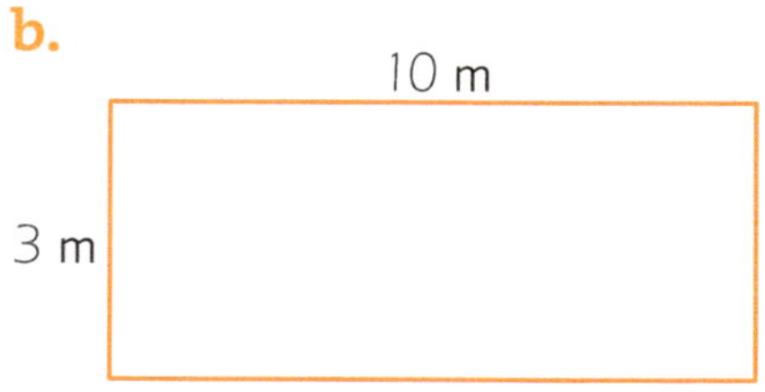

P = ____________ m

c.

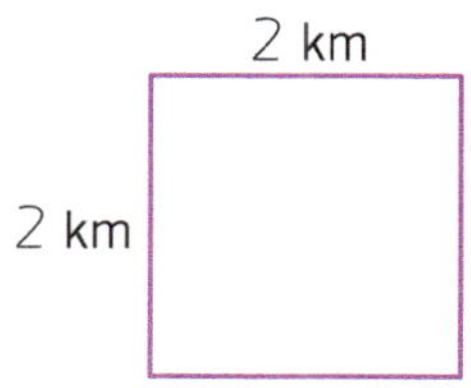

P = ____________ km

2. Calculate the lengths of the missing sides. Analyze

a.

P = 40 m

Length of segment *AB* ▸ ________ m

b.

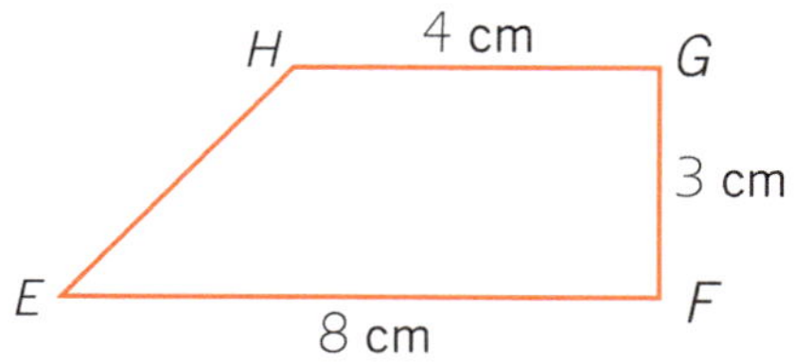

P = 20 cm

Length of segment *HE* ▸ ________ cm

c.

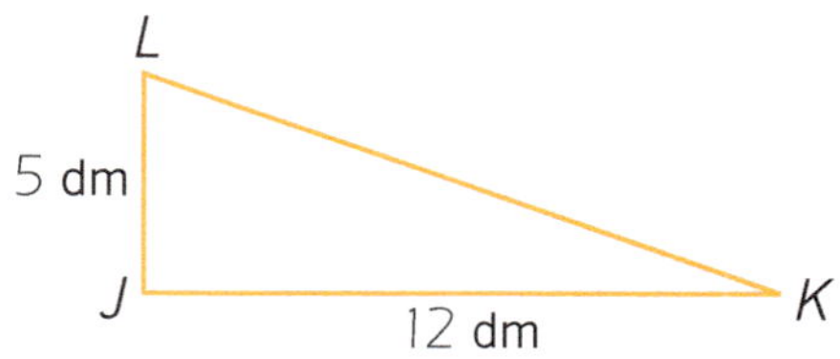

P = 30 dm

Length of segment *KL* ▸ ________ dm

3. Solve the word problems. Analyze

a. A farmer puts up a fence around the area of his land, which has a rectangular shape. If the length of the land is 350 m, and the width is half of the length, how many meters will the fence be?

b. How many different rectangles with a perimeter of 16 cm can you make if all the sides are natural numbers? Write the measurements.

Area of Rectangles

Connecting

Lucy and Samuel have rectangular bedrooms of different sizes. They both want to remodel their rooms, so they make floor plans using square meters.

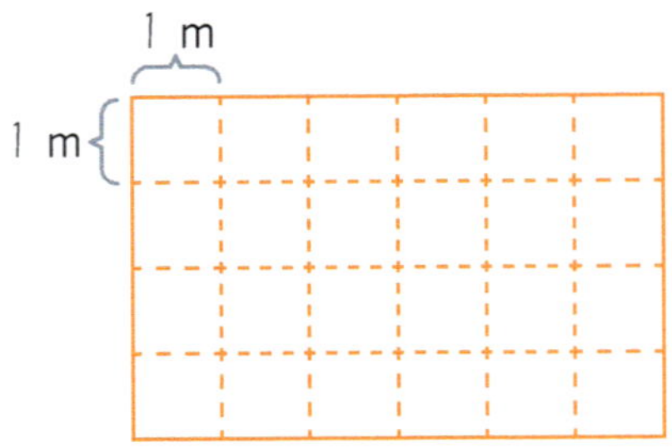

Lucy's Bedroom

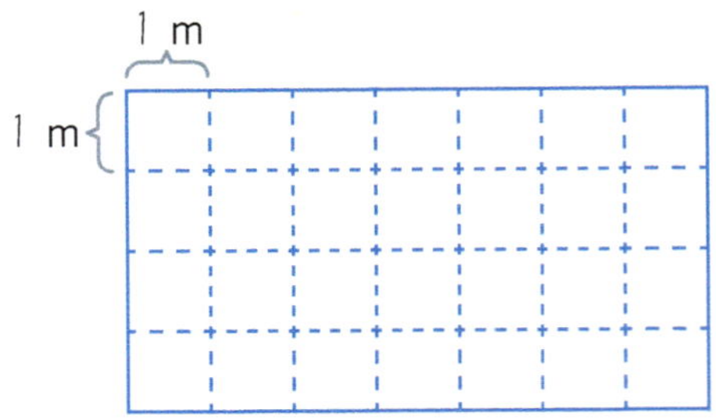

Samuel's Bedroom

- Whose floor plan has more space? ▸ ____________________
- Write the length and width of each bedroom.

Lucy	length ▸ ____________	width ▸ ____________
Samuel	length ▸ ____________	width ▸ ____________

- How many square meters does each bedroom measure?

Lucy ▸ ____________ Samuel ▸ ____________

Learning

The **area (A)** of a two-dimensional shape is the measurement of the **surface** it occupies. To measure the surface area of two-dimensional shapes you can use units such as square centimeters (**cm^2**), square decimeters (**dm^2**) and square meters (**m^2**).

To calculate the **area of a rectangle**, multiply the width by the length.

Example: To calculate the area of a rectangle, you have to:

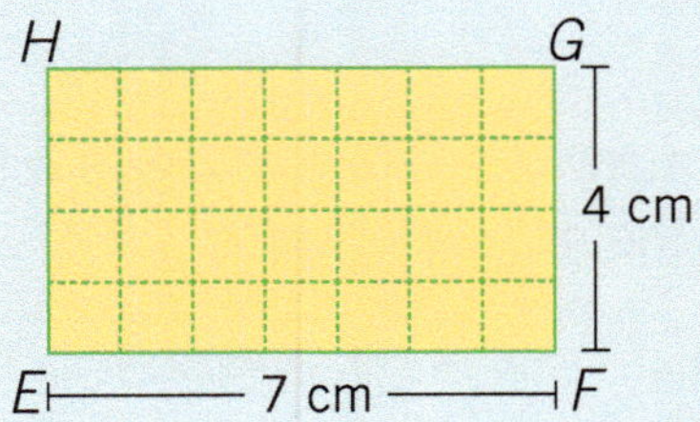

multiply side EF by side FG = 7 cm × 4 cm = 28 cm^2

Practicing

1. Calculate the areas of the rectangles. Remember that each □ is equal to 1 cm^2. Apply

$A =$ _______ cm^2 $A =$ _______ cm^2 $A =$ _______ cm^2 $A =$ _______ cm^2

2. Complete the table. Apply

	Rectangle	Calculation	Area
a.	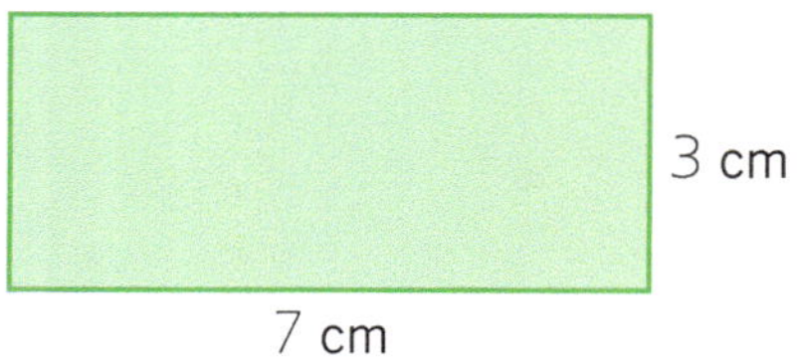		
b.		4 m × 15 m =	

3. Solve the word problems. Analyze

a. The length of one side of a rectangle is 10 cm. Its area is 50 cm^2. What are the lengths of the other sides?

b. How many different rectangles with an area of 18 cm^2 can you make using only natural numbers? Write the measurements of the rectangles.

Representing Rectangles

Connecting

Toby bought 300 m of wire to fence off an area of land that measures 5,000 m^2. Toby draws three examples of how he thinks he could build the fence.

Option 1

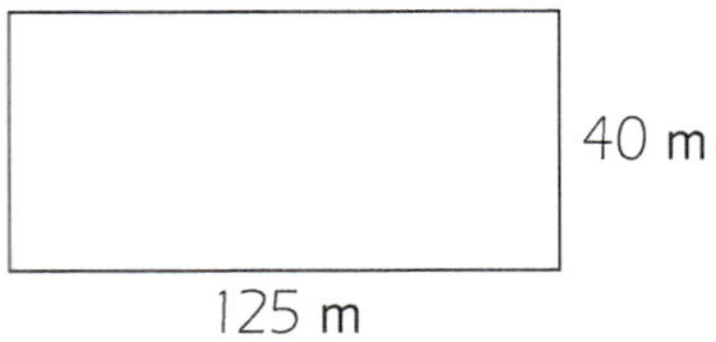

Option 2

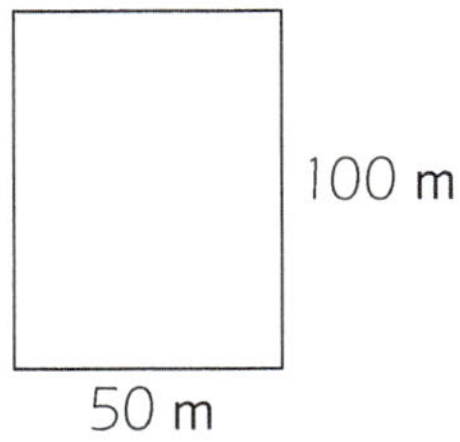

Option 3

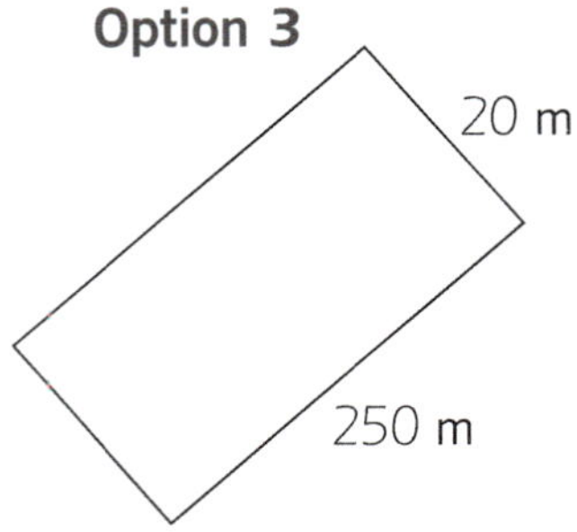

- Mark the correct statement with a ✔.

☐ The area of each rectangle is equal to 5,000 m^2.   ☐ The area of each rectangle is not equal to 5,000 m^2.

- Calculate the perimeter of each rectangle.

Option 1 ▸ ________ m   Option 2 ▸ ________ m   Option 3 ▸ ________ m

- Which option should Toby use to fence off his land? Explain.

____

Learning

To **represent rectangles** you must carefully consider the known information and the measurements. Here are two different situations:

- The sides of the rectangles are natural numbers and you know the measurment of the surface area.

  Example: If the area is 10 cm^2, you need to find all of the divisors of 10: 1 and 10, and 2 and 5. From this information, you can make two rectangles:

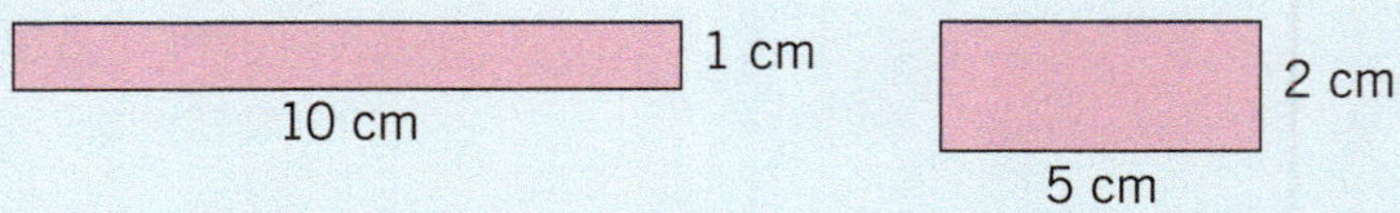

- To draw different rectangles with the same perimeter, find two numbers whose sum is equal to half the perimeter.

  Example: If the perimeter is 10 cm, the sides of the rectangle are natural numbers:

Practicing

1. Represent the rectangles in each case. Use a scale of one grid square = 1 cm^2. Apply

a. Two different rectangles that have an area of 8 cm^2.

b. One rectangle with a perimeter of 18 cm. The width is two times its length.

2. Solve the word problem. Analyze

If the perimeter of a rectangle is equal to 14 cm, and its area is 10 cm^2, what are the measurements of its width and height?

width ▶ ________ cm height ▶ ________ cm

Quiz Yourself

Read the situation and answer.

A soccer field is being replanted with sections of grass that are 300 cm long and 200 cm wide.

- How many sections of grass will be needed to cover the field?

____

____

- How should the sections of grass be positioned so that none have to be cut down in size? Explain.

____

____

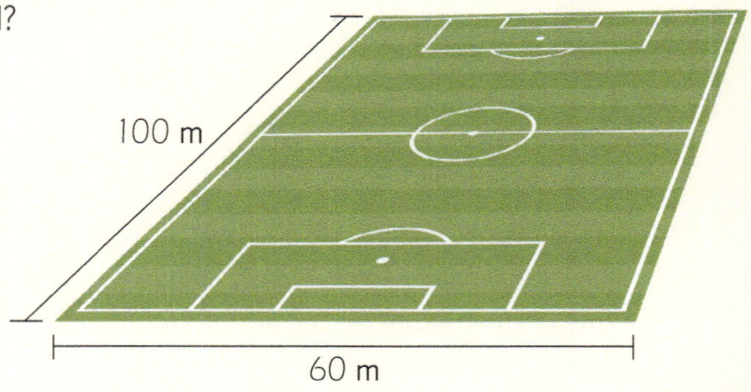

Let's Check!

Units of Length and Surface Area

1. Read the information and answer.

points
/ 3

- Annie's farm is situated 3,500 m from the main road.
- Natalie's farm is 500 m farther from the main road than Annie's.
- Kate's farm is 200 m closer to the main road than Natalie's.
- The farm that is 4000 m away from the road is mainly used for raising cows and sheep.

a. How far is Natalie's farm from the road? ______________________

b. How far is Kate's farm from the road? ______________________

c. What does Natalie use her farm for? ______________________

Conversion Between Units of Length

2. Solve the word problem.

points
/ 3

In a race, Johnny ran 1,500 m, Alex ran 15,000 dam and Rudy ran 1,500,000 cm. Convert the distances to meters, and write them from greatest to least.

Units of Surface Area

3. Circle the most appropriate unit to measure these objects.

points
/ 2

a. 

cm^2 m^2 km^2

b. 

museum floor

m^2 hm^2 km^2

Perimeter of Two-Dimensional Shapes

4. Solve the word problems.

points /4

a. The perimeter of a rectangle is 100 cm, and its width is 23 cm. What is the length of the rectangle?

b. If the width of a rectangle is 20 m, and its length is three times its width, what is its perimeter?

Area of Rectangles

5. Write **T** if the statement is **true** and **F** if it is **false**. Explain.

points /4

a. ☐ If the width of a rectangle is 5 cm, and its area is 15 cm^2, then its length is 10 cm.

Explanation ▸ ____________________

b. ☐ The area of a rectangle is 24 m^2 if its sides measure 8 m and 3 m.

Explanation ▸ ____________________

Representing Rectangles

6. Read and then answer.

points /3

On the grid, each ☐ has a surface area of 1 cm^2. The area of rectangle *ABCD* is 6 cm^2.

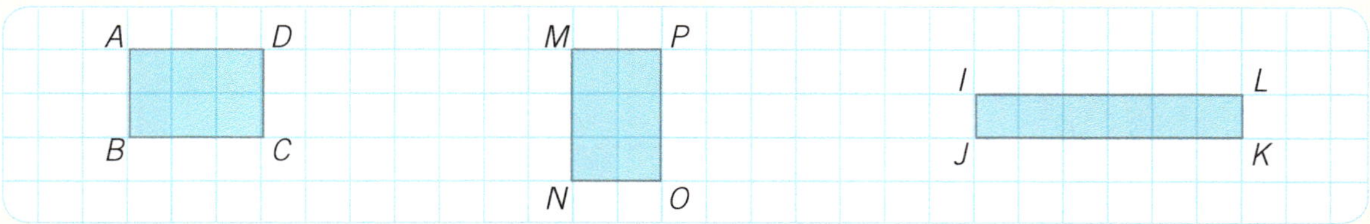

What conclusions can you make about the area and perimeter of each rectangle? Explain.

____

____

Area of Two-Dimensional Shapes

Area of Triangles Using Grids

Connecting

Triangle *CDE* is shown on a grid.

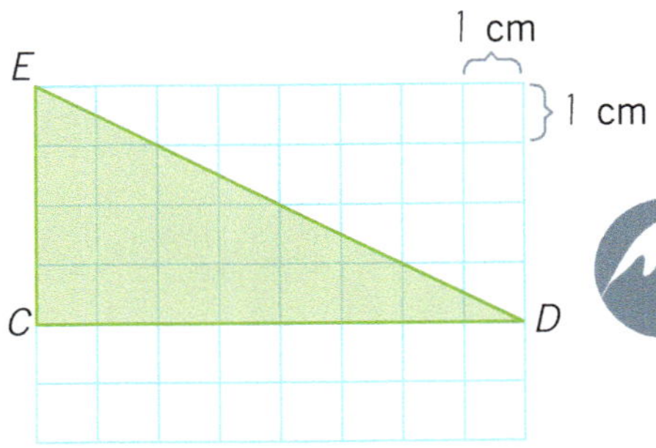

- Complete.

  Length of side *CD* = ____________

  Length of side *EC* = ____________

- The segments that form quadrilateral *CDHE* are shown in red. What two-dimensional shape is *CDHE*? What is its area?

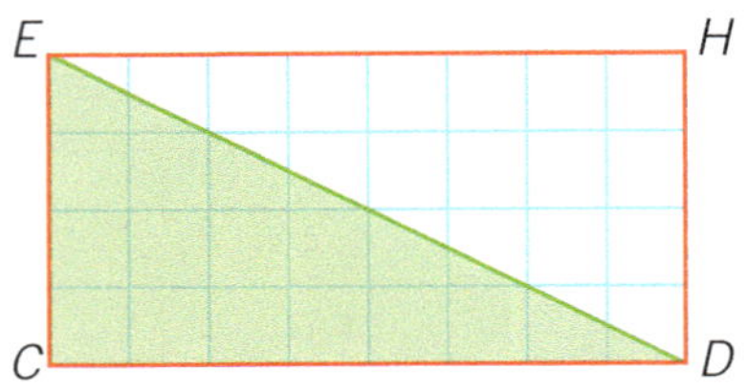

Shape ▸ ____________

Area ▸ ____________

- Using the information above, how can you calculate the area of triangle *CDE*? Explain.

____

Challenge

In construction, triangular shapes provide the greatest structural strength, and this is why you often see them used to build bridges. Research different bridges around the world that use triangles. Then, build your own bridge using ice-cream sticks and Plasticine or other materials. Test your bridge's strength by hanging different weights from the main section. Draw an accurate scale representation of your bridge.

Learning

To calculate the **area (*A*)** of a triangle, you can first think of it as half a rectangle. You can create a rectangle around the triangle using any of its sides as the base.

Example: In the triangle *ABC*, each ☐ equals 1 cm.

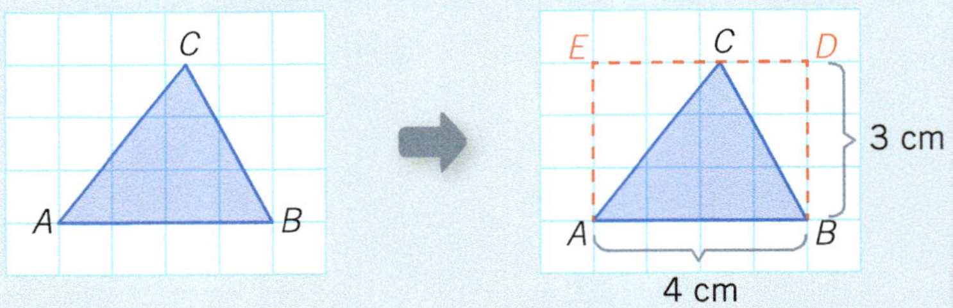

The area of rectangle *ABDE* is 12 cm^2. Therefore, the area of the triangle *ABC* is 12 $cm^2 \div 2 = 6$ cm^2.

Practicing

1. Calculate the area of rectangle *CBAD*. Then calculate the areas of each triangle. Analyze

a.

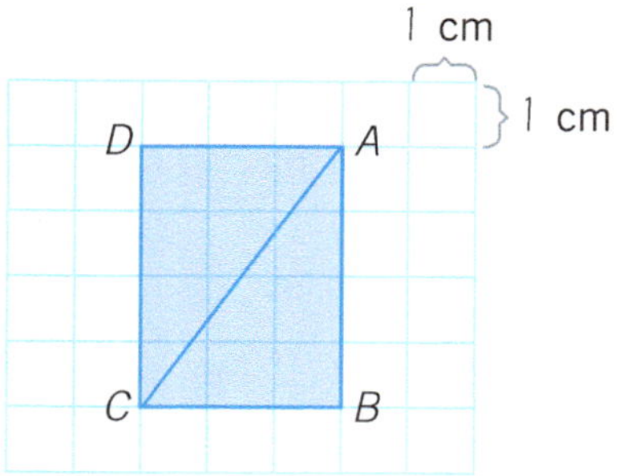

A = ______________________

b.

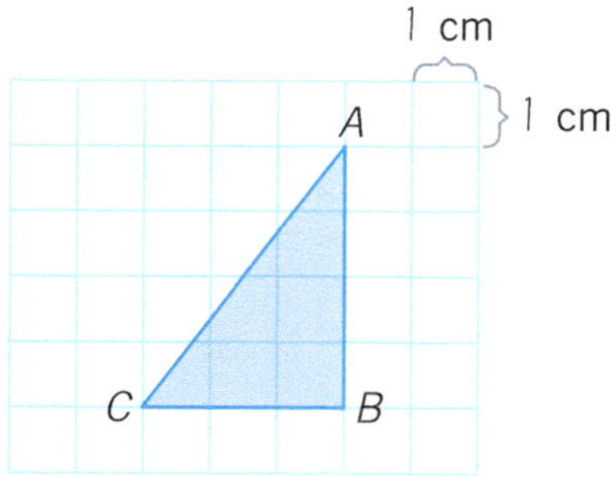

A = ______________________

c.

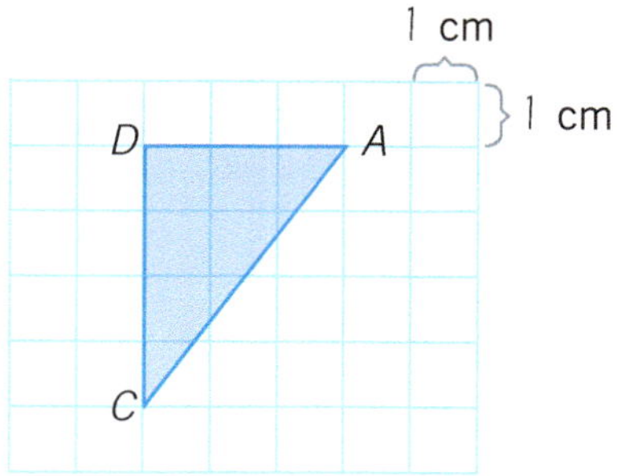

A = ______________________

2. If each ☐ measures 10 cm, calculate the areas of the triangles. Apply

a.

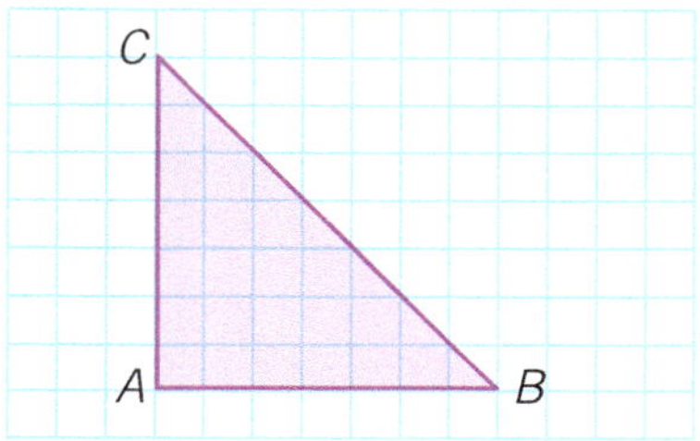

A = ______________________

b.

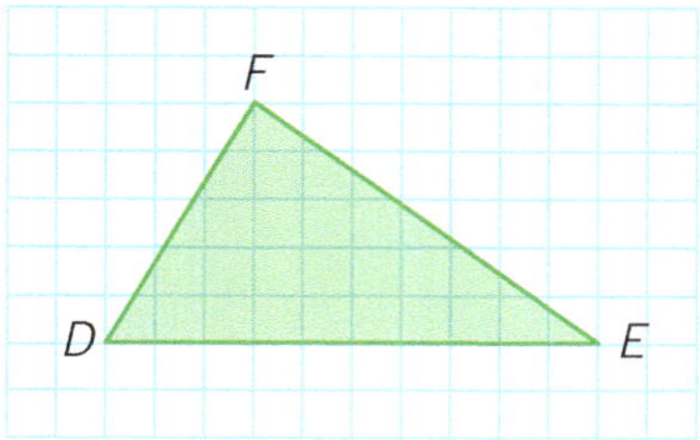

A = ______________________

c.

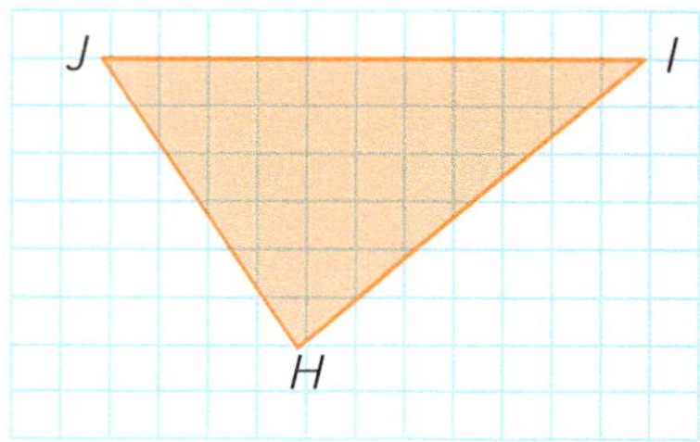

A = ______________________

3. Study the grid and then answer the questions. Each ☐ equals 1 cm. Analyze

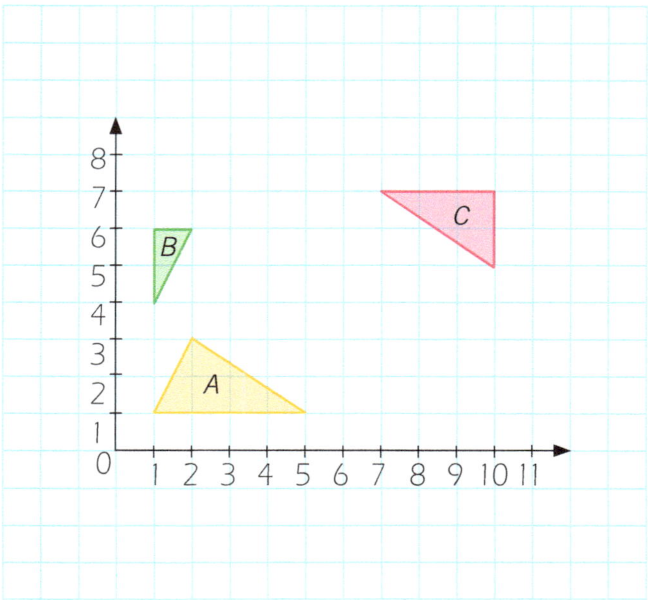

a. Calculate the areas:

Triangle *A* = ________ cm^2

Triangle *B* = ________ cm^2

Triangle *C* = ________ cm^2

b. If triangle *B* moves down 3 squares, and triangle *C* moves down 4 squares and left 5 squares, what is the area of the new shape?

Area of Triangles

Connecting

Look at triangle *ABC* drawn on the grid. Draw a red rectangle called *ABDE* around it so that point *C* will be part of side *DE*.

Use a ruler to answer:

- What is the area of rectangle *ABDE*? ▸ ____________
- What is the area of triangle *ABC*? ▸ ____________
- What is the measurement of *h*? ▸ ____________

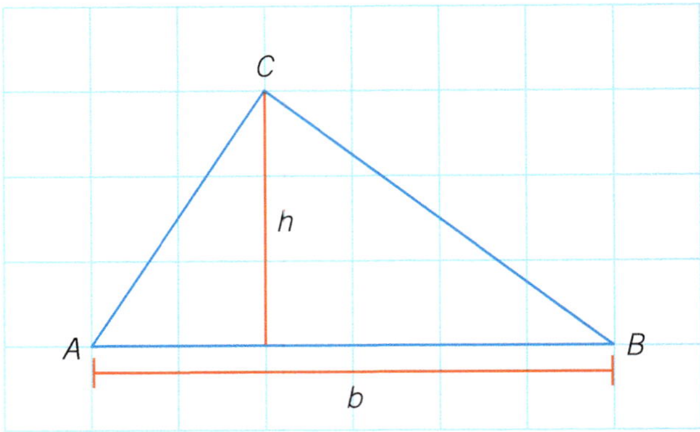

- Which operation do you use to calculate the area of triangle *ABC*? Mark the correct answer with a ✔.

☐ $\frac{b \times h}{2}$ ☐ $\frac{b \div h}{2}$ ☐ $\frac{b + h}{2}$

Learning

To calculate the **area of a triangle**, remember:

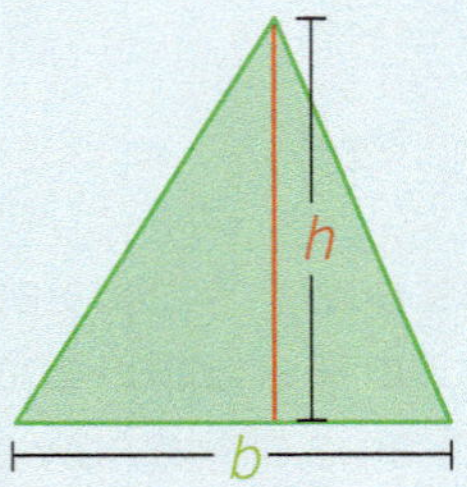

Base: *b*

Height: *h* corresponds to the perpendicular line that goes from the superior vertex to the base.

The area of a triangle can be calculated using the formula:

$$\frac{b \times h}{2}$$

Example: Look at triangle *ACB*.

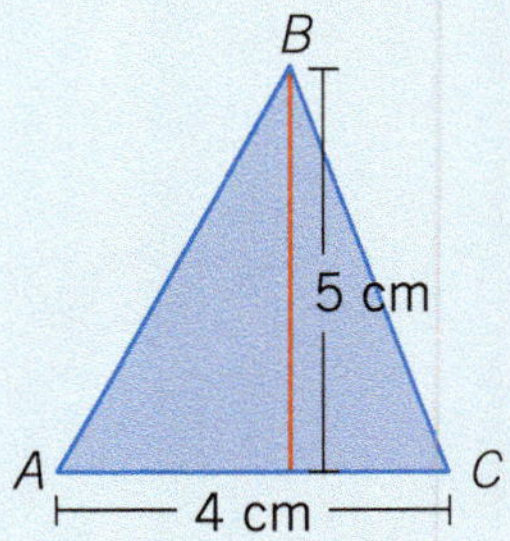

h = 5 cm

b = 4 cm

The area of the triangle *ACB* can be calculated:

$$\frac{4 \text{ cm} \times 5 \text{ cm}}{2} = \frac{20 \text{ cm}^2}{2} = 10 \text{ cm}^2$$

Practicing

1. Use a ruler to measure the base and height of the triangles. Then calculate their surface areas (A). Apply

a.

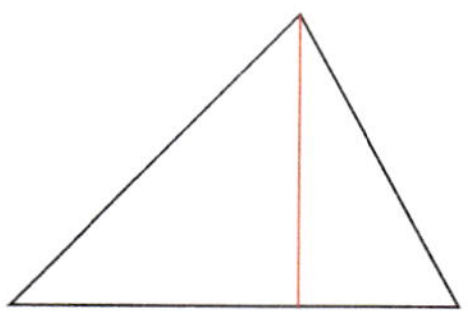

$A =$ ______

b.

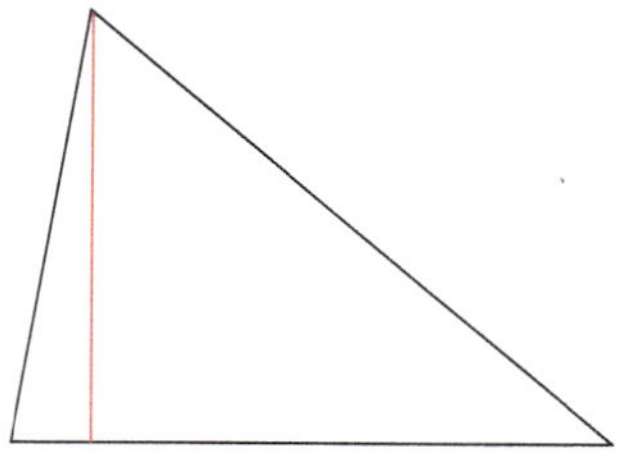

$A =$ ______

c.

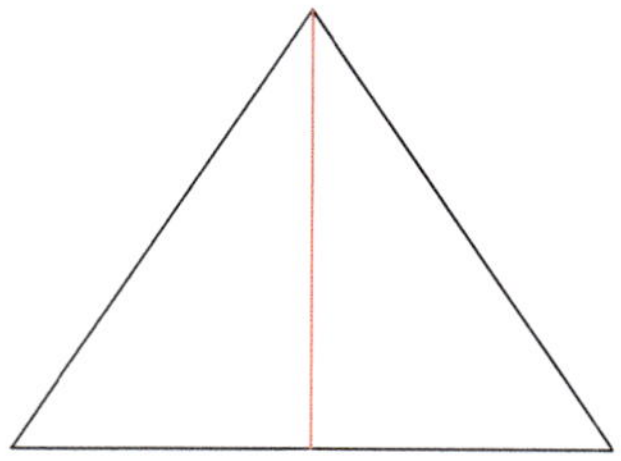

$A =$ ______

2. Calculate the surface areas (A) of the triangles. Apply

a.

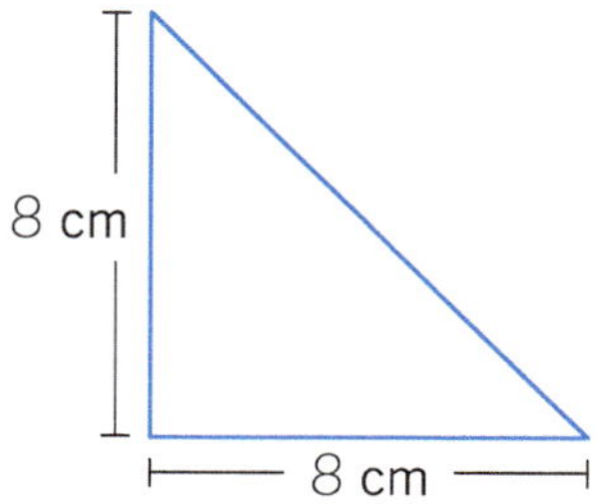

$A =$ ______

b.

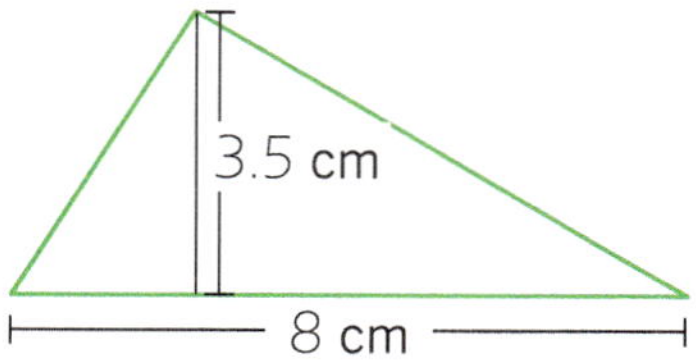

$A =$ ______

c.

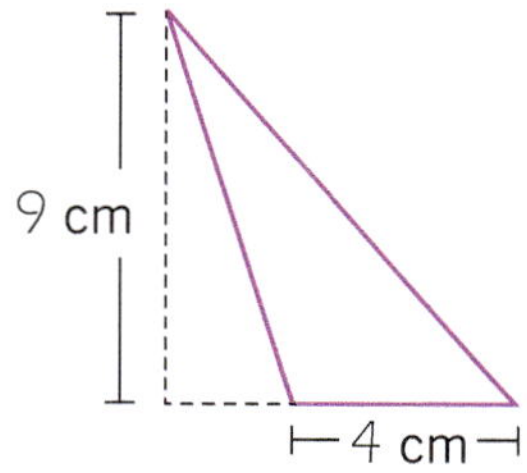

$A =$ ______

3. Look at the triangles and complete the missing measurements. Analyze

a.

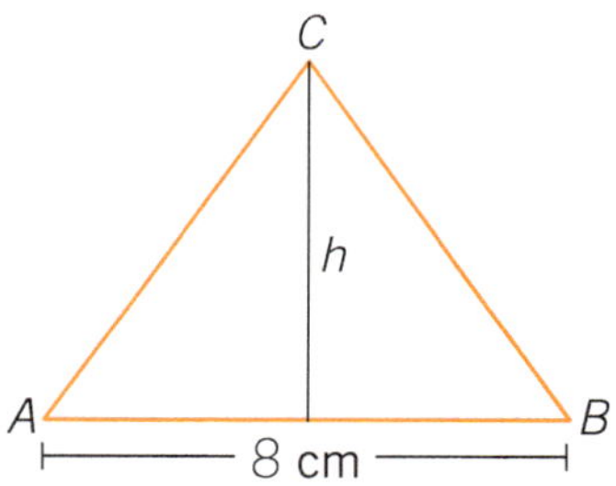

$A = 16\ cm^2$

$h =$ ______

b.

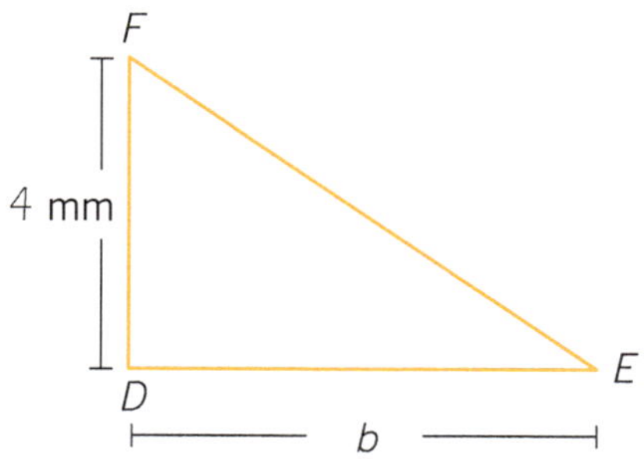

$A = 14\ mm^2$

$b =$ ______

c.

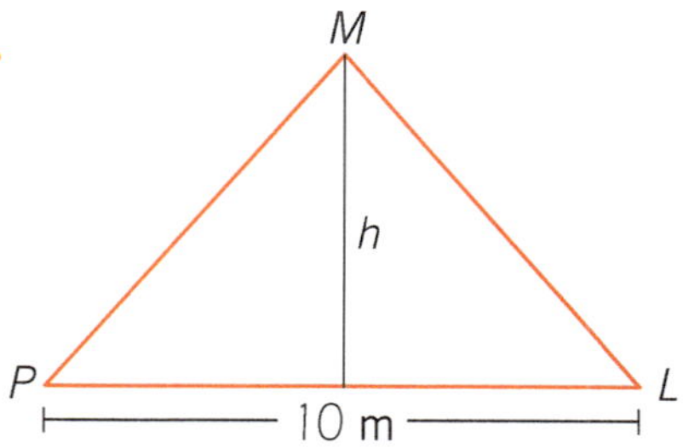

$A = 40\ m^2$

$h =$ ______

4. Look at the diagram and answer. Analyze

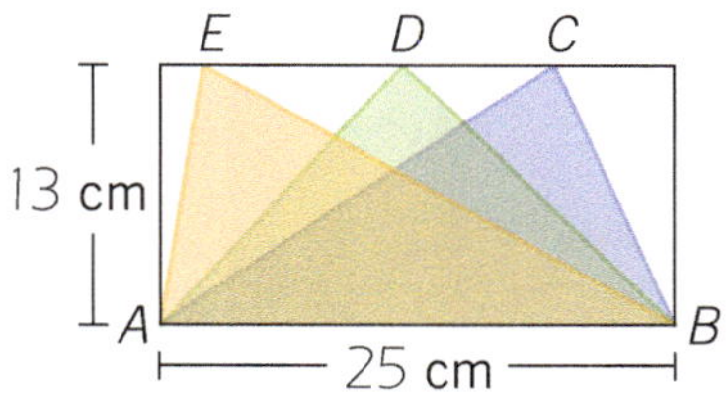

Which of the triangles has the greatest area? Explain.

______

______

Area of Rhombuses and Rhomboids Using Grids

Connecting

Some seeds are planted in a garden so that they will grow in the shape of a rhombus. Look at the garden represented on the grid. The sides of each square equal 10 cm.

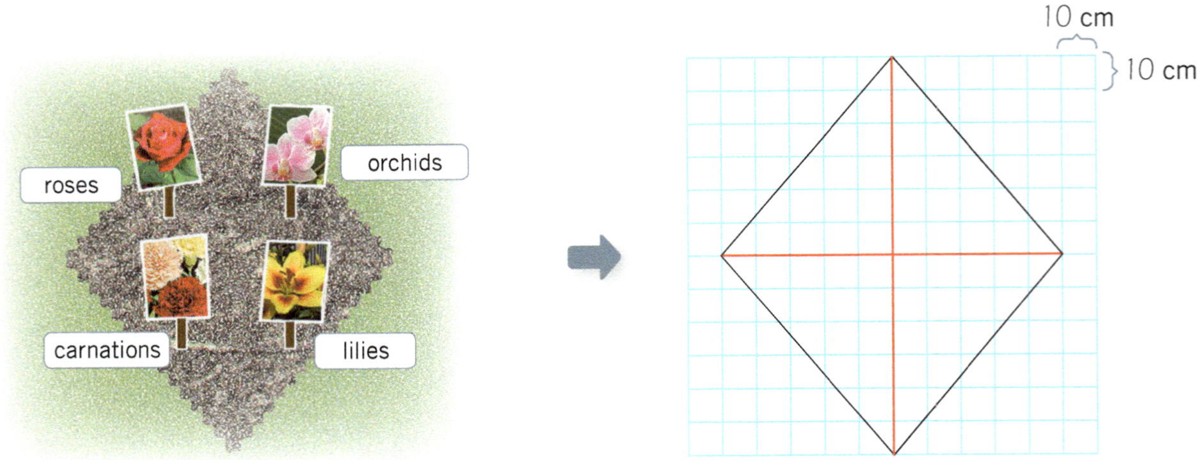

- As you can see, the rhombus is made of 4 right triangles. Circle the correct area of each of the triangles.

  ▸ 15 cm^2 ▸ 1,500 cm^2 ▸ 15,000 cm^2

- Mark the total area of the garden with a ✔.

  ☐ 60 cm^2 ☐ 6,000 cm^2

Did You Know...?

A rhombus is also called a diamond or an equilateral quadrilateral. Try saying that quickly ten times!

Learning

To calculate the **area** (***A***) of **rhombuses** and **rhomboids**, you need to break them down into different triangles or rectangles. Then add the areas of the triangles or rectangles to find the area of the shape.

Example:

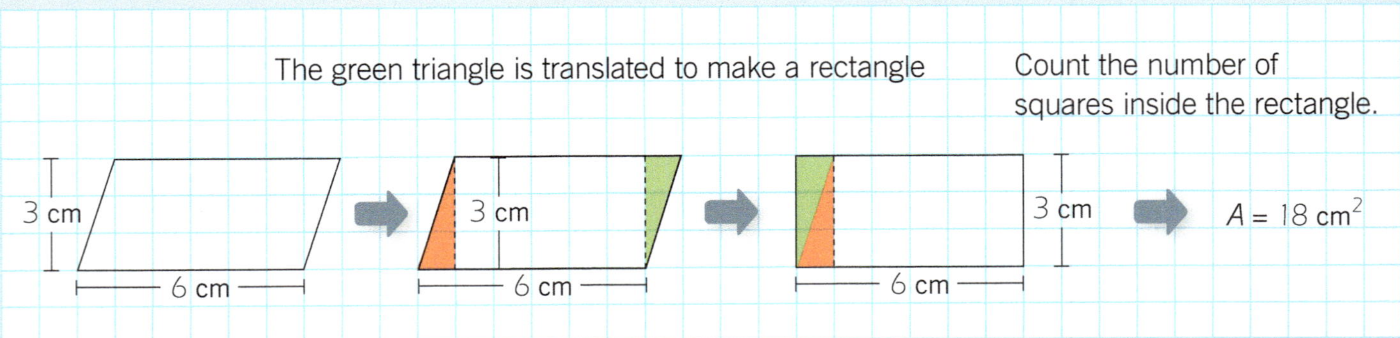

Practicing

1. Calculate the areas of the two-dimensional shapes. Each ☐ equals 1 cm^2. Apply

a.

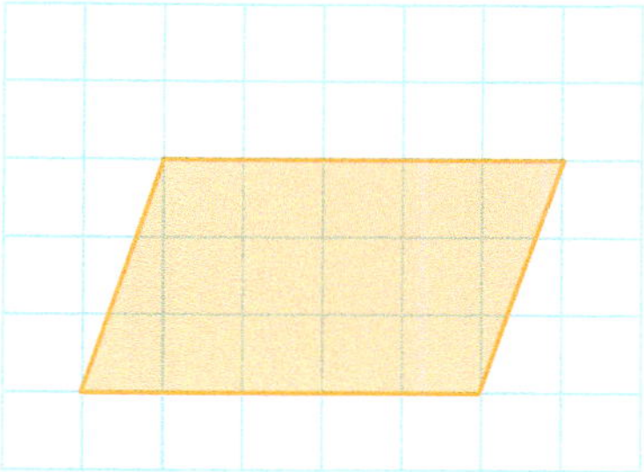

$A =$ ______________ cm^2

b.

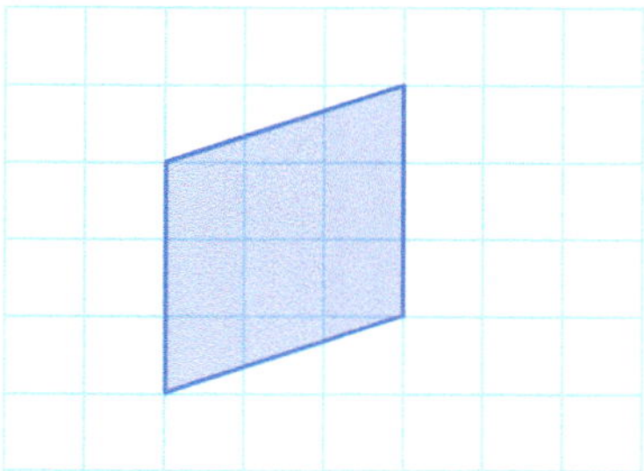

$A =$ ______________ cm^2

c.

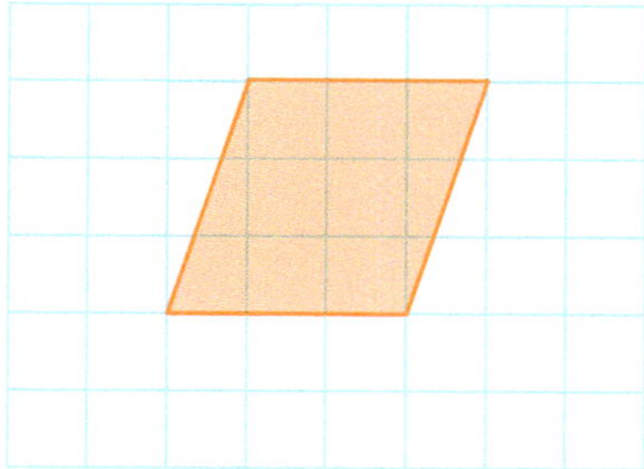

$A =$ ______________ cm^2

d.

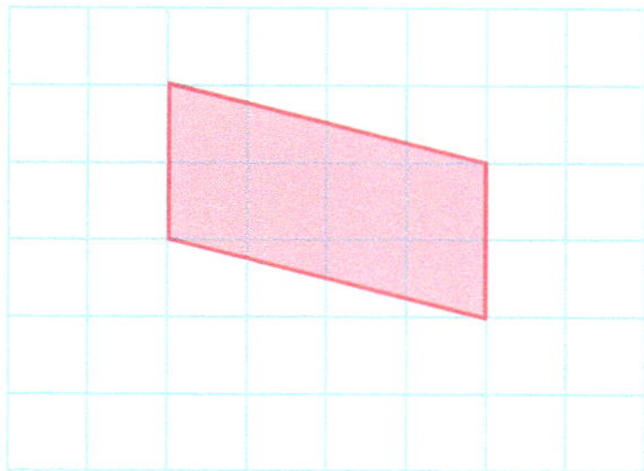

$A =$ ______________ cm^2

e.

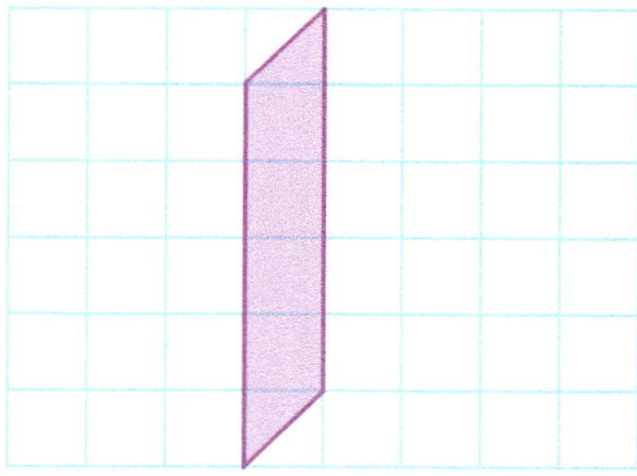

$A =$ ______________ cm^2

f.

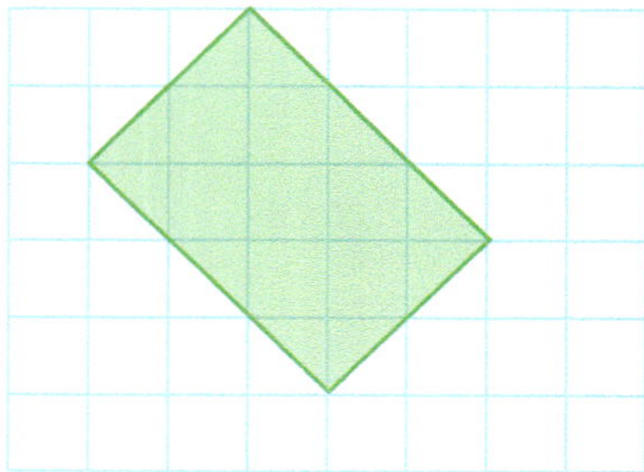

$A =$ ______________ cm^2

2. Look at the two-dimensional shapes and answer. Analyze

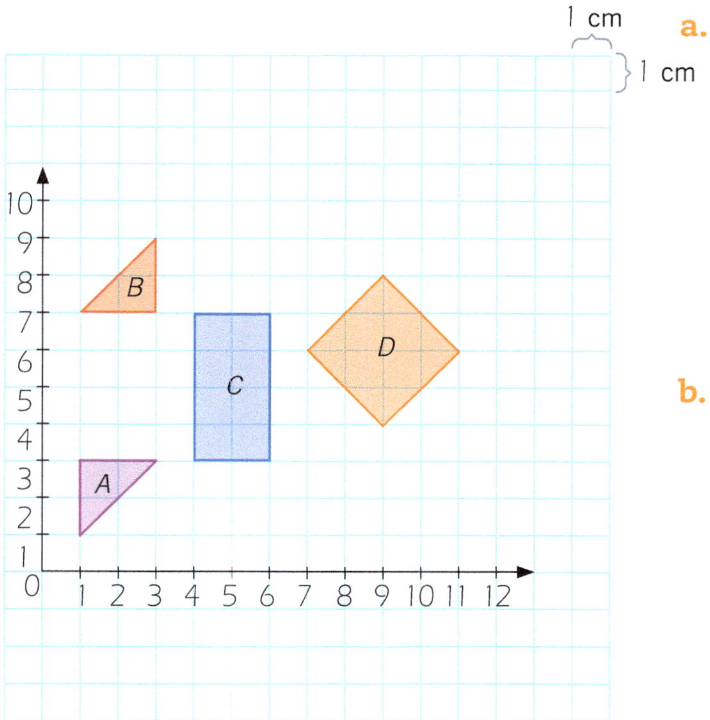

a. What is the area of quadrilateral D?

b. If triangles A and B are translated 3 squares to the right, what is the surface area of the new quadrilateral they form?

Area of Rhombuses and Rhomboids

Connecting

The teacher draws these shapes on the board in math class.

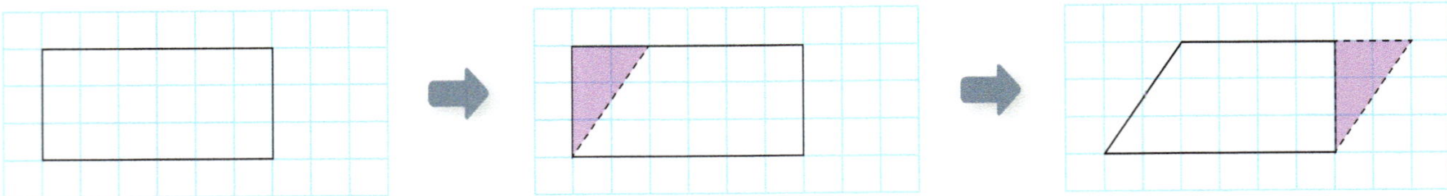

Shape 1 Shape 2 Shape 3

- Complete the statement with the words.

translated triangle

In Shape 2, one ________________ is marked. Shape 3 shows what the shape looks like after the triangle is ________________ to the right of the shape.

Mark the geometric shape shown in Shape 3 with a ✔.

☐ rhombus ☐ rhomboid

If each ☐ measures 1 cm^2 what is the area of the two-dimensional shape in Shape 3 ______ cm^2?

Challenge

Think back to the bridge you built on page 132. Were there any rhombuses in your bridge? Analyze your bridge and identify the shapes in the design. Calculate the total surface area.

Learning

To calculate the **area of a rhombus** or a **rhomboid** (a geometric figure similar to a rhombus, but having adjacent sides of unequal length), consider:

The **area of a rhombus** is the product of its diagonals, divided by two.

Rhombus

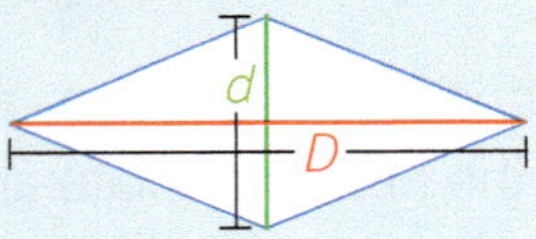

d: shorter diagonal

D: longer diagonal

Example:

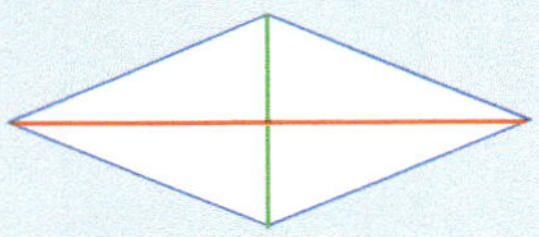

$d = 4$ cm $D = 7$ cm

$$A = \frac{D \times d}{2}$$

$$A = \frac{7cm \times 4cm}{2}$$

$$A = 14 \text{ cm}^2$$

The **area of a rhomboid** is the product of its height (h) and its base (b).

Rhomboid

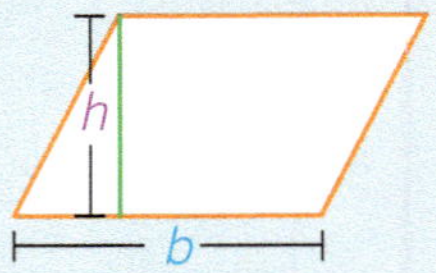

h: height

b: base

Example:

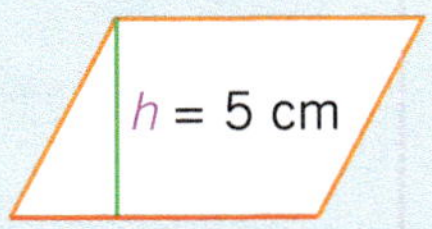

$b = 6$ cm

$$A = b \times h$$

$$A = 6 \text{ cm} \times 5 \text{ cm}$$

$$A = 30 \text{ cm}^2$$

Practicing

1. Calculate the areas of the quadrilaterals. Apply

a.

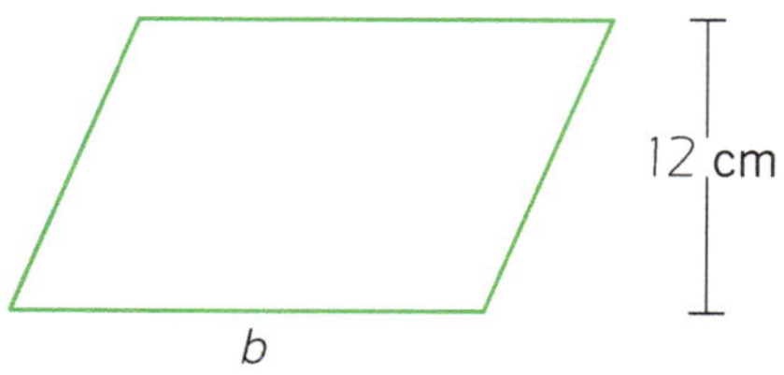

$b = 20$ cm

b.

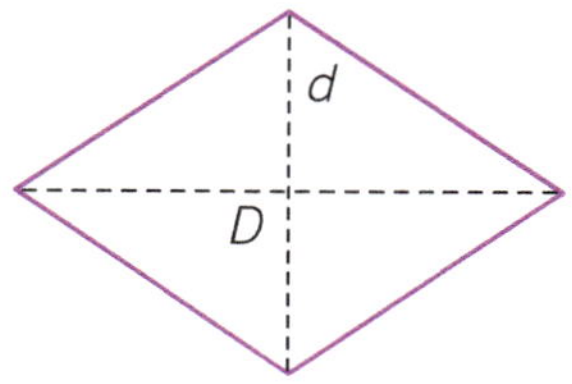

$D = 15$ m $d = 10$ m

Education through Values

Working in teams helps us to understand others' points of view and develop group strategies to solve problems together.

2. Solve the word problem. Analyze

If a rhomboid has a base of 20 cm, and its surface area is 100 cm^2, what is its height?

3. Analyze the problem and answer. Analyze

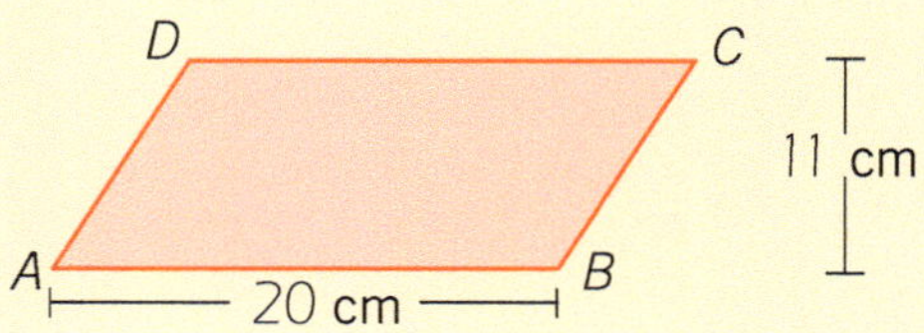

What is the surface area you could cover with eight of these rhomboids?

a. Before you answer the question, what do you need to calculate first?

b. Answer the question and share your result with your classmates.

Area of Trapezoids Using Grids

Connecting

Look at triangle *ABC*, rectangle *DEFG* and trapezoid *HIJK* on the grid.

If you translate the triangle, you can make the same shape as trapezoid *HIJK*.

So, the area of the trapezoid is the sum of the areas of the rectangle and triangle.

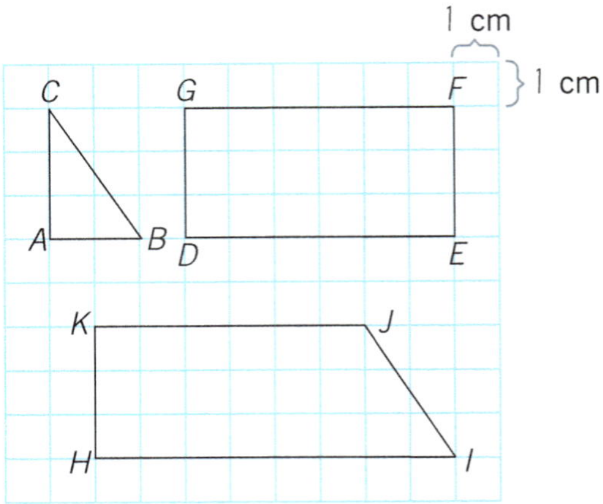

- Complete the statement with the words.

right translated congruent

To make a two-dimensional shape ______________ with the trapezoid, the triangle should be ______________ nine spaces to the ______________.

- Calculate the area of these shapes using the information above.

Triangle *ABC* = ______________ Rectangle *DEFG* = ______________

- Mark the correct answer with a ✔.

☐ The area of the trapezoid is 20 cm^2. ☐ The area of the trapezoid is 21 cm^2.

Learning

To calculate the **area of a trapezoid** you can break the shape into triangles and rectangles. Then calculate the areas of these shapes and add them together to get the area of the trapezoid.

Example: To calculate the area of trapezoid *ABCD*, break it into a rectangle and two triangles, as shown in the image.

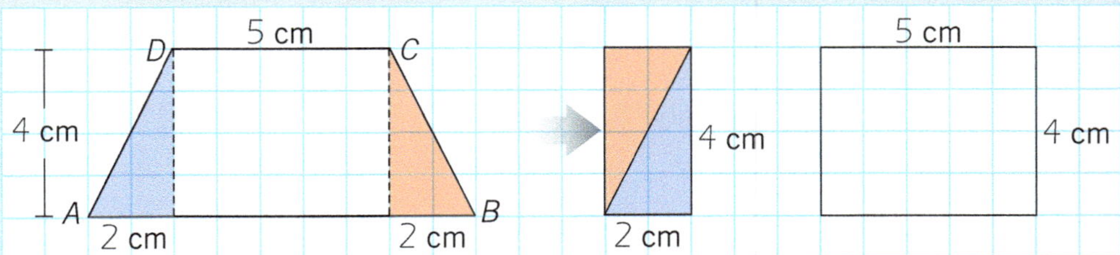

The area of trapezoid *ABCD* is 28 cm^2.

Practicing

1. Calculate the areas of the trapezoids. Imagine each ☐ equals 1 cm^2. Apply

a.

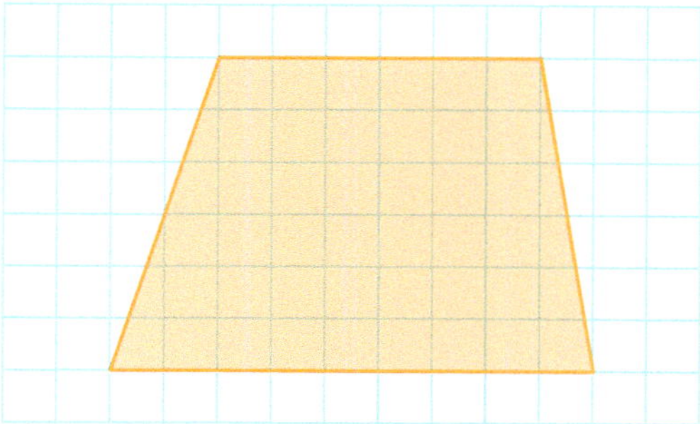

b.

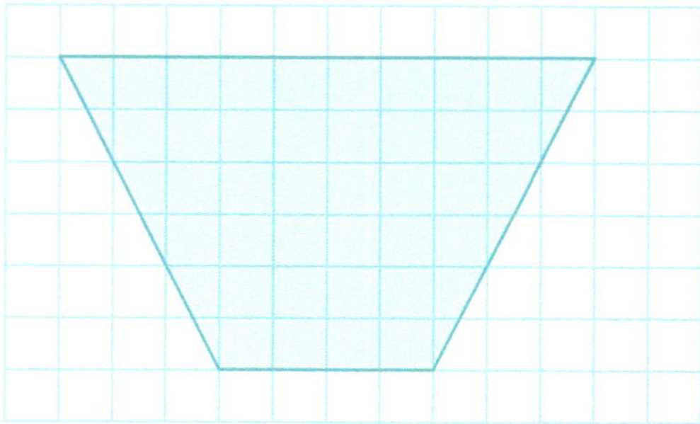

2. Analyze the two-dimensional shapes and then answer. Imagine each ☐ equals 1 cm^2. Analyze

Shape 1

Shape 2

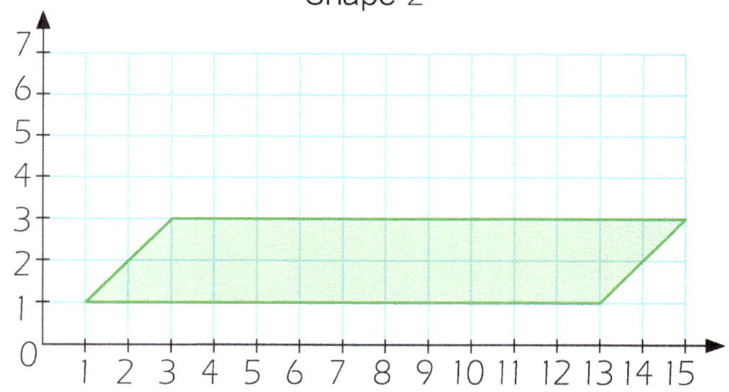

a. To make Shape 2, what transformation can you apply to one part of Shape 1? Explain.

b. Calculate the areas of the two-dimensional shapes.

Area of Trapezoids

Connecting

A furniture store is making a table in the shape of a trapezoid.

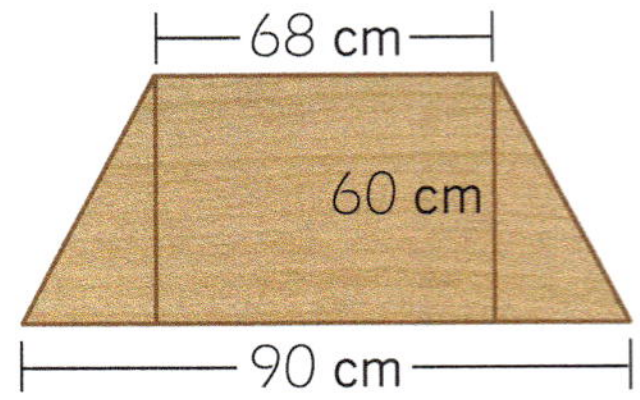

To find the surface area of the tabletop, you can break the shape into a rectangle and two triangles, like this:

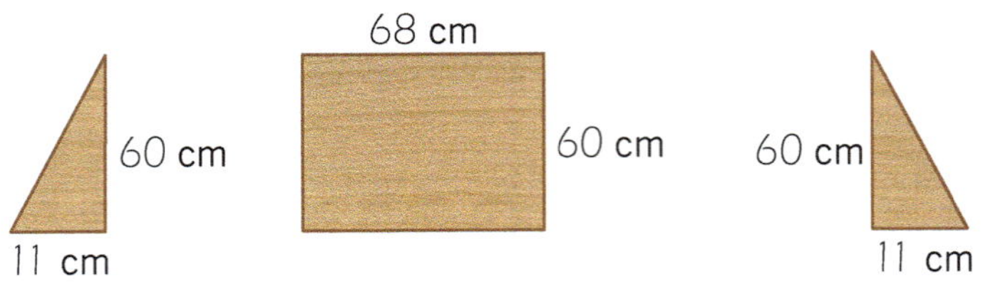

- Calculate the area of the two-dimensional shapes that form the trapezoid.

Learning

To calculate the **area of a trapezoid**, you can join the trapezoid with another that is identical to make a rhomboid.

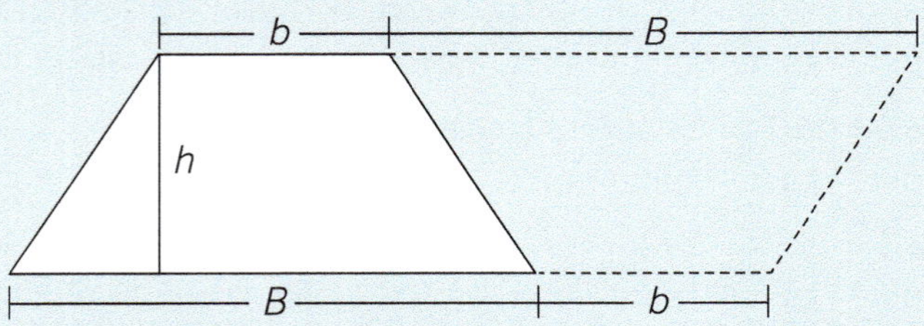

The area of the rhomboid is calculated using the formula: $(B + b) \times h$.
The area of the trapezoid is equal to half of the area of the rhomboid.

$$A = \frac{(B + b) \times h}{2}$$

Example: To calculate the area of a trapezoid you:

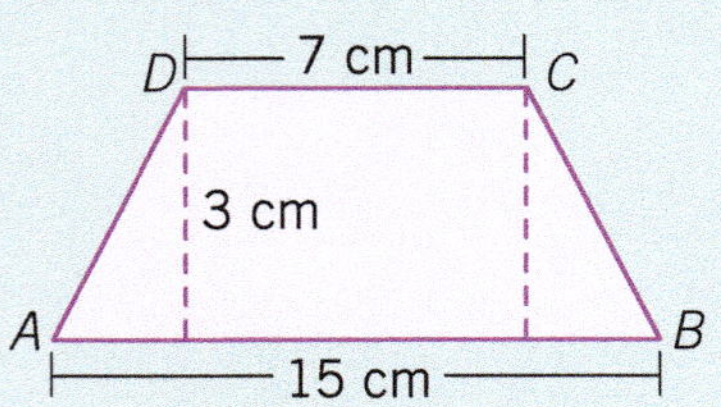

$$A = \frac{(15\text{ cm} + 7\text{ cm}) \times 3\text{ cm}}{2} = \frac{22\text{ cm} \times 3\text{ cm}}{2} = \frac{66\text{ cm}^2}{2} = 33\text{ cm}^2$$

Practicing

1. Calculate the areas of the trapezoids. Apply

a.

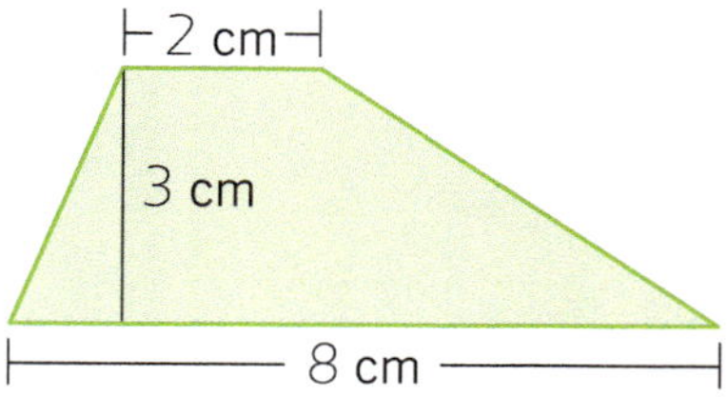

b.

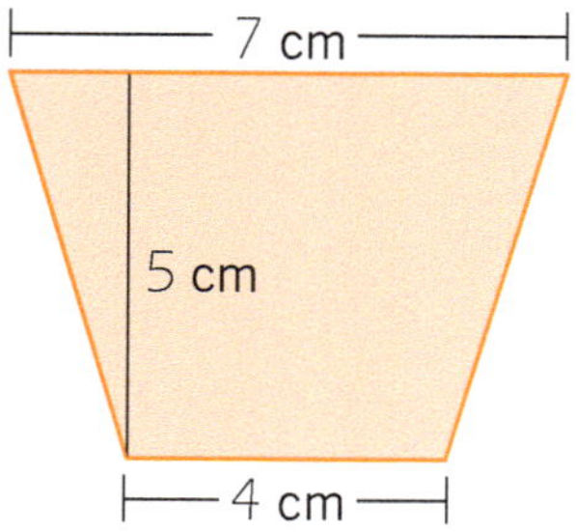

c.

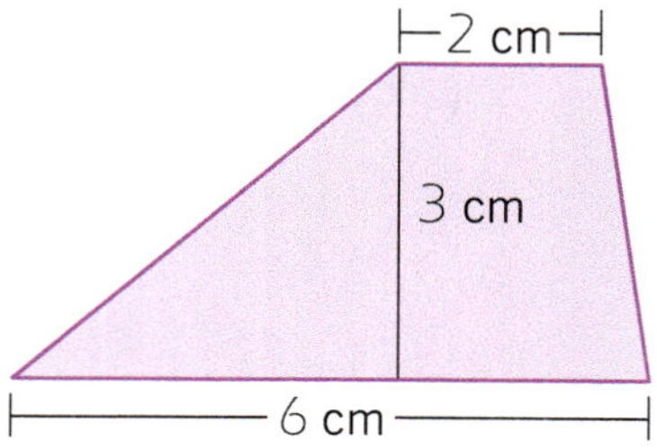

2. Solve the word problems. Analyze

a. The area of half a trapezoid is 270 m^2. What is the area of the whole trapezoid?

b. If the bases of a trapezoid measure 10 m and 5 m, and the height is 4 m, what is the surface area of the trapezoid?

c. If the sum of the bases of a trapezoid is 120 cm, and the area is 480 cm^2, what is its height?

Exam Strategies

Multiple Choice Questions

1. Sarah is going to paint her house. Before she starts painting, she needs to know the surface area of the walls to calculate how much paint to buy. If each window is 1 m^2, what is the total area of the two walls shown?

A. 90 m^2
B. 142 m^2
C. 154 m^2
D. 159 m^2

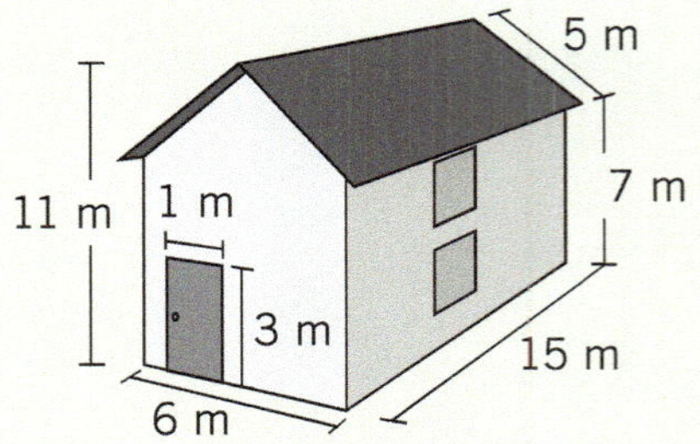

Analyzing the Answers

A. This alternative calculates the area of the floor of the house, but not the walls.

B. In this case, the area of the side wall and the rectangular part of the front wall are calculated. However, the area of the triangle below the roof is not added to the operation.

C. In this case, the area is calculated correctly using the formulas:

Wall *A* ▸ $6\text{ m} \times 7\text{ m} - 3\text{ m}^2 = 39\text{ m}^2$ (area of the door: 3 m^2; total area of the wall: $6\text{ m} \times 7\text{ m}$)

Wall *B* ▸ $\dfrac{6\text{ m} \times 4\text{ m}}{2} = 12\text{ m}^2$

Wall *C* ▸ $(15\text{ m} \times 7\text{ m}) - 2 \times 1\text{ m}^2 = 103\text{ m}^2$ (area of the windows: $2 \times 1\text{ m}^2$; total area of the wall: $15\text{ m} \times 7\text{ m}$)

Total area ▸ $39\text{ m}^2 + 12\text{ m}^2 + 103\text{ m}^2 = 154\text{ m}^2$

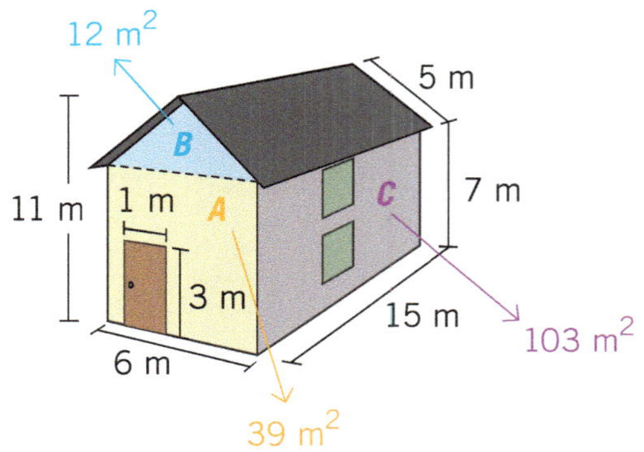

D. This alternative calculates the area without taking into consideration the area of the doors (3 m^2) or windows (2 m^2).

▸ Therefore, the answer is **C**.

1. A — B — C — D

What Did You Learn?

Final Evaluation

1. Measure the segments and answer.

points /4

a.

length in cm ▸ ____ length in mm ▸ ____

b.

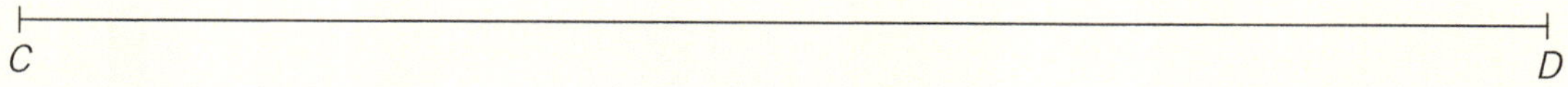

length in cm ▸ ____ length in mm ▸ ____

2. Convert the missing units of length to complete the chart.

points /6

km	hm	dam	m	dm	cm	mm
			7,000			
30						
						400,000
					80,000	
	20					
		3,540				

3. Calculate the perimeters and the areas of the shapes.

points /4

a.

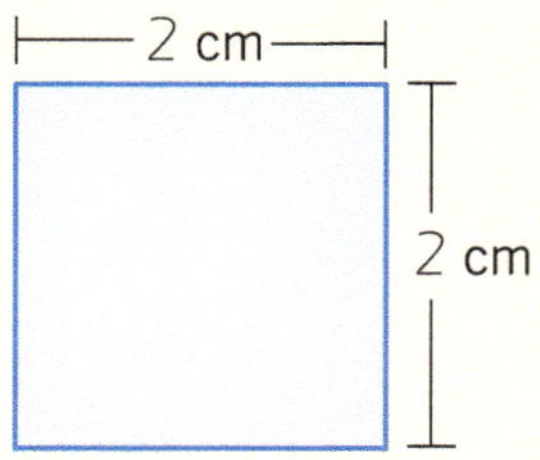

$P =$ ____

$A =$ ____

b.

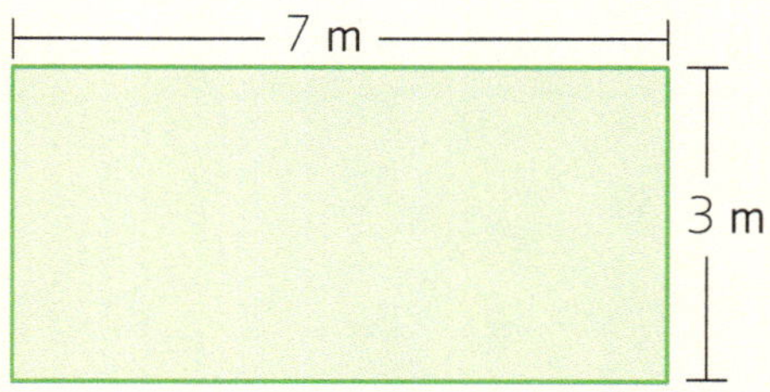

$P =$ ____

$A =$ ____

4. Calculate the areas of the two-dimensional shapes on the grid.

points
/ 4

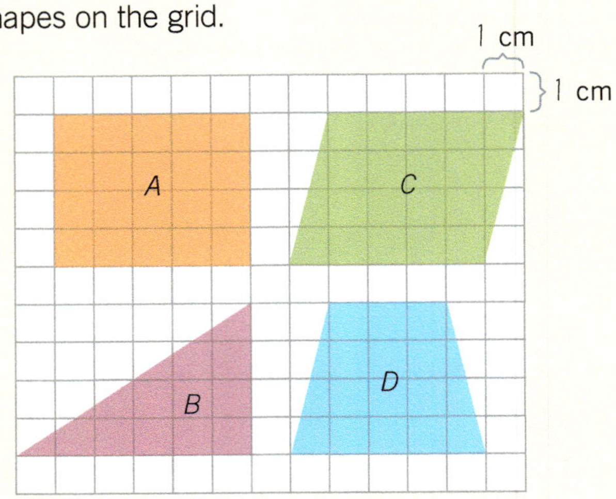

a. Area of Shape *A* = ______________

b. Area of Shape *B* = ______________

c. Area of Shape *C* = ______________

d. Area of Shape *D* = ______________

5. Calculate the area of the two-dimensional shape.

points
/ 2

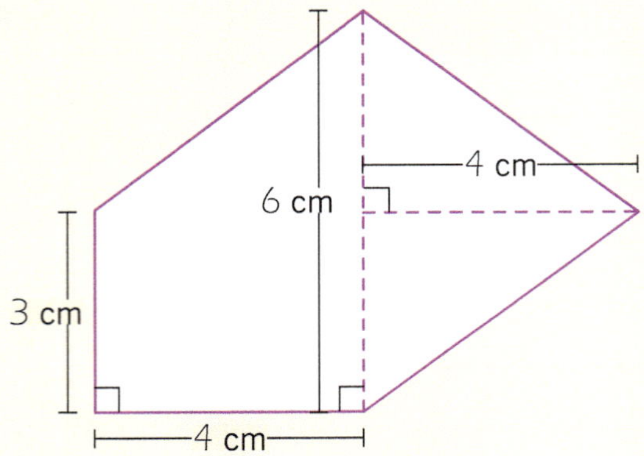

6. Look at the floor plan of the room and calculate the areas. Each □ is equal to 40 cm^2.

points
/ 2

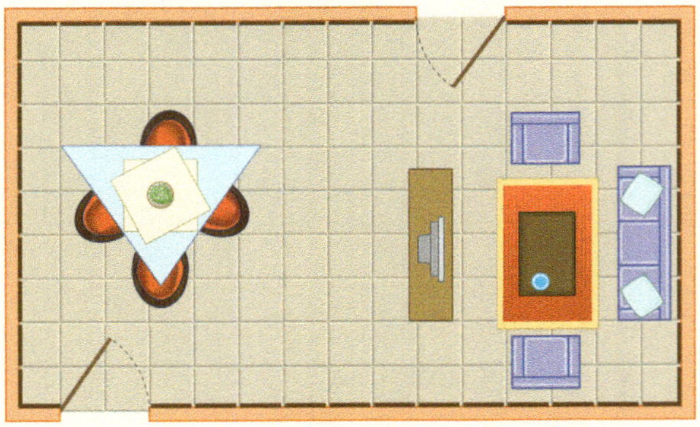

Area of the room = ______________

Estimated area of the table in the dining room (in light blue) = ______________

Mark the correct answer with an ✕.

points

/ 5

7. Which measurement is equivalent to 15 km?

A. 150 hm
B. 1,500 dm
C. 15,000 dam
D. 150,000 cm

8. Which measurement is not equivalent to 34 dam?

A. 340 m
B. 3,400 dm
C. 34,000 cm
D. 3,400,000 mm

9. If one side of a square measures 1 m, what is its surface area?

A. 10 m^2
B. 10,000 cm^2
C. 10,000 dm^2
D. 100,000 mm^2

10. If *a* is equal to 7 cm, what is the perimeter of the shape?

A. 32 cm
B. 34 cm
C. 222 cm
D. 224 cm

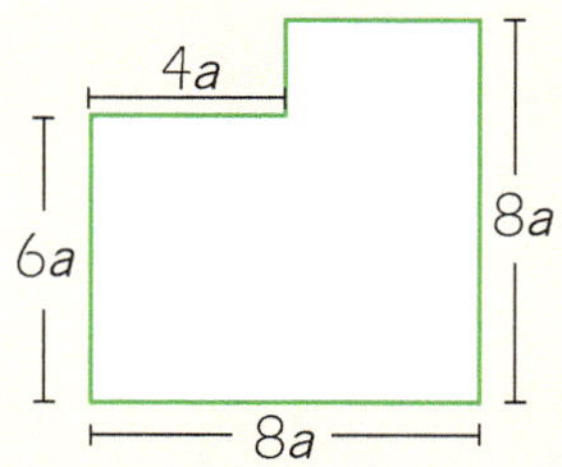

11. If the area of a rectangle is 24 cm^2, which of these measurements corresponds to its length and width, respectively?

A. 6 cm and 4 cm
B. 4 cm and 3 cm
C. 20 cm and 4 cm
D. 12 cm and 12 cm

12. If a rectangle has a surface area of 117 cm^2 and a length of 13 cm, what is its width?

points
/5

A. 3 cm
B. 6 cm
C. 9 cm
D. 13 cm

13. On the grid, how many 1 cm^2 squares make up the surface area of the triangle?

A. 20
B. 21
C. 22
D. 42

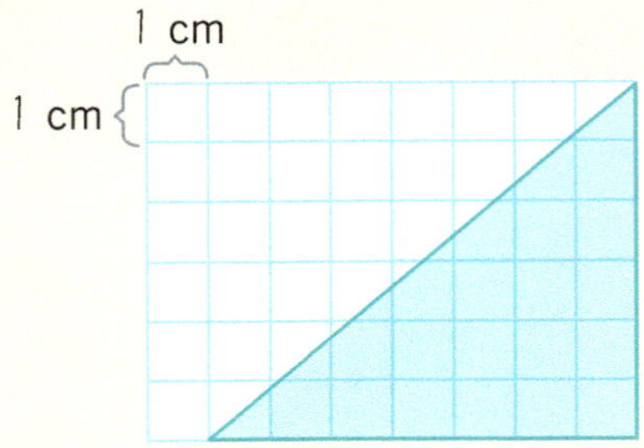

14. What is the height of a triangle if the base is 42 cm and the area is 756 cm^2?

A. 18 cm
B. 30 cm
C. 36 cm
D. 40 cm

15. What is the area of the rhombus?

A. 57 cm^2
B. 340 cm^2
C. 680 cm^2
D. 1,360 cm^2

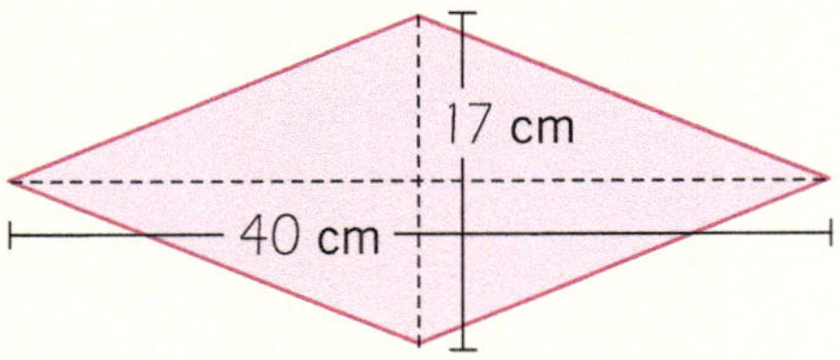

16. If the trapezoid has an area of 384 cm^2, what is the sum of its bases?

A. 12 cm
B. 24 cm
C. 36 cm
D. 48 cm

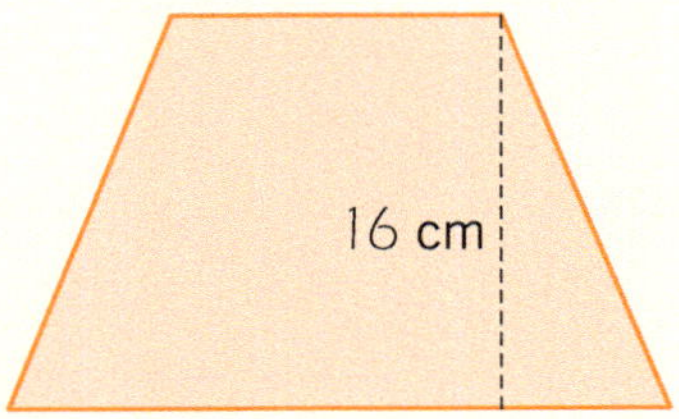

points

4

17. Look at the two-dimensional shape on the grid. Which statement is false?

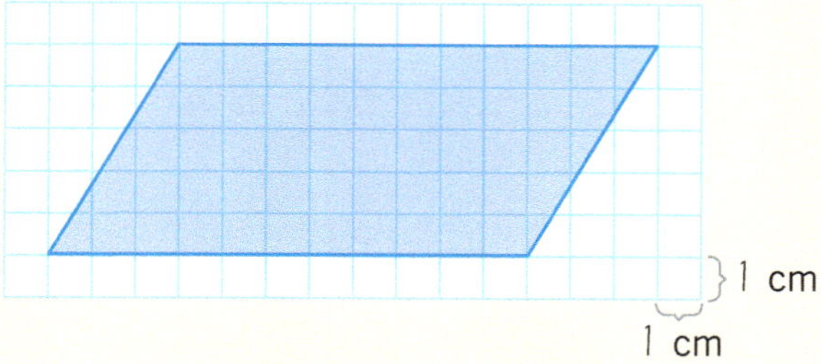

A. One of its sides measures 11 cm.

B. It has a surface area of 50 cm^2.

C. The height of the shape is 5 cm.

D. The shape is a rhomboid.

18. If the area of a rhomboid is 320 km^2 and its base is 32 km, what is its height?

A. 5 km

B. 10 km

C. 100 km

D. 288 km

19. What is the area of the trapezoid?

A. 10 cm^2

B. 35 cm^2

C. 45 cm^2

D. 55 cm^2

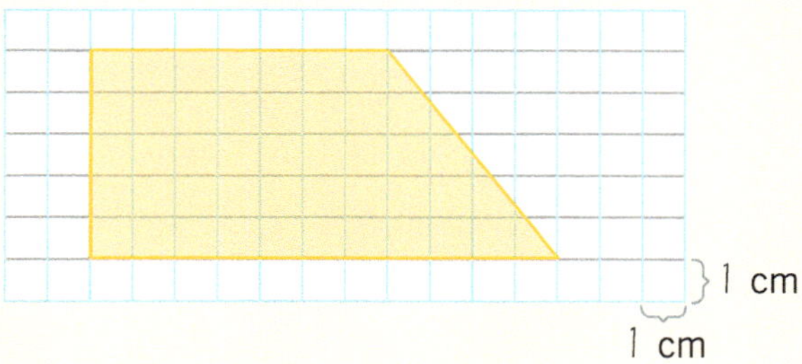

20. The composite two-dimensional shape is made of three smaller shapes. What is the total area of the shape?

A. 16 cm^2

B. 24 cm^2

C. 72 cm^2

D. 68 cm^2

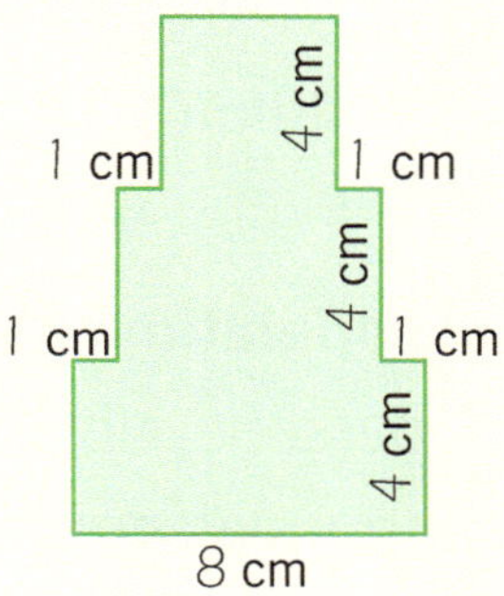

Find Test 5 Study Page

5.1 Key Words Unit 1

natural numbers – *n*, positive integers from 0 to 9

expanded form – *n*, a way to write a number dividing it into the value of each digit

number line – *n*, a line representing real numbers with marks showing integer values

rounding – *n*, a method of simplifying a number by increasing or decreasing it to the next digit

scale – *n*, a line with a series of marks at regular intervals, used to measure distances

5.2 Key Words Unit 2

simplify – *v*, to divide both the numerator and denominator by the same number to make a fraction as simple as possible

proper fraction – *n*, a fraction in which the numerator is smaller than the denominator

improper fraction – *n*, a fraction in which the numerator is greater than the denominator

mixed fraction – *n*, a number written as a combination of a whole number and a fraction

amplify – *v*, to multiply both the numerator and denominator by the same number to make the digits of a fraction bigger

equivalent – *adj*, equal to

5.3 Key Words Unit 3

double – *v*, to multiply by two; to render twice as much

halve – *v*, to divide by two; to reduce by half

distributive property – *n*, a property that states that multiplying a sum by a number is the same as multiplying each of the number's addends by the number and then adding the products

strategy – *n*, a careful plan or method for achieving a particular goal

factor – *n*, one of the numbers that is multiplied to make a product

5.4 Key Words Unit 4

average – *n*, a number that represents the overall characteristics of a set of numbers. It is found by adding two or more numbers and dividing the sum by the amount of numbers added

frequency – *n*, the number of times an item or event appears or occurs in a data set

population – *n*, a group of individual persons, objects or items from which samples are taken for statistical measurement

sample – *n*, a smaller selection of a larger population or group used to study its characteristics

statistics – *n*, a branch of math that deals with the collection, analysis and presentation of data

5.5 Key Words Unit 5

perimeter – *n*, the distance around a shape

rhombus – *n*, a shape with four sides that are equal in length and with four angles that are not always right angles

rhomboid – *n*, a shape with four sides where only the opposite sides and angles are equal

trapezoid – *n*, a four-sided shape that has two sides that are parallel and two sides that are not parallel

A

addend – *n*, a number that is added to another number

advantage – *n*, a benefit or gain; a desirable feature

axis – *n*, (pl. axes) a horizontal or vertical line on a chart

B

bar chart – *n*, the representation of information or data with rectangles (bars) placed vertically or horizontally between two perpendicular axes

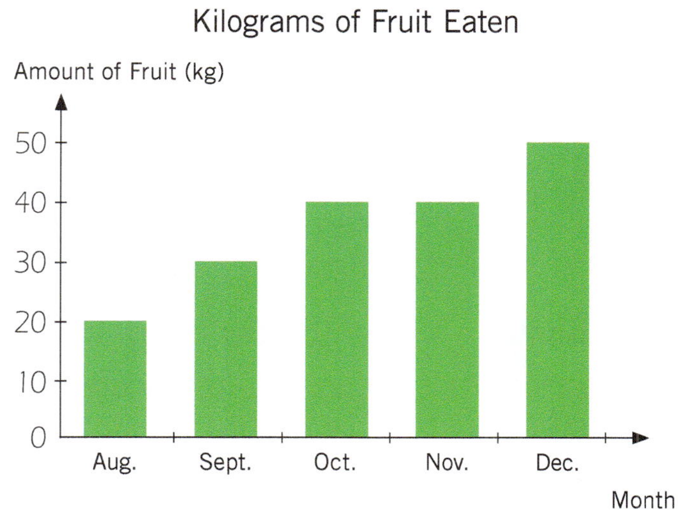

C

calculation – *n*, the process or result of adding, subtracting, multiplying or dividing

cardboard – *n*, a stiff, thick paper usually used to make boxes

category – *n*, a type or class of things

consecutive – *adj*, one after the other

convert – *v*, to change the units of something into another unit of measurement

cost – *n*, the amount of money that is needed to buy or pay for something

D

decompose – *v*, to separate a number into its parts

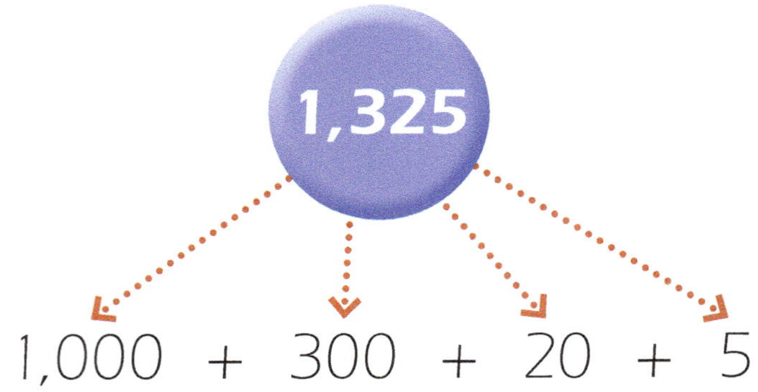

denominator – *n*, the number below the line of a fraction, that shows how many equal parts the whole is divided into

digit – *n*, a written symbol for the numbers 0 to 9

disadvantage – *n*, a bad feature or quality; something that causes difficulty

dividend – *n*, a number that is divided in a division operation

divisor – *n*, a number that divides another number

E

equivalent fractions – *n*, different fractions that represent the same part or parts of a whole number

estimate – *v*, to form a general idea about the value, cost, size or other measurement of something

expand – *v*, to break down into parts

expenses – *n*, the amount of money spent

F

factor – *n*, one of the numbers that are multiplied to make a product

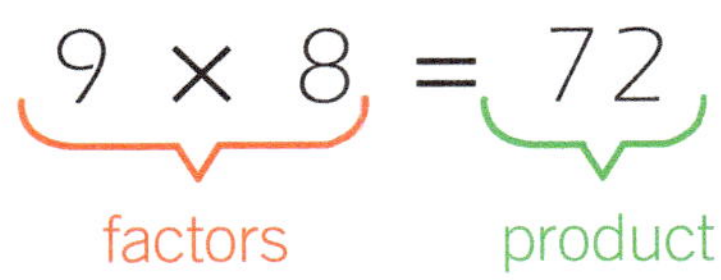

fraction – *n*, a representation of a part of a whole or, more generally, any number of equal parts

frequency table – *n*, a table that shows the frequency of events

H

height – *n*, the measurement from top to bottom

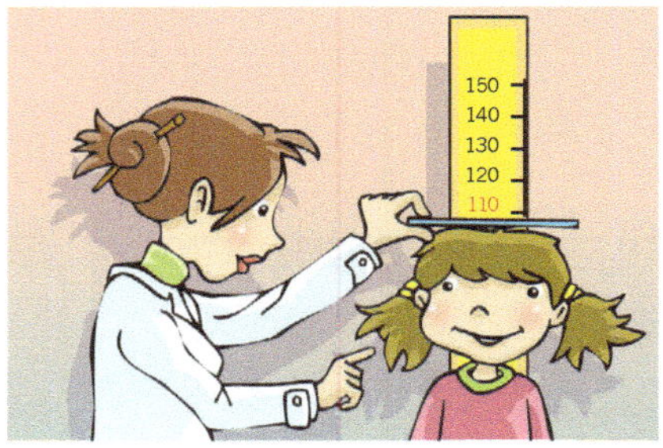

I

interval – *n*, a space between objects, units or events

L

length – *n*, the distance from one end to the other; how long something is

locate – *v*, to find the place or position of something or someone

M

minuend – *n*, the number from which the subtrahend is subtracted

multiple – *n*, a number that can be divided by another number with no remainder

N

numerator – *n*, the number above a fraction line, that shows how many parts of the whole there are

$$\frac{1}{7}$$

O

objective – *n*, a goal or purpose

operation – *n*, a math process; addition, subtraction, multiplication or division

ordinal number – *n*, a number that shows what position something has in a series

P

parallelogram – *n*, a four-sided two-dimensional shape in which the two sets of opposite sides are equal in length and parallel to each other

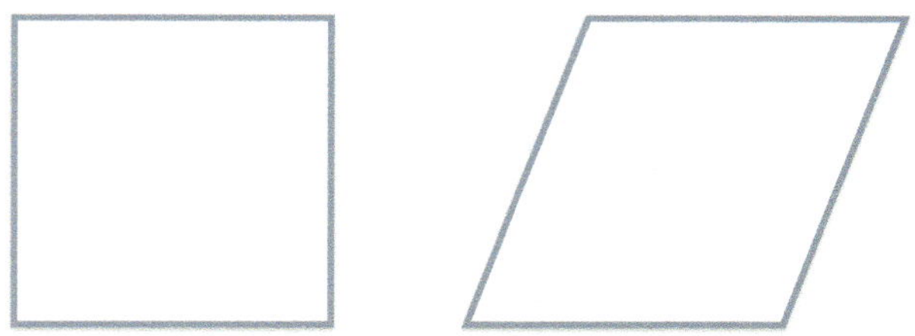

place value – *n*, the value of a digit according to the place or position it occupies in a number

polygon – *n*, a two-dimensional shape with three or more straight sides

product – *n*, the result when numbers are multiplied

Q

quadrilateral – *n*, a two-dimensional shape with four sides and four angles

qualitative – *adj*, non-numerical descriptive information

quantitative – *adj*, numerical information

quotient – *n*, the answer to a division

R

random – *adj*, not able to be predicted; happening by chance

random sample – *n*, a group that is chosen by chance from a larger population

remainder – *n*, the number that is left over when a number cannot be divided equally

round – *v*, to increase or decrease a number to the nearest whole number or indicated number

round trip – *n*, a journey to a place and back again

S

same – *adj*, exactly like someone or something else

segment – *n*, a line that passes through at least two points

snack – *n*, a small amount of food that you eat between meals

square meter – *n*, the area of a square whose sides measure exactly one meter

stalk – *n*, the stem of a plant

standard form – *n*, a way to write numbers using digits from 0 to 9

story – *n*, a floor of a building

subtraction – *n*, the process of finding the difference between one number or amount and another

sum – *n*, the product of an addition operation

T

terms – *n*, the parts of an expression that are separated by operation signs

translation – *n*, the movement of a two-dimensional shape, from one place to another, without changing anything else about it

triangle – *n*, a polygon with three sides

turn into – *v*, to change or develop into something different

two-dimensional shape – *n*, a flat, plane shape with two dimensions, such as length and width

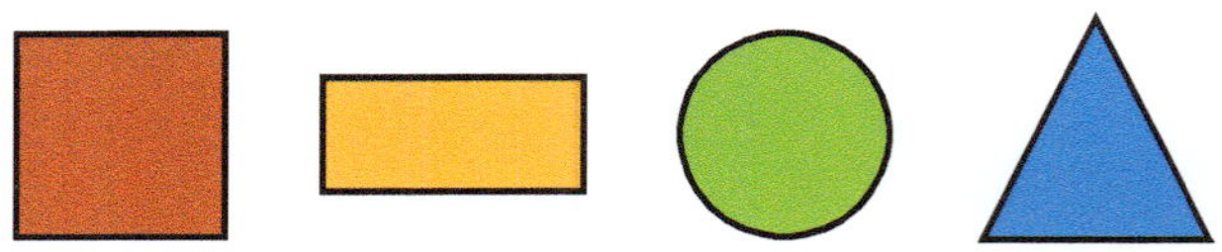

U

unit of measurement – *n*, any division of quantity considered a standardized form of measurement

V

variable – *n*, something that is counted or analyzed in an experiment

W

whole fraction – *n*, a fraction whose numerator and denominator are the same

wide – *adj*, having a specified extension from side to side

width – *n*, the distance across from side to side

withdraw – *v*, to remove money from a bank account

Place Value Chart

Example: 9,507,032,891

Billions	Hundred Millions	Ten Millions	Millions	Hundred Thousands	Ten Thousands	Thousands	Hundreds	Tens	Ones
B	**HM**	**TM**	**M**	**HTh**	**TTh**	**Th**	**H**	**T**	**O**
9,	5	0	7,	0	3	2,	8	9	1

Math Symbols

plus	+
minus	−
equal to	=
multiplication	×
less than	<
greater than	>
division	÷
height	*h*
perimeter	*P*
base	*b*/*B*
area	*A*
diagonal	*d*/D
degrees	°
square meter	m^2

Units of Conversion

10 mm	1 cm
10 cm	1 dm
10 dm	1 m
10 m	1 dam
10 dam	1 hm
10 hm	1 km

Math Formulas

Perimeter of a rectangle:

$P = (2 \times l) + (2 \times w)$

Area of a triangle:

$A = \dfrac{b \times h}{2}$

Area of a rectangle:

$A = b \times h$

Area of a rhomboid:

$A = b \times h$

Area of a rhombus:

$\dfrac{D \times d}{2}$

Area of a trapezoid:

$\dfrac{(B + b) \times h}{2}$

Test 1 Study Page • Review

Remove, answer, and glue in your notebook.

Section 1: Large Numbers

Read the information and answer.

Humans produce thousands of tons of waste every day. These are the amounts of waste generated in tons in four regions of the world.

Region 1 ▶ 169,119

Region 2 ▶ 437,545

Region 3 ▶ 254,389

Region 4 ▶ 1,566,286

1. Write, in words, the tons of waste produced by the regions.

   a. Region 2 ▶ ____________________

   b. Region 3 ▶ ____________________

2. Write the place values for the amount of waste produced by Region 4.

   a. M ▶ ____________ b. HTh ▶ ____________

3. Expand the total amount of waste produced by Region 1.

   a. Standard ▶ ____________________

   b. Expanded ▶ ____________________

4. Round the amount of waste in the regions to the hundred thousands place.

   a. Region 2 ▶ ____________ b. Region 3 ▶ ____________

5. Place the amount of waste produced by each region on the number line.

Name: ______________________________ Grade: __________

Reading Natural Numbers

9,507,032,891

billions (9) · millions (507) · thousands (032) · hundreds (891)

Comparing Natural Numbers

223,450,000 > 221,450,000

3 > 1

Rounding Natural Numbers

767,054,210 → 800,000,000

6 > 5

354,814,520 → 350,000,000

4 < 5

Expanded Forms

8,200,030

Expanded

$8 \times 1{,}000{,}000 + 2 \times 100{,}000 + 3 \times 10$

Standard

8,000,000 + 200,000 + 30

	B	HM	TM	M	HTh	TTh	Th	H	T	O	
	7,	6	5	3,	0	5	1,	8	9	2	→ addend
+	2,	1	5	3,	5	7	6,	8	0	7	→ addend
	9,	8	0	6,	6	2	8,	6	9	9	→ sum

To check the answer to a subtraction operation, add the difference and the subtrahend.

7,661,419 – 3,541,114 = 4,120,305

4,120,305 + 3,541,114 = 7,661,419

7,661,419 – 4,120,305 = 3,541,114

Test 1 Study Page • Summary

Section 1

- Large Numbers
  - Reading and Writing Natural Numbers
  - Place Value in Natural Numbers
  - Standard and Expanded Forms
  - Location of Numbers on a Number Line
  - Comparing and Putting Natural Numbers in Order
  - Rounding and Estimating Natural Numbers

Section 2

- Addition
  - Adding Natural Numbers

Section 3

- Subtraction
  - Subtracting Natural Numbers
  - The Relationship between Addition and Subtraction

Section 2: Addition

6. Solve the addition operations.

a.
```
  2,258,320
+ 9,042,689
```
☐

b.
```
  35,210,223
+ 73,899,778
```
☐

c.
```
  365,892,100
+ 752,210,992
```
☐

7. Solve the word problem.

A company made $735,350,000 last year and $56,401,320 this year. How much money did the company make in these two years?

Section 3: Subtraction

8. Solve the subtraction operations.

a.
```
  1,254,369
−   584,210
```
☐

b.
```
  325,254,210
− 284,998,100
```
☐

c.
```
  8,254,100,391
− 6,510,982,089
```
☐

9. Complete the operations and the operations to check the answers with the missing numbers.

a.
```
  7,550,134,689        ☐
+ ☐                  − 1,932,670,145
  9,482,804,834        ☐
```

b.
```
  ☐                    515,578,320
− 515,578,320        + ☐
  ☐                    638,948,772
```

glue here

glue here

glue here

glue here

glue here

Section 2: Addition and Subtraction of Fractions with the Same Denominator

4. Solve the operations and represent the answers.

a. $\frac{3}{7}+\frac{1}{7}=$ ☐

c. $\frac{4}{10}-\frac{3}{10}=$ ☐

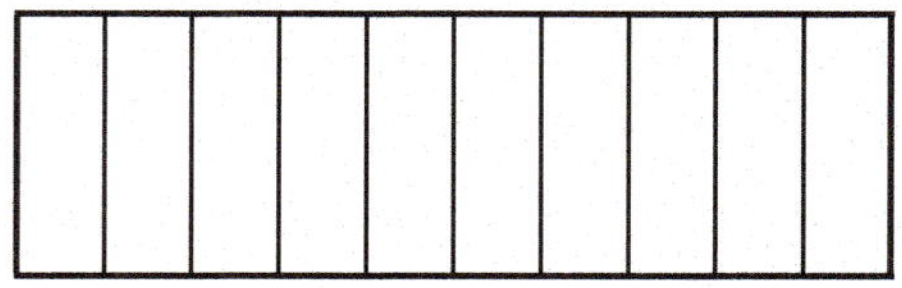

b. $\frac{2}{8}+\frac{2}{8}=$ ☐

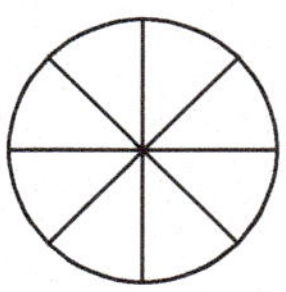

d. $\frac{8}{15}-\frac{3}{15}=$ ☐

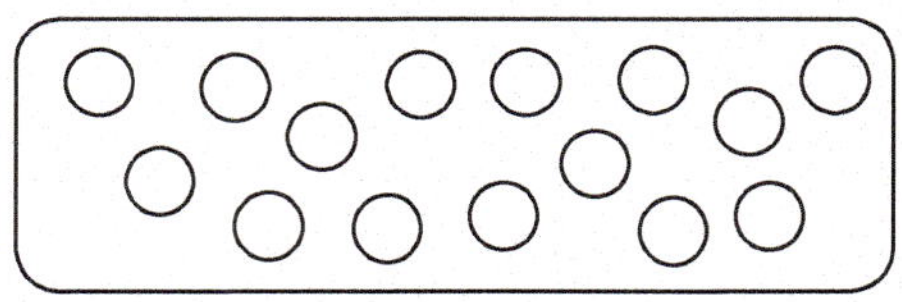

5. Solve the fraction operations.

a. $1\frac{1}{12}-\frac{12}{12}=$ ☐

b. $\frac{3}{5}+\frac{2}{10}=$ ☐

c. $\frac{8}{3}-\frac{12}{6}=$ ☐

Test 2 Study Page • Summary

Section 1

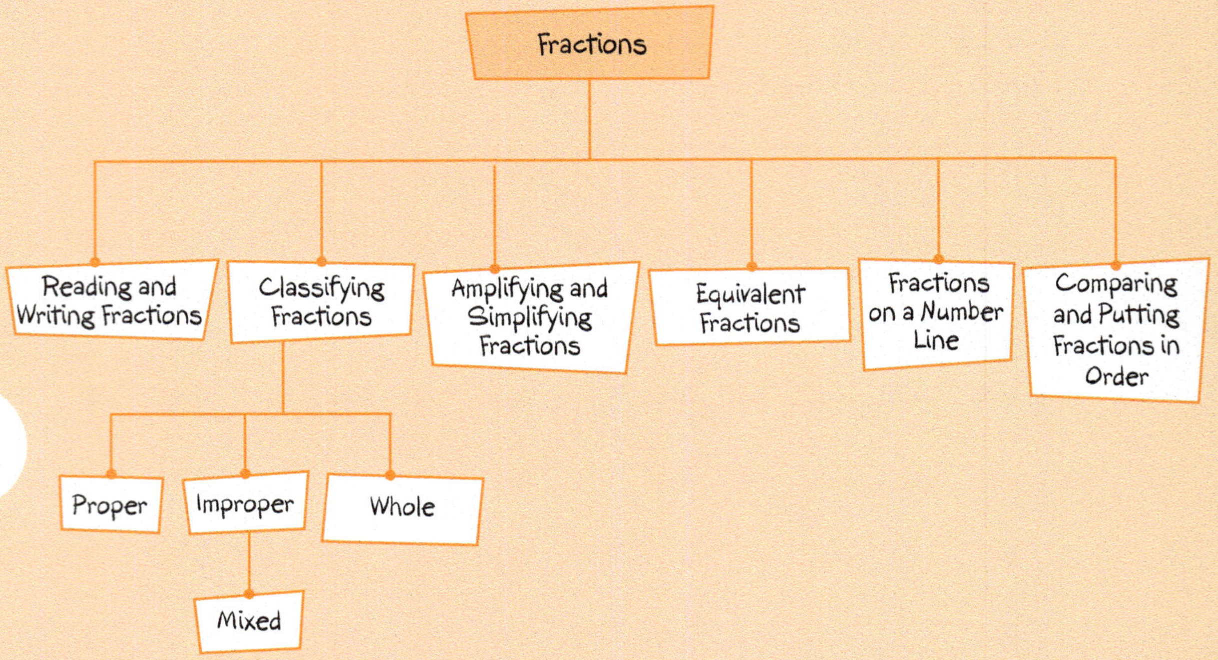

Section 2

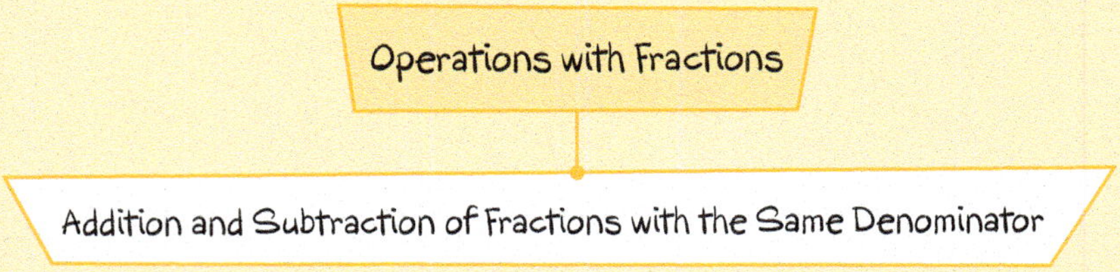

Name: ______________________ Grade: __________

Reading and Writing Fractions

numerical fraction	written fraction	graphic representation
$\frac{5}{8}$	five-eighths	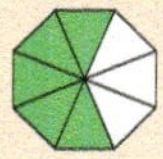

Classifying Fractions

- $\frac{2}{3}$ is a **proper** fraction, since $2 < 3$.
- $\frac{5}{5}$ is a **whole** fraction, since $5 = 5$.
- $\frac{9}{4}$ is an **improper** fraction, since $9 > 4$.

Fractions on a Number Line

$\frac{3}{8}$ on a number line is:

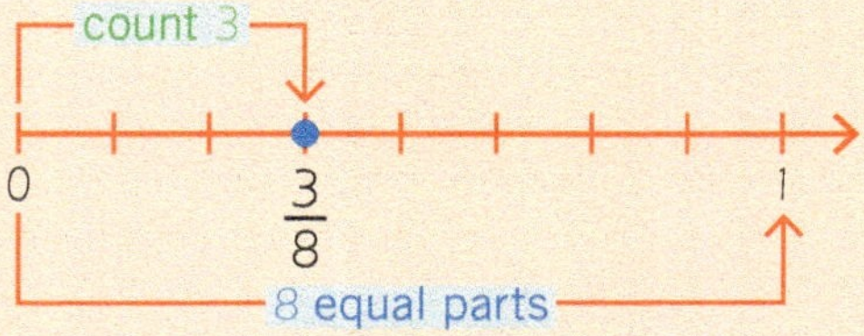

Putting Fractions in Order

To put **fractions in order**, use a **number line**.

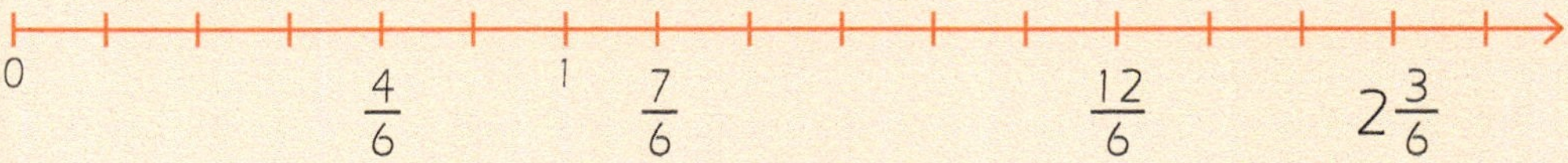

You can put the fractions in increasing order: $\frac{4}{6} < 1 < \frac{7}{6} < \frac{12}{6} < 2\frac{3}{6}$,

or decreasing order: $2\frac{3}{6} > \frac{12}{6} > \frac{7}{6} > 1 > \frac{4}{6}$.

Equivalent Fractions

$\frac{14}{12}$ — simplified by 2 → $\frac{7}{6}$ — mixed fraction → $1\frac{1}{6}$

$\frac{14}{12}$ — amplified by 2 → $\frac{28}{24}$ — mixed fraction → $1\frac{1}{6}$

Addition of Fractions with the Same Denominators

To solve $\frac{3}{6} + \frac{5}{4}$, you amplify or simplify the fractions to make the denominators equal.

$$\frac{3}{6} = \frac{3 \times 2}{6 \times 2} = \frac{6}{12} \qquad \frac{5}{4} = \frac{5 \times 3}{4 \times 3} = \frac{15}{12}$$

Then you can add the fractions and put the answer in its simplest form.

$$\frac{3}{6} + \frac{5}{4} = \frac{6}{12} + \frac{15}{12} = \frac{21}{12} = \frac{21 \div 3}{12 \div 3} = \frac{7}{4} = 1\frac{3}{4}$$

Test 2 Study Page • Review

Remove, answer, and glue in your notebook.

Section 1: Fractions

1. Write the fractions in words. Then classify them as proper, improper or whole.

	Word Form	Classification
a. $\frac{7}{3}$	________	________
b. $\frac{7}{12}$	________	________
c. $\frac{9}{9}$	________	________

2. Complete with the missing fractions.

a. When simplifying the fraction $\frac{32}{36}$ by 4, you get ☐.

b. When amplifying the fraction $\frac{8}{7}$ by 3, you get ☐.

c. When simplifying the fraction ☐ by 2, you get $\frac{5}{2}$.

3. Locate the fractions on the number line.

$\frac{7}{8}, \frac{7}{4}, \frac{3}{2}, \frac{12}{12}$

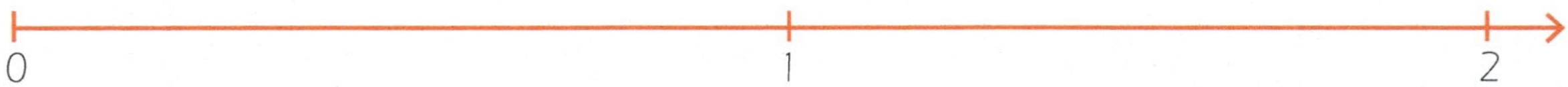

Test 3 Study Page • Review

Remove, answer, and glue in your notebook

Section 1: Mental and Written Strategies

1. Solve the multiplication operations using the strategies given.

a. Turning two factors into four

30×25

b. The double of doubles

25×8

Section 2: Multiplication

2. Solve the multiplication operations.

a. 325×3

c. 455×6

b. 689×0

d. 321×1

Section 3: Division

3. Solve the division operations.

a. $95 \div 5$

c. $95 \div 1$

b. $81 \div 3$

d. $64 \div 4$

Name: ______________________________ Grade: __________

Turning Two Factors into Four Factors

25×12

$5 \times 5 \times 4 \times 3$

$5 \times 20 \times 3$

$100 \times 3 = 300$

Doubling and Having

25×12

$50 \times 6 = 300$

Double of Doubles

25×12

$50 \times 6 = 300$

$100 \times 3 = 300$

Multiplication with 0 and 1

Multiplying by 1

$3{,}220 \times 1 = 3{,}220$

$1 \times 2{,}500 = 2{,}500$

Multiplying by 0

$5{,}641 \times 0 = 0$

$0 \times 8{,}320 = 0$

Decomposing

243×2

$(200 + 40 + 3) \times 2$

$(200 \times 2) + (40 \times 2) + (3 \times 2)$

$400 + 80 + 6 = 486$

Addition in column

$$\begin{array}{r} 243 \\ \times \quad 2 \\ \hline 6 \\ 80 \\ +\,400 \\ \hline 486 \end{array}$$

Distributive Property

$12 \times (15 + 10)$

$(12 \times 15) + (12 \times 10)$

$180 + 120$

$= 300$

Division with 1

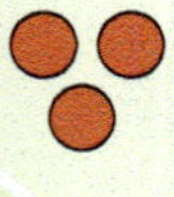

▸ If you have one group of elements and you divide it by 1, the result is the same number. ▸ Therefore, $3 \div 1 = 3$.

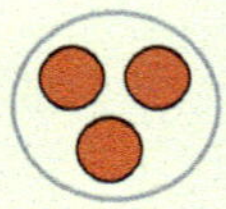

Relationship between Multiplication and Division

$25 \times 3 = 75$ → $75 \div 3 = 25$

$25 \times 3 = 75$ → $75 \div 25 = 3$

Estimating Products and Quotients

Round the factor or dividend greater than ten to the nearest tens, hundreds or thousands place.

$1{,}000 \times 5 = 5{,}000$

The estimated product

$981 \times 5 \rightarrow$ is 5,000

Word problems

1. Read the word problem and the question.
2. Identify the information that will help you solve the question.
3. Determine the operation and calculation strategy.
4. Answer the question.
5. Check your answer.

Test 3 Study Page • Summary

Section 1

Mental and Written Strategies

- Turning Two Factors into Four Factors
- Doubling and Halving
- The Double of Doubles

Section 2

Multiplication

- Multiplication with 0 and 1
- Multiplication Strategies
  - Decomposing
  - Addition in Column
- Applying the Distributive Property Using Addition

Section 3

Division

- Division with 1
- The Relationship between Multiplication and Division

Section 4

Multiplication and Division Word Problems

- Estimating Products and Quotients
- Word Problems

Section 4: Multiplication and Division Word Problems

4. Solve the word problems.

a. Vanessa is in charge of collecting money for a gift. If seven people give $15 each, how much money will Vanessa have to buy the gift?

Information ▶ ______________________________

____

Operation ▶ ______________________________

Strategy

Answer: ______________________________

b. Ivan has decided to read the same number of pages of a book each day. If the book is 117 pages long, and he has 9 days to read it, how many pages should he read each day?

Information ▶ ______________________________

____

Operation ▶ ______________________________

Strategy

Answer: ______________________________

glue here

glue here

glue here

glue here

glue here

Test 4 Study Page • Review

Remove, answer, and glue in your notebook.

Section 1: Statistics

1. Look at the bar chart and answer the questions.

a. What day did most people go to the art show?

▶ ______________________________

b. How many people went to the art show on the fourth day?

▶ ______________________________

c. How many people went to the art show in total?

▶ ______________________________

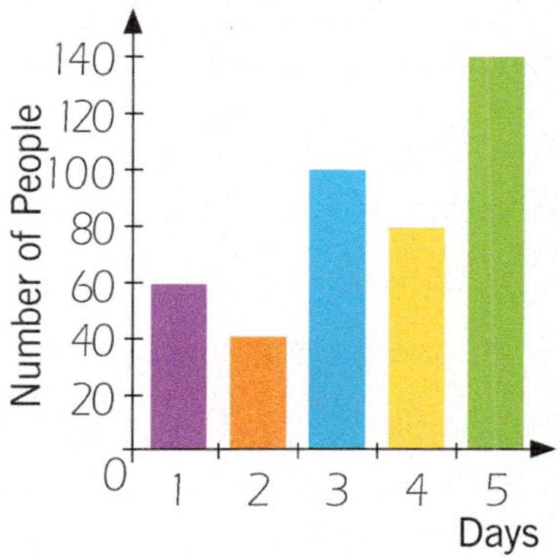

2. Label the bar chart using the information in the frequency table.

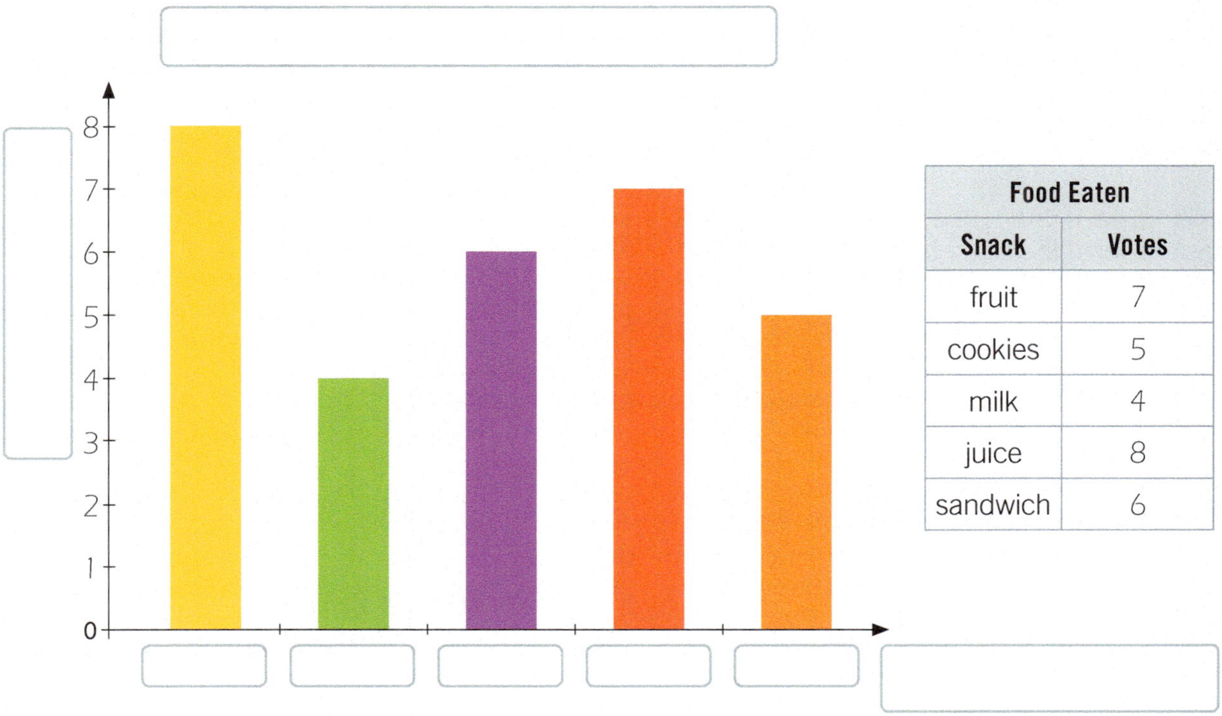

Food Eaten	
Snack	**Votes**
fruit	7
cookies	5
milk	4
juice	8
sandwich	6

Name: ______________________ Grade: __________

Reading and Interpreting Bar Charts

A **frequency table** shows data in an organized way: **population**, **sample**, **variable**, **category** and **frequency**.

The study: Survey about students' favorite sports

- **Objective:** to know students' favorite sports
- **Population and sample:** 15 students were surveyed
- **Frequency:** the number of votes for each sport
- **Variable:** sports (Categories: soccer, swimming, tennis)

Bar charts help you visualize data quickly and clearly. To read the information, look at the length of the **rectangular bars**. The bars represent the quantitative and qualitative **variables** studied. The **x-axis** is the horizontal line and the **y-axis** is the vertical line.

Reading and Interpreting Frequency Tables

Favorite Sport	
Sport	**Number of Students**
Soccer	5
Swimming	7
Tennis	3

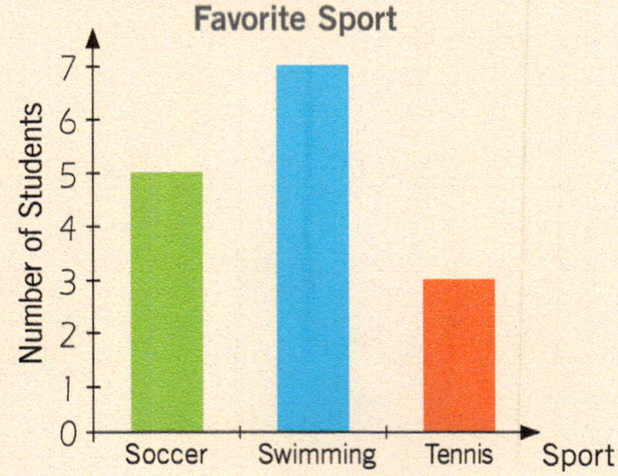

Calculating Averages

The **average** is the sum of the values of a variable divided by the total number of values.

Monday	Tuesday	Wednesday	Thursday	Friday	Saturday	Sunday
21° C	24° C	21° C	18° C	18° C	21° C	24° C

The average temperatures was: $\frac{21 + 24 + 21 + 18 + 18 + 21 + 24}{7} = \frac{147}{7} = 21°$

Advantages and Disadvantages of Averages

Advantages

- Most common numerical value used to represent a group of data.
- It is one number.

Disadvantages

- You cannot calculate the average of qualitative data.
- It is greatly affected by very small or very big values, which can make it an inaccurate represention of a data set.

Test 4 Study Page • Summary

Section 1

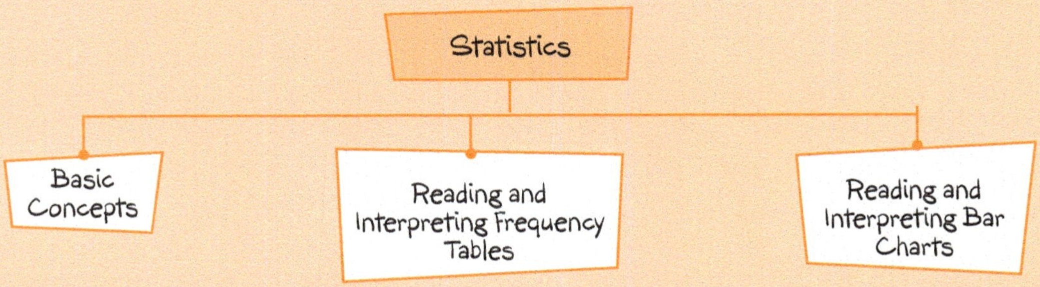

Section 2

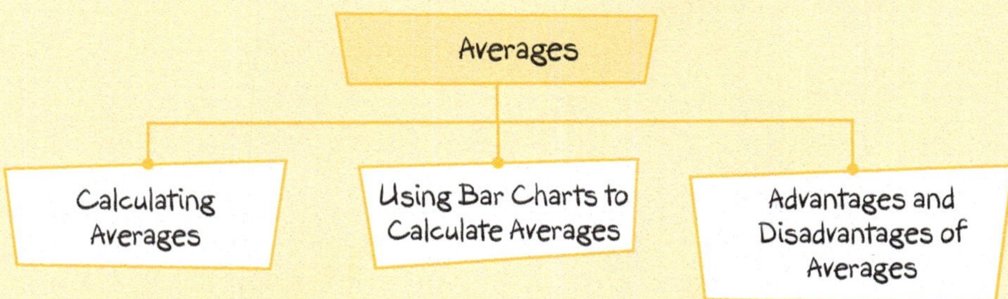

Section 2: Averages

3. Calculate the averages of the sets of numbers.

a. 4, 8, 2 and 6

b. 35, 18, 24, 12 and 25

4. Write the missing number to calculate the averages given.

a. 5, 12, 15, 8, _______, 4 = 8

b. _______, 80, 110, 220, 218 = 186

5. Look at the information and calculate the average of the data.

The bar chart shows tons of shrimp exported by a company. Calculate the average number of tons of shrimp exported during six months.

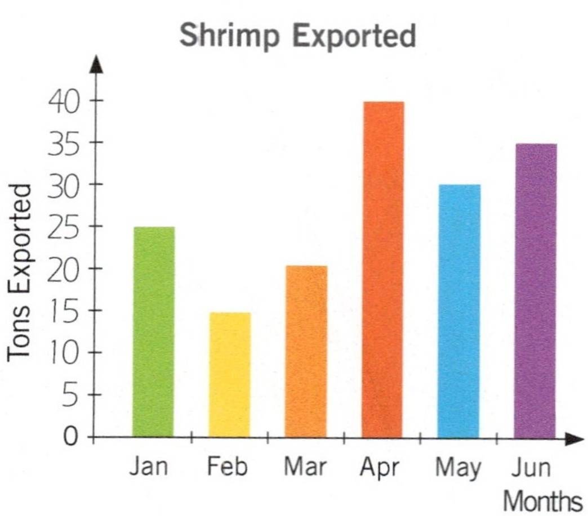

Test 5 Study Page • Review

Remove, answer, and glue in your notebook.

Section 1: Units of Length and Surface Area

1. Use a ruler to measure the sides of the triangle and complete.

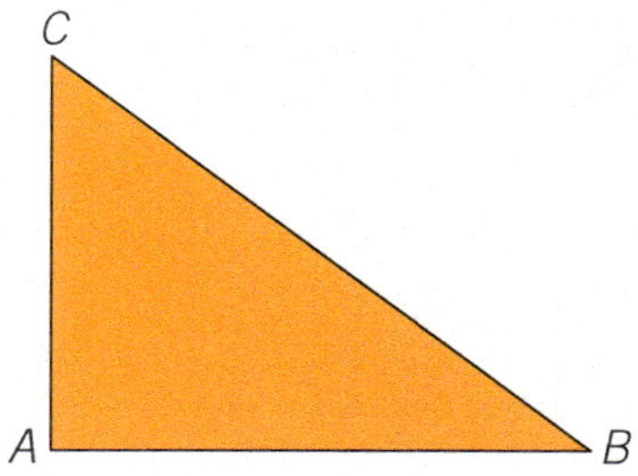

a. Side *AB* ▸ ________ cm

b. Side *BC* ▸ ________ cm

c. Side *CA* ▸ ________ cm

2. Convert the units of length to complete the equivalences.

a. 20 m ▸ ______________ cm

b. 35 km ▸ ______________ dam

c. 7 hm ▸ ______________ dm

d. 4 dam ▸ ______________ m

e. 5 mm ▸ ______________ m

f. 4 dm ▸ ______________ dam

Section 2: Perimeter and Area of Rectangles

3. Calculate the perimeter (*P*) of the shapes.

a.

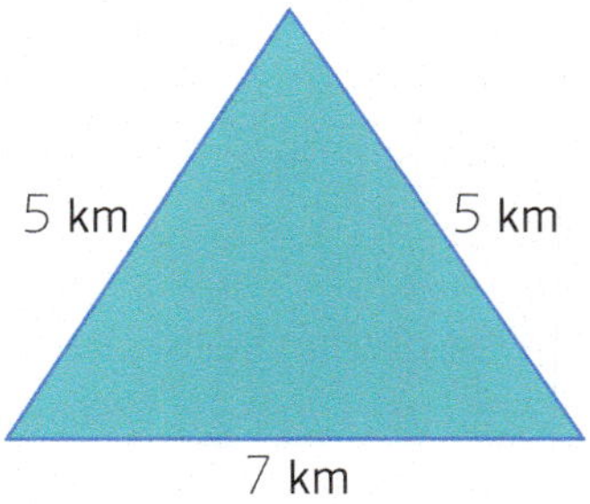

P = ________________

b.

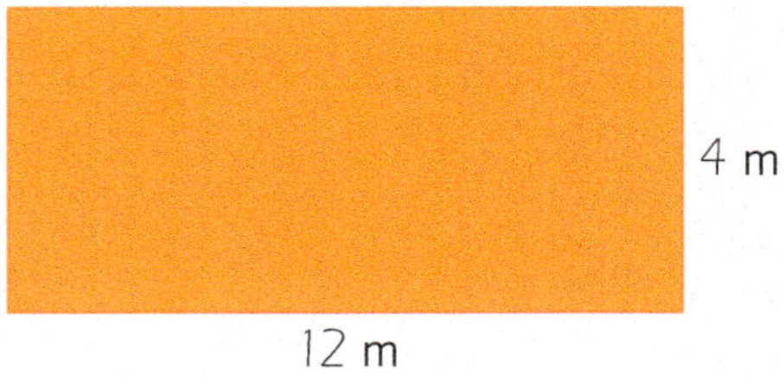

P = ________________

Name: ______________________________ Grade: __________

Conversion between Units of Length

To convert into smaller units, multiply.

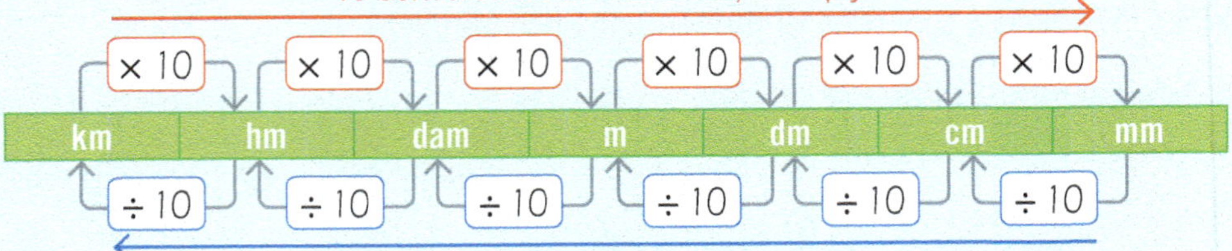

To convert into larger units, divide.

Conversion between Units of Surface Area

To convert into smaller units, multiply.

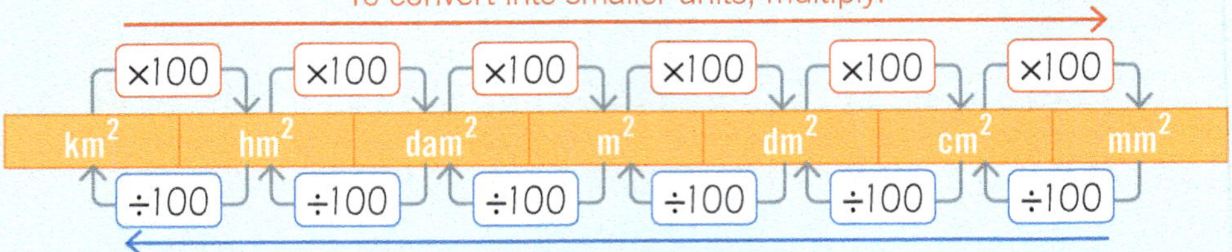

To convert into larger units, divide.

Perimeter of Two-Dimensional Shapes

The **perimeter (*P*)** of a two-dimensional shape is the total measurement of all its sides.

Area of Rectangles

To calculate the **area of a rectangle (*A*)**, multiply the width by the length.
If the area is 10 cm^2, you need to find all of the divisors of 10: 1 and 10, and 2 and 5. From this information, you can make two rectangles:

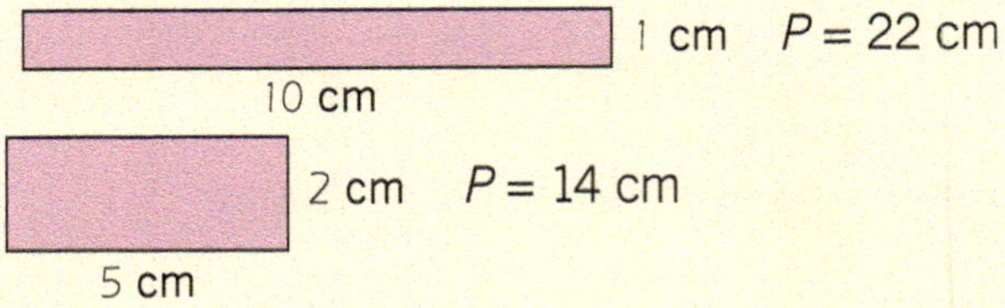

Area of Two-Dimensional Shapes

The shape in the grid can be broken down into a rectangle and a triangle to find the area. Each square is equal to 1 cm^2.

Area of triangle: 4 cm^2
Area of rectangle: 20 cm^2
4 cm^2 + 20 cm^2 = 24 cm^2
Surface area: 24 cm^2

Formulas to calculate the areas of two-dimensional shapes:

Triangle: $\frac{b \times h}{2}$ Rhombus: $A = \frac{D \times d}{2}$

Rhomboid: height (*h*) × base (*b*).
Trapezoid: break it into a rectangle and two triangles.

Test 5 Study Page • Summary

Section 1

- Units of Length and Surface Area
  - Units of Length
  - Conversion Between Units of Length
  - Units of Surface area

Section 2

- Perimeter and Area
  - Perimeter of Two-Dimensional Shapes
  - Area of Rectangles
  - Representing Rectangles

Section 3

- Area of Two-Dimensional Shapes
  - Area Using Grids
    - Triangles
    - Rhombuses and Rhomboids
    - Trapezoids
  - Area of Triangles
    - Area of Rhombuses and Rhomboids
      - Area of Trapezoids

4. Solve the word problems.

a. If the perimeter of a rectangle is 20 cm, and one of its sides is 3 cm long, what is the area of the rectangle?

$A =$ ____________________________

b. If the area of a rectangle is 15 m^2, and one of its sides is 5 m long, what is its perimeter?

$P =$ ____________________________

Section 3: Area of Two-Dimensional Shapes

5. Analyze the shapes and answer.

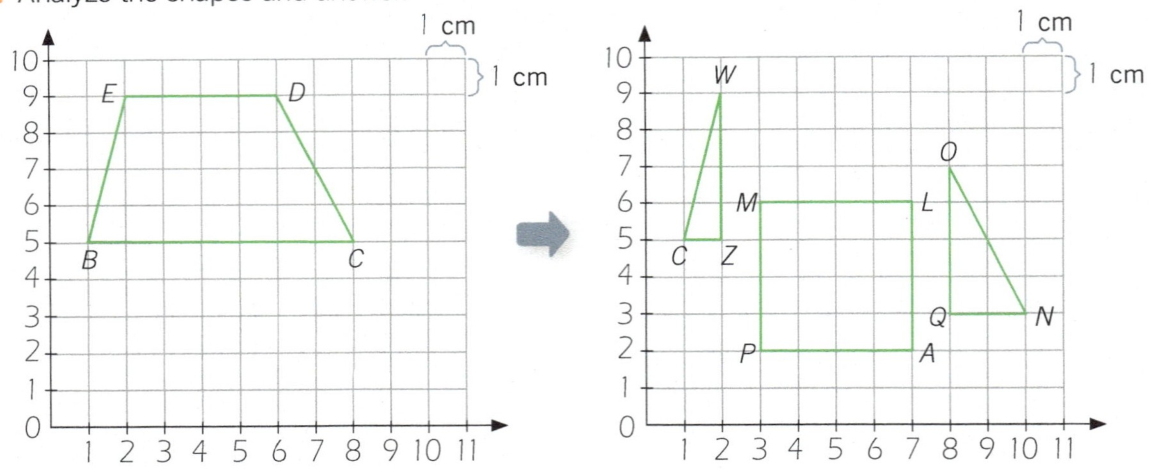

a. Calculate the areas of the polygons represented above.

BCDE ▸ __________________ *PALM* ▸ __________________

CZW ▸ __________________ *QNO* ▸ __________________

b. Explain the relationship between the areas of the polygons.

____

____

glue here

glue here

glue here

glue here

glue here